Sarvahi Vyapaka Sai
All Pervasive Sai

S. Seshadri

STERLING

STERLING PUBLISHERS (P) LTD.
Regd. Office: A1/256 Safdarjung Enclave, New Delhi-110029.
CIN: U22110DL1964PTC211907
Phone: +91 82877 98380/ +91 120-6251823
e-mail: mail@sterlingpublishers.in
www.sterlingpublishers.in

Sarvahi Vyapaka Sai - All Pervasive Sai

ISBN 978-93-93853-44-8

Printed and Published by

Sterling Publishers Pvt. Ltd.,
Plot No. 13, Ecotech-III, Greater Noida - 201306, Uttar Pradesh, India

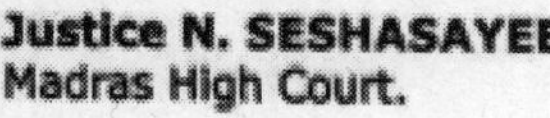

FOREWORD

Om Shri Sai Ram.

A rare call from the divinity blessed me with an opportunity to share the opening page of the compilation of essays and articles of a nonagenarian author on and about Shirdi Sai Baba.

Sai is not a mere name, nor does Baba signifies any cult. He is symbolic, if not synonymous with the faith that comforts His devotees of His constant presence. He assures and comforts that not one of his devotee is alone, nor are their challenges permanent. He who surrenders to Him without reservation is the safest and the most blessed. Baba is always on time, never behind and never ahead. Only we need the patience and the trust in Him.

I understand that this compilation of articles have earlier appeared in the journal '*Sai Sudha*'. The author has not made it a story of Baba's miracles, but allows Him to move in the company of his ardent devotees, and also has let other spiritual masters share space with Him. What is particularly appreciative of the work is the author's ability for articulation, choice of expression which makes for a comforting readability to humble every reader and to render surrender a spontaneous process.

Justice N. SESHASAYEE
Madras High Court.

My father was a subscriber of '*Sai Sudha*', and as a boy I had collected them from the postman only to leave them at my father's table. Not once I remembered to have touched it even accidentally. And, today, humbled by the grace of Sai, I get an opportunity to read what I had missed decades ago.

On reading the various articles from the draft compilation provided to me, my respect for the author turned into reverence, and I visited him to get his blessings. He is an amazing person with a remarkable power of articulation with an unbeatable memory at 94 years. My *pranams* to the author.

I wish that everyone from every walk of life from every religious group possess a copy of the book for its humbling experience, for securing inner peace and garnering a rare courage that we are not alone. After all Sai is universal and so is the peace that we are constantly searching for.

PREFACE

Today there can hardly be any person who is not familiar with the name 'Sai Baba'. While there are temples and shrines for Sai Baba not only in India but all over the world, there are devotees of Sai Baba in almost every country. Baba lived as a fakir in a dilapidated mosque in a remote hamlet, Shirdi, in Maharashtra. As predicted by Sri Narasimhaswamiji as far back as 1940, Shirdi became a place of pilgrimage at par with Tirupati. Everyday thousands of devotees visit Shirdi, which is now connected well by road, rail and air. The reason is not for to seek. Swamiji wrote in 1950, "Baba found that the one central or common factor that would bind the various religionists in this country into a common bond of unity was and is supreme faith in a common cause who remained unidentified and unidentifiable with any particular Race, Religion, Sect, Creed or Caste. Baba was himself the best proof, the best instance and best means of founding such a faith". In the valuable book, "Life of Sai Baba" Sri Narasimhaswamiji has presented exhaustively the manifold nature of Sri Sai Baba with authentic authority.

It was Sri Sai's unparalleled grace that enabled me to write Editorials in 'Sai Sudha', the monthly magazine published by All India Sai Samaj, Chennai for nearly twenty years. It was my endeavor to present in the articles, as much as possible, the solution given by Baba to various problems assailing us from time to time. Over hundred such articles are being presented in this book. My daughter Sow. Usha Parthasarathy, an ardent devotee of Sai and the Founder-Secretary of Sai Vruksha Trust in Madurai, carrying out humanitarian services as a token of Sai worship, wished that the articles by me should be brought out in book form. I thank Justice Sri N. Seshasayee for having kindly given a Foreword for this book. I am thankful to Sri S.K.Ghai of Sterling Publishers, Delhi who readily agreed to publish this book. He has to his credit the grace of Sai and privilege to have published several books by various authors on Sri Sai Baba.

It is my hope that a study of the articles covered in the book would give the reader the benefit and pleasure of understanding Sri Sai Baba's nature to some extent.

Jai Sairam

S. Seshadri

CONTENTS

SARVAHI VYAPAKA SAI

(Sai Sudha – May, 2010)

Sai devotees should be familiar with the Arati song '*Aisa Yei Ba Sai Digambara'*. Gurudeva is hailed as *Sarvahi-Vyapaka* – all-pervading, present everywhere. In this song Sai is invoked as Dattatreya. Every day in the morning he bathes in the holy waters of Kashi, in the noon for bhiksha he is at Kolhapur (the abode of Mahalakshmi) drinking the waters of river Tungabhadra and in the evening he reaches Mahur mountain for night yoga-nidra or yogic sleep. How is this possible? His form is just not a physical sheath as possessed by ordinary humans, but is '*akshaya*', imperishable. With that subtle form he can at will move anywhere, be present at various places at the same time.

In the song *'Jaya Deva Jaya Deva Datta Avadhuta O Sai Avaduta'* Sai is hailed as the manifestation of Lord Dattatreya. In the Kakada arati (morning) song it is said '*bhu-kechara vyapuni avaghe hritkamalee rahasi tochi Datta Deva tu Shirdi rahunipavasi*'. i.e. 'pervading the entire universe, you also make your abode in every living being's heart. You are also Lord Datta living in Shirdi and blessing us.

Large number of devotees who had the good fortune of having contact with Sri Sai Baba before his Mahasamadhi firmly believed that after Akkalkot Maharaj, Sri Sai was the latest manifestation of Lord Dattatreya. There are incidents in the lives of some Sai devotees to corroborate this view.

Sri Vasudevananda Saraswati (Tembe Swami), a contemporary of Sri Sai Baba, was met by Das Ganu Maharaj and his friends at Rajahmundry on the banks of River Godavari. The Swami sent through Das Ganu a coconut to be offered to Sri Sai Baba, his elder brother. When Das Ganu went to Shirdi without the coconut (his friends having eaten it away), Baba reprimanded him for not delivering the valuable offering sent by his 'brother'. Vasudevananda Saraswati is a follower of Datta Sampradaya. It is told that H.H. Chandrasekara Bharati Swami of Sringeri hailed Sri Vasudevananda Saraswati as the very manifestation of Lord Datta. It is also said that he authored the beautiful Sanskrit work "*Samhitaayana Guru Dwisahasri*" being a Sanskrit adaptation of the original Marathi Parayana Grantha *Sree Guru Charitra* of Sri Gangadhara Saraswati and that it was done at the specific command of Lord Dattatreya.

Books and publications on Sri Sai reveal several instances to show that like Lord Dattatreya he also appeared in several places in the same form or in a different form, although people of Shirdi were quite positive that Baba never moved out of Shirdi.

An anecdote in the life of Mother Krishnabai of Anandashram is reported in April 2009 issue of *The Vision.* Smt. Devitai, one of the closest disciples of Sri Upasani Baba and Godavari Mata of Sakori came to Anandashram in June 1987; she was talking to Mother Krishnabai about Sri Upasani Baba, Godavari Mata, Shirdi etc. The conversation between them was on the following lines.

Mataji: I think I have seen Sai Baba.

Devitai: When was that, Mataji?

Mataji: It was in Bombay. I was then 15 or 16. I was standing in a corner near the Gamdevi temple when Sai Baba came that way. At that time I did not know who he was. But, from the description, I later came to know that he was none but Sri Sai Baba of Shirdi.

Since Mataji is reported to have been born in 1903, the year she met Sri Sai Baba in Bombay should be 1917 or 1918. If at that young age Krishnabai had the privilege of having Sri Sai's darsan at her place, it was clearly an indication of her future – to be a loving mother to thousands of devotees offering solace and spiritual guidance on the path of love.

Baba once told Mrs. T., a lady from Bandra (Bombay) that he had to go thrice a day to her house. A lady of Shirdi who was present was astonished at this statement as she saw Baba daily at Shirdi. She asked

Baba, "What is this strange thing you say?" Baba turned to the Bandra lady and asked her whether what he said was not true. Did she not give him things to eat? The Shirdi lady asked the Bandra lady, 'Truly does Baba go to you and do you feed him?" The Bandra lady and her son answered in the affirmative. Baba spoke to the Shirdi lady then: "Yes, mother, I go easily to Bhav's house (i.e. Bandra House). In the middle there is a wall. Jumping over it, next comes the railway line and then Bhav's house. I have to fly across walls and excavations."

Baba once declared, "He who thinks that Baba is in Shirdi alone has totally failed to see (to know) Baba."

Baba appeared before Mahlsapathi at distant Jejuri. He told Megha that he did come into Megha's room which was bolted inside. 'Bolted doors do not bar access to me' he told him.

Baba appeared in the places of other devotees like S.B. Nachne, Mrs. Chandrabai Borkar, B.V. Dev and several others as a fakir or a sadhu. He went to Adam Dalali at Bombay in the guise of a Marwadi and asked him for food. Dalali gave him some money and sent him to a Marwadi hotel at Bandra. Later when Adam Dalali went to Shirdi, Baba said, pointing to him, 'I went to this man. He sent me to a Marwadi for food."

There are several instances which reveal the All-pervasiveness (*sarva Vyapaka* power) of Baba. Let us conclude with one striking incident (Sai Baba's Charters & Sayings, No.532).

In March 1913 Raoji Balakrishna Upasani Bahalkar's younger son had high fever for 5 or 6 days. The doctor gave up hopes. Then R.B.U. sat and prayed to Baba.

Baba appearing at 2 a.m. in his room at Dhulia and applying udhi to the boy, said, "Now, have no more anxiety. In two hours, your boy will perspire. In the morning he will feel better. After he gets well, bring him to me".

In the morning the boy was better. This was about 6-3-1913.

On 8.3.1913 Shyama wrote to Raoji: Baba said 'I have been to your Dhulia friend's house'. I asked him, 'Who is that friend?" Baba replied, 'Upasani Bahalkar Raoji. *I am daily going to his house.* You better write to him'. Therefore I have written this letter.

Fifteen days later Raoji and his son were going to Shirdi. On the way at Kopergaon the tonga driver was delaying them. At Arati time Baba told Shyama, 'Wait a bit for the Arati to start. Your Dhulia friend is coming. The tonga driver is troubling him.'

On their arrival in time for receiving *Prasad*, Baba said (to the boy): "When you were ill, I came to Dhulia. Do you remember?"

In 1968, at the time of the Golden Jubilee Celebration of Sri Sai Baba's Mahasamadhi at Chennai, we had the rare privilege of having in our midst Baba's ankita bhakta, Sri Rege Maharaj. With the presence of other Mahatmas like Pujyasri Gopalakrishna Bhagavataswami, Swami Abhedananda and Sri Purushottama Goswami Maharaj the whole atmosphere in the Sai Mandir was aflame with divine fervour. At that time Sri Rege Maharaj exclaimed, "Who says that Baba is only in Shirdi?"

Let us bow down to Sai, the *Sarvahi Vyapaka Samartha*.

WHY WORSHIP SRI SAI BABA?

(Sai Sudha – January 1966)

No doubt the name of Sri Sai Baba has become a household word and Sri Sai Baba is worshiped as Ishtadevata by thousands of devotees in India. Still the doubt whether lie is to be identified with God lingers in the minds of some. They ask, "Is he to be worshipped as God because he possessed some supernatural powers?" Sri Narasimhaswamiji has dealt with this subject and profusely answered questions of this nature in many of the articles and editorials written by him in Sai Sudha. If one glances through the pages of the four volumes of the Life of Sri Sai Baba written by the Swamiji with an unbiased and open mind, one is sure to get convinced of the divine nature of Sri Sai. According to Srimad Bhagavad Gita (Chapter X- Verse 41), "Whatever is powerful, beautiful or glorious in this world, has come forth from a fraction of the Lord's power and glory".

Many incidents narrated in the Life of Sri Sai Baba and the direct personal experiences of numerous devotees, collected and presented to us in the form of books by Sri Swamiji, reveal to us beyond any doubt that Sri Sai Baba could not be an ordinary Siddha who attracts the mass by exhibition of his powers. Many of the persons who possess and exhibit siddhis have to acquire these powers by constant religious practices and discipline. These persons do not always have these siddhis at their command and frequently they retire into solitude to accumulate their powers. In the case of Sri Sai Baba, it has not been like that; Siddhis came to Sri Sai of their own accord. Sri Sai is one who is far above all these siddhis. The epithets *siddhesai* (Lord of psychic – siddhi – powers), *siddha sankalpa* (One whose very thought becomes an accomplished fact), *siddha avangmukha* (One who is indifferent to siddhis), in Sri Sai Sahasranamavali clearly show Baba's position with regard to Siddhis. A complete chapter has been devoted to the subject of Baba and Siddhis in the fourth volume of 'Life of Sri Sai Baba'.

Baba did not perform miracles to attract crowds. After all what are miracles? If anybody does something out of the ordinary that the vast majority cannot normally do, it is termed as extra-ordinary and miraculous. If anyone is able to perform such acts often, many are attracted to him. But what remains to be seen is the purpose behind such performances of miracles. One who is not affected by praise or blame, who always lives in God and is verily a Godman, does not perform such miracles to attract people to him. By mere sankalpa, a fleeting thought in his mind can bring thousands of people to his feet. The advent of such a Mahapurusha in this world is to redeem humanity and if any time he exhibits some superhuman powers it is just in the process of fulfilment of his mission. Strongly propelled by his bargainless love for his devotees, those who look to him, the innate' daivi prakriti in him asserts itself and manifests in the form of a superhuman and supramundane act to help the devotees. Sitting in one place, he is able to see and know what transpires at distance places and hear and respond to the prayers of his devotees even though they are hundreds of miles away from him physically.

A Mahapurusha like Sri Sai continues to carry out his mission of helping his devotees even after giving up his body. He becomes one who continues to carry out the will of the Creator by remaining in a subtle form even after giving up his physical *frame Apantaratma rupena srashturishta pravartakaha* (Sai Sahasranamavali). Those who have experienced and are experiencing the continuous unfailing grace of Sri Sai, who acts in the form of apantaratma, naturally clings to him, identifies him with Parabrahman and worships him as his Ishtadevata.

It will be rather difficult, nay it is rather wasting one's precious time to try answering perverted objections born out of idle curiosity. All doubts are however dispelled very easily from the minds of serious-minded devotees and eventually they find no difficulty in identifying Sri Sai with the one whom they have been all along worshipping as Sri Rama, Sri Krishna and Sri Siva or Allah or the Christ.

SAI IS LOVE

(Sai Sudha – February 1966)

"Numerous germs abide forever on and around the cow's udder; while they suck the cow's blood they are not able to taste the sweet milk that the cow can give. Nay, they are even ignorant of the existence of such milk. But it is the person who knows and wants to draw the milk from the udder, gets the milk and tastes it. Similarly, all persons who pride themselves in having visited Shirdi many times and staying there for a number of days cannot be deemed to have enjoyed the Grace of Sri Sai Baba. One who knows what really Sai can give approaches Him in the right spirit and gets it." This is the essence of what Sri Rege Maharaj said when someone told him that he had visited Shirdi ten times.

Out of the fifty odd devotees who participated in the pilgrimage to Shirdi arranged by the All India Sai Samaj in January last, the few who had the company of Sri Rege most were doubly blessed. Every moment's stay with this great devotee of Sri Sai revealed the glory of the Master in larger and larger dimensions. How to describe the Mercy of the Lord who condescended, in the form of Sri Rege Maharaj, to take the few devotees to the various places connected with His earthly life at Shirdi! Hearing about the greatness and glory of the Master from the lips of Sri Rege Maharaj was like hearing from the Master Himself and it was by itself a unique spiritual experience. In particular, the devotees could not but feel the living presence of the Master when they stood at the Dwarakamayee (the mosque where the Master stayed during his earthly life), listening from Sri Rege with rapt attention and awe to the account of the Master's unparalleled love for His devotees.

As directed by the Master, whenever he visited Shirdi, Sri Rege stayed with Mother Radhakrishna Ayi, who was called by the Master as Ramakrishni. Sri Sai told Sri Rege, "She is my Mother and yours too". No other child's love for its mother can be more intense than that Sri Rege has for Mother Radhakrishna Ayi. Whatever advancement he has made spiritually, he owes it to his association with this Mother, Her regard for Sri Sai was unique. When the Master walked along the street passing her door, she would have His darshan through her window only, lest she might thrust her 'unholy' face before the Master! Whenever she swept the street, she used to walk backwards lest her feet might tread on the swept passage before the Master walked over it! The Master who was sending her a roti (bread) every day as Prasad would double the quota whenever Sri Rege stayed with her. Some day if the Mother got double the quota, she would understand that Sri Rege was expected to arrive shortly that day. When Sri Rege talked about the 'Mother', he was visibly moved.

The divinity of Sri Sai manifested itself more in His unequalled love for His devotees rather than in His miracles (chamatkars). How many got the benefit of this Motherly Love of the Master? The Master proclaimed, "I am keeping the treasury (spiritual) open. Come and take as much as you can," But how many really cared to take it? Most of the people came only to get their worldly desires fulfilled, to get a son, a job, relief from some ailment and so on. Those who wanted only the Master's Love did get it and their experience could not be put in words.

Once when Sri Rege was proceeding to Shirdi (perhaps on a Guru Poornima Day) he saw other devotees carrying garlands and flowers for the Master. Poor man, he forgot to buy anything. He tried to get one from his brother-devotees but failed. Feeling very sorry for his omission, he slowly walked to the Mater and bowed to Him. The Master, the Embodiment of Love, looked at him affectionately and lifting all the garlands that were put on His neck by other devotees told him, "Why are you feeling sorry, child? All these garlands are yours."

Devotees used to bring clothes to be worn by the Master. After Sri Sai wore them for some time, one of the attendants standing nearby would call out the person who brought the cloth and give it back to him. Sometime the Master used to give the cloth brought by one person to another and vice versa. Sri Rege once brought a nice Dacca muslin cloth about 5 feet square, purchased at the price of about Rs. 75/-. It was very nice and could be folded like a handkerchief. Sri Rege though that if it were true that the Master had such abounding love for him, He should wear it and should not return it. Without anyone observing, Sri Rege while bowing before the Master thrust the cloth underneath the gadi (mattress) on which Sri Sai was sitting, and walked away. After some time, Sri Sai exclaimed, "What! Something is pricking me from underneath the gadi. Please see what it is." So saying, He got up and when the gadi was removed, Sri Rege's cloth fell down. Sri Sai immediately got hold of it and said, "This is mine. I am not going to return it to anyone." He wore the cloth all along and asked everyone, "Do I not look very nice in this?" Sri Rege got reassured of the Master's love for Him.

On another occasion someone brought some red plantains and offered them to Sri Sai Baba. Sri Rege had a special liking for this variety of plantains and as the Master would normally distribute all offerings to those who were present, he thought he would get his turn and share also. But the Master peeled off the plantains one by one, distributed the fruits to all others and threw the skin to Sri Rege asking him to eat it. Hiding his mouth with a kerchief, Sri Rege without any hesitation ate away all the skins which was very bitter. But when there was only one plantain left, the Master turned to Sri Rege and told him. "What! Did I not give you any fruit? Let's both eat this fruit." Saying thus, Sri Sai asked Sri Rege to bite off one portion of the fruit and He bit off the other portion and between them they both ate one fruit. Perhaps the Master wanted to teach a valuable lesson to His ankita child, that one should not be enamoured of appearances and hanker after things! The lesson is really to us!

When Sri Rege narrated all the above and numerous other incidents tears rolled down his eyes. One could see that the Master has transfused the Love that He was and is into the veins of His devotee! If one cannot see the Master in His dear child, where else can he?

BABA DEFEATED?

(Sai Sudha – September 1966)

"There was a wrestler in Shirdi, by name Mohdin Tamboli. Baba and he did not agree on some items and both had a fight. In this Baba was defeated". – Shri Sai Satcharitra, page 26.

A genuine and natural doubt has arisen in the mind of one Sai Bhakta. When Baba's nature is divine, how could he be defeated? The ways of Great Ones like Baba are inscrutable. Neither logic nor reason can comprehend the meaning and purport of their acts. One thing we can be sure of is that whatever they do is only for the universal good, for the good of humanity as a whole and totally selfless. It will not therefore by any means be an easy task to answer why Baba happened to be defeated in a wrestling bout with Mohdin Tamboli.

In the first place whether Baba really engaged himself in a wrestling bout with Tamboli is not certain. Shri Sai Satcharitra says that it is one of the 'stories' told about Baba's early days in Shirdi. There is no authenticity about it, nor has any mention been made about this by Sri Narasimhaswamiji in any of his numerous works on Sri Sai. Granting that there is some truth and authenticity in the story, let us see what the author of Shri Sai Satcharitra writes further: "Gangagir was also very fond of wrestling. While he was once wrestling, a *similar* feeling of dispassion came over him and at the proper time he heard the voice of an adept, saying that he should wear out his body playing with God", (page 26) Gangagir was a saint who lived in Baba's time. The author of Shri Sai Satcharitra attributes Baba's defeat to a feeling of dispassion by referring to the incident of Gangagir's wrestling. This may perhaps be true also. When the wrestling was going on, the thought that it was a futile venture and that it would not help anyone in any way could possibly have crossed his mind and made him give it up and this could have been taken for a defeat.

When Mahlsapathy started worshipping Baba ritualistically, the infuriated Moslems decided to prevent him from doing so using force. Accordingly a very stout, muscular, powerful and well-built Muslim by name Tambuli and four or five others went up to the entrance to the Mosque and stood there with clubs one morning. Tambuli gave notice of their intention to Mahsapathy who was scared and did the worship to a part of the compound wall invoking Baba there! Baba understood the situation and asked Mahlsapathy to carry on the puja coming inside and thundered forth, "Let me see who will beat you". "So saying he dashed his satka, a short club, which he had in his hand on the ground with such thunderous sound that the few Muslims at the entrance trembled. They found that they would have to reckon with Baba Himself if they wished to pursue their plan, and Baba, individually and physically would be more than a match for them. Besides Baba was a weird personality who could turn water into oil and they had therefore still greater fear in trying to oppose Baba. So they considered discretion the better part of valour and retreated quietly". (*Life of Sai Baba* by H.H. Narasimhaswamiji, Vol. I, pp.30-31) 'How could Baba have been defeated by Tambuli in a wrestling?

One Rohilla (a powerful Muslim could not appreciate Baba's 'heterodox' ways in allowing Hindus to worship him in the mosque, etc., although he considered Baba to be Paygambar (God). One day it occurred to him that he should put an end to this heterodoxy by making short work of Baba. "One day as Sai Baba was going out walking, the Rohilla came up from behind with a stout club in his right hand and reached striking distance. Baba turned towards him and touching or seizing his left wrist cast a glance at him, beneath which the poor Rohilla cowered and sank like a lump of lead, - powerless to lift his club or even to lift himself. Baba left him there and went away. Later the man had to be raised up with someone's help". (*Devotees' Experiences*, Part I). If Baba could make a powerful Rohilla sink on the ground by the mere touch of a wrist, why did he allow himself to be defeated in a wrestling bout?

Baba's particular affection to Rao Bahadur H.V. Sathe aroused the jealousy of a few people, particularly one Nana Wali. One day this Nana Wali intended to manhandle Sathe with a hatchet and was standing near the entrance to the mosque awaiting the arrival of his victim. Cautioned in time by his father-in-law, Sathe left Shirdi once and for all and settled in Poona. Some people jeered at him for his continuous faith in Baba who did not protect him from the persecution of Nana Wali and others. Sathe's reply was characteristic: "I pointed out that the same argument could be used against Vittal of Pandharpur. Gangadhar Shastri, the lawyer of Gaekwad, was a Vittal Bhakta and sought help and refuge in the temple of Vittal. But there right in the temple itself, before the face of Vittal, he was murdered by his enemy. I find that leaving Shirdi and settling here at Poona ultimately have been for my good. Sai Baba is protecting me here as he did at Shirdi". (*Devotees' Experiences*, Part II). Can we conclude that Baba was unable to control Nana Wali and others?

Bayyaji Apaji Patel was a hefty man. He used to lift Baba up. He was very proud of his physique and boasted that he had the strength of Bhima. One day when massaging Baba's feet, this thought passed the mind of Bayyaji. Baba, being *sarvantaryami*, understood what was going on in Bayyaji's mind. He wanted to free Bayyaji from this pride and vanity. That night Bayyaji, as usual, tried to lift Baba up. But, lo! He could not move Baba an inch in spite of his summoning up all his energy! Sri Ṇarasimhaswamiji, therefore, hails Sri Sainath as *Balathidarpa Bayyaji mahagarva vibhanjanah* in Sahasranamavali.

We have all read and heard about the valiant death of Abhimanyu at the hands of the enemies when he fought single-handed with all the great warriors like Karna, Bhishma, Drona and others. Can we say that Krishna, the Eternal Friend and Guide of Pandavas, did not know what was in store for Abhimanyu? Why did He not save Abhimanyu?

God and Godmen accomplish what they want by mere sankalpa. Sri Krishna told Arjuna in the Gita, "I have already destroyed all these people; you just be an instrument". The same Krishna, in His dual with Kalayavana, was said to have taken to flight, chased by Kalayavana who was ultimately reduced to ashes by the King Muchukunda whose sleep was disturbed. Jarasandha invaded Mathura several times with the object of avenging Kamsa's death at the hands of Krishna. Instead of defeating

Jarasandha and killing him, Krishna settled in Dwaraka, created by His will, in the midst of the vast ocean where no enemies could come and give trouble. Will it not be silly to imagine that Krishna could not put an end to Kalayavana and Jarasandha?

Godmen like Sai Baba are *dvandvadheetha* – i.e. who are beyond the pairs of opposites, dualities, like pleasure and pain, success and failure, victory and defeat etc. It is only ordinary mortals like us who are caught in the web of dualities and struggling like a fish out of the water. In the long run it will help us a great deal to think of the Lord's leelas and teachings without wasting our time in trying to analyse same by our intellect the scope of which is limited.

BABA REINCARNTED?

(Sai Sudha – October 1966)

Doubt raises its hood in the minds of some of our members/ devotees and the All India Sai Samaj has very rightly been approached to throw some light. But this question first arose in 1944 and after making thorough enquiries and completely satisfying himself about the bonafides of those who claimed to be "Baba-reincarnates", Sri Narasimhaswamiji wrote an editorial on this subject in Sai Sudha (July 1944).

According to Sri Narasimhaswamiji, there is no question of anyone taking the place of Sri Sai Baba. Sri Sai Baba was and is present everywhere. This is felt and experienced by many even today. The chapter "Succession to Sai's Seat" in Vol.II of Life of Sai Baba by Sri Swamiji, is worth reading. This was written by him sometime in 1954. This is as much true now as it was then. Swamiji has given a firm and final reply to all doubters: "Sai's (God's) seat is never vacant. There is absolutely no question of someone else occupying Sai's seat".

This question was again put to Sri M B Rege (Retired Judge of Indore High Court), who had the privilege of sitting at the feet of Sri Sai Baba at Shirdi from 1910 to 1918. In fact Sri Rege is one who got the assurance from Baba that he would always be with Sri Rege, protecting him birth after birth. An article containing his views on this issue was published us in Sai Sudha, August 1965 already.

While we are not inclined to enter into any controversy on the merits and demerits of the persons claiming to be the incarnation of Sri Sai Baba, we make haste to set out in unambiguous terms the stand taken by the All India Sai Samaj:

1. The All India Sai Samaj has been founded to propagate the life and teachings of Sri Sai Baba, which work it has been doing for over 25 years now.
2. That Sri Sai Baba is still living and helping His devotees is the personal experience evidenced by many devotees connected with the All India Sai Samaj.
3. Following the stand taken by Sri Narasimhaswamiji, our Founder-President, the foremost among Sai's Apostles and the pioneer of Sai Movement and also the views expressed by Sri Rege, the All India Sai Samaj does not recognize a reincarnation of Sri Sai Baba in any person now.
4. Worship, however, depends essentially on one's faith. If anyone is able to see Sri Sai Baba, we see nothing wrong in that.

In conclusion we wish to reiterate that it is needless to enter into any controversy or academic or any other kind of discussions on this issue. We can only appeal to all devotees of Sri Sai Baba to cast away all their doubts and have sustained faith in the teachings of Lord Sai *who is still active and helping his devotees*. It will, however, be a great pleasure to us to answer genuine questions, if any, regarding the life and teachings of Sri Sai Baba, like the one raised and answered in the article - 'Is Baba defeated?'

QUESTIONS AGAIN

(Sai Sudha – September 1967)

Now and then questions are raised as to why Baba did such and such thing and why he did not do such and such a thing. Earlier, in an editorial of Sai Sudha we dealt with the question "why Baba allowed himself to be defeated in wrestling bout with one Tambuli, when he was divine in nature". The human intelligence can never find answers to such questions; it is never possible for the human brain to discern the purport of the actions of Avatarapurushas like Baba. But whatever they do are for the ultimate good of the devotees approaching them in particular, and to the universe in general.

When Nana Chandorkar asked Baba why calamities like the loss of his son-in-law, grandchild, etc. should befall him when he and his family were under the care of Baba, Baba replied that he could do nothing about it and for that matter, even Parameswara could not change the effect of karma. But when positive danger to life was predicted to the millionaire Buty by astrologers, Baba proclaimed, 'Let me see how Death strikes him!' and saved the devotee from being struck by a vicious serpent.

Dixit's daughter Vatsali had to die prematurely at Shirdi itself, whereas when Dixit's brother at distant Nagpur was seriously ill and Dixit was anxious that he could be of no use to his brother, Baba said, "I shall be of use (i.e. I shall save him)" and he did save him by going there at the same moment in the guise of a sadhu and administering udhi.

When some Muslims wanted to manhandle Mahlsapathy for dragging Baba into heterodox ways by worshipping him in the Hindu fashion, Baba roared waving his chatka (short staff), 'Let me see who harms you! You come inside and do puja as usual' and the frightened Muslims left the mosque. Baba even assured Mahlsapathy of permanent protection. But, Baba did not prevent Sathe from being assaulted by Nana Wali and Sathe had to run away once and for all from Shirdi and think of Baba from Pune itself.

Such paradoxical instances can be endlessly cited in recounting Baba's leelas, but one can never answer their 'whys'. The Divine Will is incomprehensible. Normally, all acts are governed by the law of karma; one enjoys or suffers according to the merit or demerit he earned in previous lives. No one denies this. But great ones like Sri Sai Baba can change even the effect of karma. Baba is *karmabeejakshayam kartha, karmanirmoolanakshamah, karmavyadhi vyapohi* and *karma bandha vinascakah*, i.e. One who destroys the very root of karma, one who can eradicate karma (altogether), removes diseases due to karma and cuts off the bondage of karma (vide Sai Sahasranamavali). As long as one has completely surrendered himself at the feet of a Samartha Sadguru like Sri Sai Baba, he need not worry in the least about the effects of karma. If one tries to find out the reasons for the actions of personages like Sri Sai Baba, not only will he find himself landed in utter confusion but also lose the essential faith.

It will therefore be wise to stop wasting our precious time in finding out answers to endless questions and pray to the Most Merciful Lord Sai to endow us with complete faith and fortitude to think of Him always.

MIRACLES AND SRI SAI BABA

(Sai Sudha – December 1967)

In the present day world we find that people in large numbers are attracted to great saints depending upon the miracles they work and paradoxically enough Sri Sai Baba's name is associated with miracles. However much spiritually advanced a saint may be, people do not generally go and fall at his feet unless he exhibits some miracles. If a person exhibits some siddhis like producing articles out of empty hands, reads the thoughts of people by clairvoyance, people generally consider him to be divine. But does divinity constitute only miracle working? Sri R R Diwakar in his foreword to "*Sources of Sai History*" (G.S. Khaparde's Shirdi Diary) writes: "Miracles, a host of them, are associated with him (Sri Sai) as are usually associated with so many saints and sadhus. But few realise that miracles are not necessarily and always the criteria of spirituality. Miracles and occult powers are quite different from spirituality. Sai Baba should not be looked upon as a mere miracle-monger nor should his name be used as a talisman for curing evils and fulfilling common and mundane desires. That would be like using Amrit for getting rid of one's cold!" Divinity asserts itself and attracts people wherever they are and does not need the medium of miracles. If a person is really divine in nature, people are attracted to him automatically as bees by the honey and iron particles by magnet. With all his spiritual attainments, Sri Narasimhaswamiji, in Life of Sai Baba (Vol.II) pronounces that mere power to read thought, mere clairvoyance and mere production of articles from empty box or hands will not constitute one into an Avatar (i.e. Divine)

Did Sai not work miracles? The answer can be 'yes' and 'no'. Sai did not work miracles as understood commonly, he actually advised persons like Khusa Bhav to abstain from exhibiting such siddhis. These miracles generally do not go farther than satisfying the curiosity of people. Sai did work some miracles which are too subtle to be understood, but which not only turned baser material into pure unalloyed gold but also empowered such converted material to transform other base materials coming into its contact as gold. Among many we shall take two instances.

Police Constable Ganapatrao Dattatreya Sahasrabuddhe did not have much faith in Baba's divinity nor did he care much for any spiritual advancement when he first came to Baba as an orderly with Deputy Collector Nana Chandorkar. The spiritual alchemist Sri Sai turned his baser nature into the gold of saintliness capable of moulding the spiritual destinies of tens of thousands by his wonderful kirtans as the famous Das Ganu. His great love to the Master rings through the arati songs sung at Shirdi such as "*Yaho yaho avaghe jana kara Babasi vandana, Ganu mhane Baba Sayee ahamva pava majhe Ayi*", i.e. All you people, come up, come up and do reverence to Sai Baba. Ganu says, "Oh Sai Baba, Mother mine, run up and catching me in your arms, caress me!"

Next is Kasinath Govinda Upasani Sastri, a most orthodox Brahmin to whom going to Sai, a Muslim Fakir, sounded repulsive. Well versed in scriptures, highly learned, his ego was too hard to melt away. But the Wondrous Master made this Sastri stay at Shirdi for three years, completely annihilated his ego and transformed him into a great spiritual dynamo to attract thousands of people and shape their spiritual lives. How Sai revealed Himself to Sri Upasani Baba during the latter's three years tutelage is brilliantly borne out in his Sai Mahimna Stotra out of which a verse which appealed to Sri Narasimhaswamiji most is given below:

Aneka ascruta atarkya leela Vilasaih Samavishkrita Iscana bhasvatprabhavam Ahambhavahinam prasanna atmabhavam Namami Iswaram Sadgurum Sainatham

"I bow to Sadguru Sainath, who is God, who manifested His divinity by many inscrutable, unheard of, miraculous leelas, who yet has no egotism and who is benignly gracious".

Instances of this nature can endlessly be recounted from the life of Sri Sai Baba. Can there be greater miracles than these? When one is attracted by a miracle like production of articles, thought reading etc., the attraction does not last long and dies as quickly as it came. But when one is attracted to a person like Sai, which can only be through *rinanubandha*, the attraction never dies as the Master absorbs the attracted person's soul unto Himself. Such a person develops a Sai-complex, becomes always Sai-conscious and nothing of the world can detract him.

BABA'S POWERS

(Sai Sudha - May 2000)

Once a Theosophical lady thought whether Baba's extraordinary powers were cases of black magic. In response Baba shouted, "Black! This is a Brahmin, a pure Brahmin, a white Brahmin. He will lead thousands on to the Subhra Marga, i.e, white or pure path (to God). No (Black) Kala Yavana can put his foot here". When Baba said "Brahmin", he could not have referred to the caste, but he was Brahman himself having realised Brahman.

Sri Narasimhaswamiji clarifies; "Baba's powers were not acquired one after another by dint of repeating mantras and going through rites intended for such acquisition. His powers were part of his nature, as developed by the Guru's grace after a course of prolonged and intense love and devotion to the Guru God. Srimad Bhagavata narrates how the saint Rishaba in proceeding with his blissful God-realisation, i.e, realisation of Vasudeva as God external to himself and as his self, developed siddhis such as (1) *duragrahana* – seeing things happening at any distance, (2) *antardhana* – sudden appearance and disappearance, (3) *manojava* – quick flash of thought, achieving all feats of intellect or reason – intuition intensified, (4) *parakayapravesa* – entering other bodies living or dead and (5) *Vaihayasa* – travelling with a physical body through air despite obstruction like walls, etc.

Baba had all the siddhis and utilised them exclusively for the welfare of mankind.

It was not the Theosophical lady referred to above alone who doubted that Baba's powers were cases of some magic. When Sri Narasimhaswamiji started publishing about Baba's lilas in an English journal in the hope that the public would be impressed and benefited, one esteemed sadhu told him that the net result of his reading was that Baba was only a son of a juggler who had various mystic powers and that there was nothing particular for one to go to Baba for, in Swamiji's own words, "When asked whether Sri Krishna's chamatkars would not be equally styled jugglery, the sadhu replied that in the case of Sri Krishna, the chamatkars were seen to be directly connected with His divinity and to be serving a divine purpose, and as these were not found in the narration of experiences in the journal the impression of jugglery was produced. Then this writer internally prayed to Baba for enlightenment, and he got an internal direction, 'Think and write in your own mother tongue, Then the writer started thinking and writing out in Tamil an account of Baba and noting step by step what Baba's spiritual and physical origins were and how powers were retained by him and utilised by him. The illumination came that Baba attained divinity by the grace of his Guru in whom his entire soul was concentrated for very long periods, not ordinarily possible to the mass of mankind or even to the mass of sadhus, and that these powers were utilised by Baba in the promotion of his activities for the benefit of humanity and not for ulterior or other purposes. Therefore it was clear to the writer that alike in the case of Sri Krishna and Sri Sai Baba, the powers resulted from divinity and were used for divine purposes."

SAI, SIDDHESA

(Sai Sudha – July 2001)

Akhanda Satchidanandah, Akilajivavatsalah and *Akhilavastuvistarah* are the first three namas in Sri Sai Sahasranamavali. The One whose nature is Supreme Bliss has appeared in the earth as Sri Sai Baba as He is kind and affectionate to all jivas. He is able to take care of all the devotees because He is All Pervasive; He pervades all animate and inanimate beings. That is *Akhilavastuvistarah*.

Sai Sahasranamavali has in the end the three namas, *Kshitipalatisevitah, Kshipraprasadadata* and *Kshetrikrutaswashirdikah*. Sri Sainatha who is Satchidanandaswarupa is worshipped even by Rulers of the country and instantly grants his blessings to his devotees. For this purpose he chose Shirdi for his stay and made it a place of pilgrimage.

Thus we see that the first three namas and the last three namas in Sahasranamavali give us a glimpse into the true nature of Sri Sai Baba and the purpose for which he took birth as Sri Sai Baba. The remaining 994 namas portray the various attributes of Sri Sai, instances as to how he gave succour to his devotees, his messages and above all his readiness to take care of all those who surrender unto him. Recital of Sai Sahasranamavali will have the effect of doing parayana of Sri Sai Satcharitra, the Life and Teachings of Sri Sai.

If we take Sai Ashtotrasata Namavali, we can see that it is an abridged version of Sai Sahasranamavali. In Ashtotra, the first name is Sri Sainatha and the last one Samartha Sadguru Sainatha. By being a Samartha Sadguru he possessed all the powers, siddhis, which were at the command of God.

Therefore, the first nama is followed by the namas Sri Lakshminarayana, Krishna Rama Siva Marutyadirupa, Sri Seshasayee. So Sri Sai is identified with the Supreme Lord, Purushottama, Sri Lakshminarayana who appeared as Sri Rama, Krishna and who is immanent in all Divine Manifestations. This Seshasayee out of love for humanity condescended to appear in the Earth and took abode at Shirdi, on the banks of Godavari, *Gotavaritatashirdikah*. While His stula sareera, physical body, dwelt in Shirdi, He, at the same time, dwelt and continues to dwell even after His Maha-samadhi, in the hearts of His devotees, nay, in the hearts of all! Not only *Bhaktahrudalayah*, but also *sarvahrudvasi* and *bhutavasi*.

How did Baba get his powers, siddhis! Writes Sri Narasimhaswamiji, "His Guru had divine powers in him, and by saktinipata, at the time of parting from him, the Guru had passed them over to Baba either potentially or in full force, or perhaps partly potentially and partly in full force. He could involve the Guru's own power to raise the dead as he did about the time when he parted from his Guru". But Baba did not choose to display his powers because, there was nothing to be gained by him by a display of powers, for his desires were all controlled, and his barest necessities were met by his going about with his begging bowl in the streets, and, from there calling out for roti or dhall, and returning to the Masjid which gave him shelter". He observed his duties and observances as a Yati (a hermit) very well, *yatidharmasupalakah*. His senses, mind and intellect were firmly restrained, *yatendriyamanbuddhih* Sri Swamiji writes that all siddhis or powers were at Baba's command and formed a full panoply and perfect equipment for his work as Samartha Sadguru for those whom he wishes to lead on their path to God. 32nd stanza in chapter XV, Ekadasa Skanda of Srimad Bhagavata clarifies this.

Jitendriyasya dantasya Jitasvasa atmano maneh
maddharanam dharyatah Ka sa siddhih sudurlabah

Sri Krishna says, "What power is beyond the reach of the sage who has controlled his mind, senses, nerve currents and disposition, and concentrates on Me?" Sri Swamiji elucidates: "Whether it is the Krishna form or Guru form or any other form, God is one and the same. The only requisite is that the concentration should be powerful and prolonged so as to bring on the properties of the contemplated form on the contemplating soul".

Bow to Samartha Sadguru Sri Sainath, Siddhesa!

BHAVA AND ANUBHAVA

(Sai Sudha – June 2010)

Jaya mani jaisa bhava
Taya taisa anubhava
Davisi dayagana

"You grant experience suited to each one's faith and mental attitude. Such is your way, O Merciful one". – From Arati song by Madhav Adkar.

Thousands of devotees approached Sri Sai Baba. Let us leave alone the vast majority whose approach was only to have some material want or desire fulfilled. There were some who came to Sai with a spiritual bent of mind. They wanted to have a glimpse of the Master's Divinity and gain some push in their spiritual progress. For them the Master was gracious enough to grant experience suited to each one's bhava, mental attitude or standing.

Dr. Pandit had intense devotion to his Guru Raghunath, a sage from Bhopeshwar, popularly known as 'Kaka Puranik'. When Dr. Pandit accompanied Dada Bhat on his way to Dwarakamayi to offer Pooja to Sri Sai, he abruptly took away the plate containing the Pooja materials from Bhat's hands, took sandal from the plate and drew three parallel lines (tripuntra) on Baba's forehead. Till then no one was allowed to apply sandal or kumkum on Baba's forehead. Why did Baba give this privilege to Dr. Pandit? At the sight of Baba Dr. Pandit felt that it was his own Brahmin Guru Kaka Puranik of Dhopeshwar who was seated in the mosque; he, therefore, unhesitatingly applied Tripundra with sandal on Baba's forehead as he usually did for his own Guru. Baba, in appreciation of this devotee's bhava, appeared to him in the form of his own Guru and also graciously condescended to his applying *Tripundra* on his forehead, breaking away from the normal practice.

Mule Sastry was a very orthodox Brahmin. He was staying in the wada; he took his bath, wore the special silk cloth (*Madi Vastra*) and started doing Agnihotra. At the same time, Baba who was on his way to Lendi said enigmatically that he would like to wear Geruva (saffron-coloured) cloth. Who could fathom the meaning of Baba's words! At the time of Arati, Jog asked Mule Sastry to accompany him to the Masjid. Sastry who had his bath and wore silk cloth was of the opinion that going out and mixing with people could cause pollution and harm his purity. He told that he would have darshan later in the afternoon. Just before commencement of Aarti, Baba wanted Dakshina to be got from the newly arrived Brahmin (Mule Sastry) and brought to him; Buty Saheb undertook this errand. Mule Sastry's mind wavered. 'Why should an agnihotri, a pure Brahmin, give Dakshina?' Nevertheless, Mule Sastry accompanied Buty, with Dakshina, to the masjid. When he stood at a distance and threw flowers at Baba's feet so that his purity might not be affected, he had a wonderful experience. In the gadi, it was his own Guru Golap Maharaj in saffron clothing and saffron upper garment worn by a Sanyasi; Baba was not seen. Gholap Maharaj seated in a Masjid! Sastry ran forward and fell at his feet. Baba assumed the form of Sastry's Guru who had long before attained Samadhi, thus giving him anubhav (experience) as per his *bhava*.

There are other instances that one read in books on Sri Sai Baba where Baba appeared as Rama, Krishna and Vithala satisfying the particular devotee's Bhava. It was similar to Sri Krishna and Sri Rukmini giving darshan to Anjaneya as Sri Rama and Sita Devi to fulfil the wish of the foremost among Sri Rama Bhaktas.

However those are all episodes that we read from the various books written on Sri Sai. This writer had the privilege of witnessing directly an incident where Baba appeared in different forms, nearly thirty two years after his Mahasamadhi. It is a pleasure to share this experience with other Sai devotees.

It was sometime in 1960. There was a grand Divyanama Sankirtana in the Sai Mandir at All India Sai Samaj, Mylapore, conducted by Pujyasri Gopalakrishna Bhagavataswami in which several eminent Bhagavatas

from Chennai participated. In those days, in front of the shrine, the hall had only a zinc sheet roofing open on all sides. In the outer wall of the main shrine on top a picture of Baba was kept; *this picture had the figures of Rama, Krishna, Siva and Maruti at the back of Baba's figure (*Krishna-Rama-Siva- Marutyadi Roopah*). When the Namasankirtan reached a crescendo, producing an aura of thrill, the whole atmosphere became charged with devotional fervour. Sri Bhagavataswami, who was chanting the Nama ecstatically dancing suddenly lost consciousness and went into a divine stupor; after a few minutes he regained his composure. The next day during a conversation with him, when asked about the rapturous experience he had in the previous night during the Bhajan, he said: "While singing, I was looking at Baba's picture on top; suddenly I saw Baba coming down towards me, followed by Rama, Krishna, Siva, Maruthi. I was overwhelmed by that wonderful sight and became oblivious of the surroundings, of the whole world."

Sri Narasimhaswamiji hails Baba himself as a Mahabhagavata. Baba loved bhajans, music and dance. It is, therefore, not surprising that he enjoyed the enchanting bhajan of the foremost of Bhagavatas in the Twentieth Century and was gracious enough to give him darshan as *Krishna-Rama-Siva-Marutyadi Roopah* Sai. The devotees who were privileged to be present at that time had the unique experience of enjoying a sort of spiritual ecstasy, albeit for a very short period. That was the benefit of being in satsang, being in the company of a Mahabhagavata in a hall sanctified by a great tapasvi Sri Narasimhaswamiji, in the divine presence of his Master Samartha Sadguru Sainath Maharaj.

Sri Sai continues to attract devotees of various sorts, gives them experiences suited to their mental attitude and helps them in their progress on the spiritual path.

---

* When the main hall was provided with pucca RCC roofing in 1966, this picture was shifted to the rear of the shrine under the Aswatta-Neem tree, kept in a niche specifically built.

SRI SAI BABA'S NATURE - I

(Sai Sudha – August 2002)

When Sri Narasimhaswamiji started Sai Prachar, he was writing articles in English in Newspapers like "Sunday Times". He was also giving lectures at various places, which covered mostly the wonderful lilas and chamatkars of Sri Sai Baba and the benefits he conferred and continues to confer on those who approach him. When Sri Swamiji was staying in Sri Ramakrishna Paramahamsa's Ashram (some time during 1936 to 1937), the President of the Ashram once declared that he could not understand how Sai Baba went on like a juggler performing miracles and what the use of all that was, and what Baba could be supposed to be teaching. He also asked what Baba's marga might be. Swamiji was puzzled and mentally appealed to the Master to throw light and answer the questions. With Baba's help, thoughts were rearranged and aspects of Baba were revealed to him in a harmonious connection; then the truth gradually dawned upon the Swami that Baba was a teacher of the highest sort and trainer also, and not merely a teacher by utterances, but a Bhagavatothama, a Samartha moulding the completely dedicated and surrendered devotees so as to turn their souls into his own likeness.

When we read the four volumes of Life of Sri Sai Baba and other literature, a veritable treasurehouse bequeathed to spiritual aspirants as a whole, not merely to Sai devotees, by Sri Narasimhaswamiji, we can find the authority, the basis, for his conclusion and conviction that Sai is Divine, a Great Sage, that he is primarily what Sri Krishna spoke to Arjuna, the Bhagavad Gita – and to Uddhava – The Uddhava Gita in the Ekadasa

Skanda of Srimad Bhagavata. We can also see that Swamiji has quoted as authority profusely from the Vedas, Upanishads, Puranas, the Guru Gita and other works to substantiate his view. From a study of the Ekadasa Skanda or Krishna Uddhava samvadha or Uddhava Gita in Srimad Bhagavata, 11th Canto, Swamiji discovered that Baba was the same as Sri Krishna. He discovered the answers to the posers and conundrums put to him. He discovered that Baba's teaching is the same as the teaching of Sri Krishna in Bhagavad Gita and in Uddhava Gita. Sri Swamiji says: "Studying these Gitas one sees that there is no meaning in any one marga expounded by the Divine Person. Saints expound all the margas and find which marga or combination of which margas would suit each approaching devotee, and give the same to him". Swamiji further writes: "As a result of study, aided by His own grace, one sees at last that he was an adept of all the margas, though his chief marga was the Bhakti marga, that special form of it that is described as 'Guru Marga' in the Guru Gita, and that jnana and siddhis including yoga siddhis came in the wake of Guru Bhakti".

The highest form of Guru bhakti, absolute surrender to the Guru, pure unalloyed bargainfree love to the Guru, selfless dedicated service to the Guru, endowed Baba with all divine powers or siddhis, which he used from time to time to help the devotees who came to him for relief. Baba helped people in worldly matters so as to infuse faith in them and gradually turn them in the spiritual path. Sri Swamiji says that as stated by Sri Krishna in Chapter 15 of Ekadasa Skanda of Srimad Bhagavata, all the siddhis in their entirety wait upon the sage who worships Him through yogic concentration. "What is the siddhi which is unattainable by a sage who, having conquered his senses, tamed his mind and controlled his breath and body, concentrates on Me?" asks the Lord. The Lord further emphatically declares that He is the Source (bestower), the Custodian and Controller of all Siddhis (*sarvasamapi siddhinam hetuh patiraham prabhuh*). Though Baba was seen to be engaged in worldly activities, He was always in Krishna- Consciousness. Though he was seen to be moving amidst objects of the senses, Baba had neither attraction nor revulsion to sense objects, and had attained tranquility. Baba is hailed as ragadvesha viyuktatman (Bhagavad Gita 11-64). Baba was one of those rare Great Ones, who endowed with divine virtues, could understand Sri Krishna to be the Immutable and Source of all beings and adore Him with undistracted mind.

Mahatmanastu mam partha daivim prakritim ascritah
Bhajantyananya manasa jnatva bhutadi mastyayam

(Bhagavad Gita, Chapter IX – 13)

Baba was endowed with daivi sampath (divine heritage) – *daiveesampat prapoornah.* In verses 1 to 3 of Bhagavad Gita, Chapter 16, the nature of one who is endowed with *daivi sampath* is described as: Fearlessness, purity of heart, steadfast in knowledge and devotion, benevolence, control of the senses, worship, study of scriptures, austerity, uprightness, Non-violence, truthfulness, freedom from anger, renunciation, tranquility, aversion to slander, compassion to living beings, freedom from sensuality, gentleness, modesty, steadfastness; vigour, patience, fortitude, purity, harmlessness; freedom from vanity – all these are the gifts with which a person of *daivi sampath* are endowed with.

SRI SAI BABA'S NATURE - II

(Sai Sudha – September 2002)

Whoever delights in the Self (Atman) alone, is content and satisfied in the Self, for him there is no obligatory duty to discharge (Gita III – 17). Baba was *atmanubhava santushtah* (delighted with the realization of Self); *atmavidya viscaradah* (well versed in the Science of Knowledge – Jnana Yoga); *atmananda prakascah* (beaming with the Bliss of being one with Atman). Baba's nature being such, he had no object to gain in this world by action nor had he anything to lose by abstaining from action; he was not obliged or indebted to any created being for anything (Gita III – 18). Sri Krishna tells Arjuna, "In all the three worlds there is nothing that binds Me as duty; I have nothing to gain nor is there anything that I cannot gain. Yet I am always engaged in action". Sri Krishna says that if He were not to work, all the worlds would have perished. Therefore, out of *daya* or compassion for the jivas, the Lord is engaged in work. Baba was doing the same. He was the repository of all auspicious qualities having become one with the Paramatma and he had nothing to gain by action. Yet, out of compassion for mankind, Baba ceaselessly worked for their redemption, for giving them the much sought after relief. Baba is *avaapta sarva kamo api karmanyeva pratishtitah* (continues in action, though he has nothing to gain, having attained everything).

Sri Krishna says, "One's own duty, though devoid of merit, is better than the duty of another well performed. Even death in the performance of one's own duty brings blessedness; another's duty is fraught with fear" (Gita III – 35). Baba exhorted many of the devotees who came to him to stick to their own *dharma* (be it Hinduism, Christianity or Islam) and cautioned them against the danger of switching over to some other *dharma*, i.e. conversion. Baba is hailed as "*screyan svadharma ityuktva sva sva dharma niyojakah*" and "*paradharma bhayat bhaktan sve sve dharma niyojakah*" (one who made each devotee stick to his own faith as change of faith is dangerous). "Better is one's own dharma, though devoid of merit, than the dharma of another well-performed; for, performing the duty ordained by his own natural evolution is good" – Gita XVIII – 47.

Baba was a Karma Yogi par-excellence, conforming fully to the yardsticks prescribed by Sri Krishna in Chapter IV of Bhagavad Gita. Baba is *karma akarma vichakshanah* – one who discerns what is fruitful action and what is baneful action; *kamasankalpa varjitah* and *jnanagnidagdha karmanah* – the Sage whose undertakings are all free from desire and thoughts of the world, and whose actions are burnt up by the fire of wisdom. Baba is *tyakta karma phalasangah* – has given up attachment to actions and the fruits that accrue therefrom; *nitya truptah* – is ever satisfied and content and *nirascrayah* – free from expectations; *niraasci* – free from cravings; *tyakta sarva parigraha* – renounced ownership to all possessions. Being content with whatever comes his way unsought (*yadruchcha labha santushtah*), he is *dwandvatheetah* (transcended the pairs of opposites).

In Verse 34 of Chapter IV of Gita, Krishna advises Arjuna to approach illumined souls – jnanis, prostrate at their feet, render them service and question them with an open and guileless heart; these seers of Truth will instruct on the Right Knowledge. Baba expounded in detail to Nana Chandorkar the correct interpretation of Sri Krishna's advice. Baba is a jnani, a *tatvadarsin* (an illumined Soul, a Seer of Truth) referred to by Sri Krishna. He is *jnana sanchchinnah samscyah* – a Karma Yogi whose doubts have been torn to shreds by Right Knowledge or wisdom.

Baba is hailed as *sarvabhutatma bhutatma* (one who had identified his soul with the souls of all beings). "Baba had achieved that position and he declared that he was the *antaryami* of all creatures. He was coaching up his best disciples to view him as the *antaryami* of themselves and of all others, and gradually to deem themselves also the *antaryami* of all, just as Baba is the *antaryami* of all. By constantly thinking of Baba as the antaryami of all, the devotee becomes the *antaryami* of all", writes

Sri Narasimhaswamiji. Like Sri Krishna, Baba is *antaryami, antaratma* of all living beings.

In verses, 30, 31 and 32 of Chapter VI of Gita, the Lord says: "He who sees Me (the Universal Self) present in all beings, and all beings existing within Me, never lose sight of Me, and I never lose sight of him. The highest of Yogis is one who is established in union with Me, and worships Me as antaryami of all beings, always abides in Me, who looks on all equally, identifying himself with others, and looks upon the joy and sorrow of all with equal vision". Baba is, therefore, deemed to be the highest of Yogis, yogiraja. As stated earlier in the same chapter by Sri Krishna, Baba is *vidya vinaya sampoornah* (his vast knowledge is clothed in absolute humility); *sarva bhuta hite ratah* (always keen on the welfare of all beings); *jitatmanah* (conquered the Self); *seethoshna sukha dukheshu samah* (unperturbed by heat or cold); *maanapamaanayos tulyah* (unmoved by honour or ignominy); *jnana vijnana truptatmah* (his mind is sated with jnana – knowledge of Nirguna Brahman and vijnana – knowledge of saguna Brahman); *samaloshtashaa kanchanah* (to him earth, stone and gold are all alike, being a God-realised soul). He is kutasthah (tranquil being the antaratma of all); *prasantatma* (always steeped in serenity) and *brahmachari vrate sthitah* (firmly established in the vow of continence). Thus, Sri Sai Baba, as Sri Krishna said, always remained in Eternal Bliss of being one with Brahman; always merged in identity with the all–pervading Infinite Consciousness, seeing unity everywhere (in diversity), this Yogiraja could behold the Self present in all beings, and all beings within His own Self. Chapter VI of Gita concludes with the Lord's proclamation that, "Of all Yogis, the one who devoutly worships Me with his mind focused on Me is considered by Me to be the best among Yogis". Baba is *sakshatkruta hari preetya sarva scakti yutah* (endowed with all powers, siddhis, by Sri Hari, i.e. Sri Krishna, who appeared before him being pleased with his nama japa).

KSHETRIKRUTASVA SHIRDIKAYA NAMAH

(Sai Sudha – September 2004)

Pranams to the One that made Shirdi a Kshetra or a place of pilgrimage. The Sai Sahasranamavali concludes with this epithet.

A little known Fakir transforms a little-known hamlet into one of the largest pilgrim centres of the country, a veritable paradise on earth for millions of ardent devotees.

Before acquiring this unique status, the tiny village had only 80 to 100 mud houses, occupied by unsophisticated, poor and simple folk, mostly Hindus and a few Muhammadans. It had absolutely no religious merit, no significant place of worship to attract people. The Maruti temple next to the mosque, a mud and brick temple of Vittal in the heart of the village and the Khandoba temple outside the village, all mud and brick construction, are the only religious buildings.

In this obscure village in the early part of Nineteenth century a youthful nondescript fakir entered with a marriage party. The nameless lad was christened 'Sai' as he was so invited into the village by Mahlsapathi. That this place would be chosen as abode by a great Mahapurusha should have been known to all holy men and sadhus of the day. Devidas came into Shirdi well in advance. Sai enjoyed his company. He was then joined by another sage, Janakidas. Gangagir, a famous Vaishnavite house-holder saint from Puntambe was a regular visitor to Shirdi seeking the company of Sai. It was he who first proclaimed, "It is the good fortune of Shirdi that this precious gem has associated itself with Shirdi. Blessed is the soil of Shirdi on which he has set his foot".

Another saint Anandnath of Yeola, a disciple of the great saint Akkalkot Maharaj, who came to Shirdi, on seeing Sai, exclaimed, "This is indeed a diamond, a real diamond. Though today he is seen to be lying on garbage heap, it is not just a flint but a diamond".

Sri Sai Baba's perfect purity, asceticism, general benevolence, harmlessness, non-attachment and other virtues evoked the respect of the saints Devidas, Janakidas, Gangagir, Anandanath, Bidkar, etc. The villagers of Shirdi, in general, considered him to be a pagal fakir, except noble souls like Mahsapathy, Appa Bhil and Tukaram Darji, who regarded Baba as a saint, an Acharya or Guru Deva, long before he exhibited any siddhi power.

The villagers of Shirdi recognized the saintliness, the divinity, in the mad fakir after they chanced to witness the chamatkar unintentionally performed by him in lighting the lamps in the mosque with water instead of oil and making them glow for long hours. Even today with a very high degree of scientific evolution and the growing tendency to perceive things rationally, many highly educated persons – professors, lawyers, doctors, engineers and the like – assess the greatness of a Messiah like Sri Sai only after they come across a chamatkar or superhuman event. This fact can be substantiated by the large number of articles appearing in various journals and magazines, contributed by people from such higher echelon of society. These miracles or chamatkars, the out-of-the-ordinary acts by a person alone cannot form the basis to call him a Mahapurusha, a chalthe bolthe god, walking talking god. These are only sparks. What is the real nature of the Divinity that took residence in Shirdi? How powerful is that Divine Nature to make that place of residence a Kshetra or a place of pilgrimage? What made Sri Sai to make his residence holy – thirtheekrutha nivasah?

The greatest service that Sri Narasimhaswamiji has done to spiritual aspirants is his thorough and analytical exposition of the various religious texts that establish beyond doubt that Sri Sai Baba is just not one more saint, but an Avatara Varishta, Divinity descended on earth with a specific mission, the Mission of Love and Harmony, Peace and Amity. Every devotee who desires to see the real Divinity shining forth as Sai Baba should read at least the Life of Sai Baba and the Glimpses of Sai Baba written by Sri Narasimhaswamiji.

SAI, THE MOTHER

(Sai Sudha – January 2008)

"Man is bound to make mistakes. One should not notice them. If one does not follow this rule, it harms oneself alone. By constantly observing the faults of others, in the end one will become a mere fault-finder" said Holy Mother Sarada Devi. On another occasion she declared, "The Master used to say, 'Look upon people as worms'. By this he did not mean all kinds of men. He was referring only to faultfinders and people of mean tendencies".

Sri Sai, the Mother, revealed the same loving nature of the Holy Mother. When a devotee of Baba was reviling another behind the back, Baba went out and met him near Lendi. Baba asked him what he was seeing there. The man replied 'a pig'. Baba then asked him what it was doing. 'Eating filth' was the answer. Baba then told him, "You see with what gusto the pig is gorging itself on night soil. Behold how it revels on human ordure. But we feel it disgusting. That is your conduct. People fret and fume against their own brethren and kinsmen to their hearts' content. After performing many deeds of merit, one is born a man. Is he to go to Shirdi and yet commit moral suicide?"

One devotee was indulging in idle gossip, scandalising the conduct of other people. Baba summoned him and admonished him, "The good and the wicked alike come here. Why draw their frailties and foibles to public notice by depicting them?" A mother shows no distinction in her love and affection towards her children, both good and bad. Baba exhibited this mother's nature on several occasions.

Baba repeatedly advised his devotees to be patient and tolerant. "If you avoid rivalries and bickerings, God will protect you. Return not evil for evil. Return good for evil. Others' words cannot pierce you", said Sai.

Mother Sarada Devi once said, "Women should not get angry so easily. They must practise forbearance. In infancy and childhood their parents are their only protection and in youth their husbands. Women are generally very sensitive. A mere word upsets them. And words also are so cheap now-a-days. They should have patience and try to put up with parents or husbands in spite of difficulties".

Baba's advice to Mrs. M.W. Pradhan, who was wanting in patience, was, "If anyone talks ten words of us, let us reply with one word – if we reply at all; and do not quarrel or vie with anyone in order not to be outdone".

Another intimate devotee of Baba, Purandhare says: "I was very passionate, i.e. hot-tempered. Baba told me often, "if anybody comes and abuses you or punishes you, do not quarrel with him. If you cannot endure it, speak a simple word or two or else go away from the place. But do not battle with him and behave like that. I feel sick and disgusted when you quarrel with others'. He said this to me and to others also several times".

Mrs. Chandrabai Borkar, talking about Baba's compassionate nature, says, "Sai Baba has often said that we should not harbour feelings of hatred against any, nor entertain feelings of envy, rivalry or opposition or a combative disposition towards others, and if others hated us, we should simply take to nama-japa and avoid them".

From the experiences narrated by several contemporary devotees of Sai Baba, one can see what motherly care and love he showered on his devotee-children. Mrs. Tarabai Sadasiv Tarkhad, a recipient of that love declares, "It is not merely his power that endeared him to his devotees. His loving care combined with those powers made Shirdi a veritable paradise to the devotees who went there. Directly we went there, we felt safe, that nothing could harm us. Is this not the feeling of a child when it is with its mother?"

Baba did not like his devotees to be haughty and be rude to others. When Ramadasi got wild on hearing Baba had given his sahasranama book to Shama and abused Shama very rudely accusing him of having stealthily taken his book through Baba when he was away, Baba reprimanded the Ramadasi strongly. "Why are you always ready to fight? Can you not speak soft and sweet words? Every day you read the Adhyatma Ramayana and recite the Sahasranama. Yet you have not discarded your passions which are uncontrolled. And you call yourself Ramadasi!" "A true Ramdasi should have no attachment but look at the young and old with equality. You are harbouring enmity for this boy and coming to blows for this book!"

Mother Sarada Devi, the personification of the compassion of Guru Maharaj, Sri Ramakrishna, very endearingly exhorts her children to eschew rude talk, "Should one speak such words as would hurt the feelings of another? Even if it is truth, it should not be told in an unpleasant manner. Finally, you will end up with that kind of nature. If one's sensitivity is lost, then nothing will control one's speech. The Master used to say, 'if you have to ask a lame man how he became lame, you must only say: How did your leg get bent this way'?"

As a universal Mother, Baba showed the same uniform love, affection and consideration to the devotee-children of different faiths, different communities and different dispositions. It is the Mother's Nature of Sri Sai Baba that could bring together into a homogenous group called "Sai devotees" people belonging to the two major communities, Hindus and Muslims at Shirdi. As it would be the endeavor of every mother to foster love and affection among her children, Baba's mission also was to see that all his devotees show love and affection to each other.

Hail Mother Sai!

BABA: HINDU OR MUSLIM?

(Sai Sudha – March 2008)

In connection with a suit, once Sri Ramana Maharshi was examined on commission. One question was "To which asramam does Sri Bhagavan belong? Bhagavan Ramana's reply was "Atiasramam" (beyond the four stages). *Bhagavan* further explains that it is beyond the four commonly known *asramams (Brahmacharya, Grihasta, Vanaprasta and Sanyasa*).

Nearly three weeks later, a devotee goes on raising questions seeking clarification about '*atiasrama*' referred to by Sri Ramana Maharshi. Is there any authority for it? Is it mentioned anywhere? "Yes", replies *Bhagavan*, "in the Upanishads, the Suta Samhita (Skanda Purana), Bhagavata, Bharata and other works". Is there any *Karma* for them? *Bhagavan* says, "Their conduct is not regulated according to rules or codes". Is there a Guru for *atyasrami*? "Yes", says *Bhagavan*, "The SELF is my Guru" and adds that the Guru may be internal or external and he may reveal Himself internally or communicate externally.

Sri Sai Baba is also an '*atyasrami*'. He does not belong to any of the four commonly known asramas. When he was first noticed in Shirdi, he could not be classified under any of the four known asramas, nor afterwards till his Mahasamadhi. As Bhagavan Ramana clarified, Baba's conduct was not regulated according to any rules or codes. From what Baba was saying, it was assumed that Baba had a Guru and he could be Venkusa or Roshanshah. It can at best be a conjecture only. May be for Baba also, the Self was his Guru and for him the Guru could have been internal or external; he could have revealed himself internally or communicated externally.

Bhagavan Ramana came to Tiruvannamalai as a lad of sixteen to be transformed into a Maharishi. No external Guru, and as stated by him his "Self" was his Guru, he realized his Guru and he got himself merged in his Guru, The Self. Perhaps, considering this only Sri Narasimha Swamiji gave the title "Self Realisation" to the biography of Sri Ramana Maharishi authored by him.

In the vast literature created by Sri Narasimha Swamiji, in one place he says that Sri Sai Baba was also an *atyasrami*. Baba also appeared in Shirdi as a lad of about sixteen, clad like a youthful Moslem Fakir.

Was Baba actually a Muslim or was he a Hindu? Baba never liked any devotee of his to entertain this question. What does it matter whether he was Hindu or a Muslim, when he was accepted as a Samartha Sadguru, a Godman or an Avatar of God. When obstinate people persisted with their 'research' on this aspect, one day in the year 1916 Baba grew angry and expressed his total resentment at such behaviour in a peculiar way, as narrated by no less a person than Anna Saheb Dabholkar in "Sri Sai Satcharitra" – Chapter 42.

In the year 1916, at the time of Seemolanghan of the Dasara festival, when the procession returned in the evening, this strange incident happened. The clouds thundered in the sky and on and off lightning struck. In that manner, Baba manifested as a real incarnation of Jamadagni. Untying the piece of cloth from his head, removing the *Kafni* suddenly, taking off the loin cloth, threw them all in the *dhuni* which blazed into flames. The fire was already very bright and when it was fed by these offerings, it became more brilliant. The upsurge of flames rose high and mighty, and cracked loudly. The devotees were confused. All this happened unexpectedly. It was difficult to know what Baba had in mind. His way of behaviour at the time of Seemolanghan was very frightening. The fire's brilliance increased. But Baba appeared more lustrous than the fire. The people's eyes were dazzled and they averted their faces.

Agninarayan, Lord of the Fire, was propitiated by this offering at the hands of the saint. Blessed were the eyes that beheld the Digambar Jamadagni! He glared with his eyes, red with anger. He said 'Decide for yourself now, whether I am a Muslim or a Hindu; In a thundering voice Baba said: 'Look! Decide today itself whether I am a Hindu or a Muslim, unrestrainedly, and remove all your doubts'.

Because of the uncertainty about the community to which Baba belonged, some prominent Hindu devotees had to miss the opportunity of taking Baba's tirtha or Prasad. It was the physical appearance of Baba, like a Muslim Fakir seated at a Mosque, that caused some repulsion in the minds of some Hindu devotees even though they felt that Baba was a saint who could help them. Prejudices die hard, says Narasimha Swamiji.

Sri Rege, an intimate devotee of Baba who had no such reservations about his Master writes: "To me he had no limitations. Of course, when he was with us, there was the fleshy tabernacle. That was prominently brought to our notice at times. But mostly the infinite aspect of this was what remained before me ……. . Now that the body has been cast off, the infinite alone remains as 'Sai Baba'

One essential truth about Sri Sai Baba, a unique world teacher, if borne in mind by every Sai devotee, will be of immense benefit in spiritual march. Baba belongs to no particular community and Baba belongs to all communities, the whole universe. A Hindu can approach Him in a Hindu way, Moslem in his own manner and a Christian as per his tradition. There is nothing wrong if a Hindu is of the conviction that Baba is a Hindu Saint, but it will be totally wrong to expect a Muslim to accept that, because a Muslim has every reason to be convinced that Baba was a Moslem Fakir. Here again he should not try to impose that conviction on a Hindu or Christian.

SAI, SARVADEVASWARUPA

(Sai Sudha – August 2000)

The month Sravan (according to Chandramana Year) is replete with festivals, Sri Krishna Jayanthi. Sri Vinayaka Chaturthi. Sri Varalakshmi Vrata being some important ones.

All the festivals are celebrated with delight and devotion by devotees of Sai since Baba identified himself with all forms of the Lord.

A Bandra lady on her first visit to Shirdi was told by Baba that he was being fed by her for several years. To the lady who replied that it was her first visit to Shirdi, Baba said that he had been seeing her ever since her infancy. The lady was greatly puzzled. Baba asked the lady what worship she had in her house and earlier in her mother's house. The lady answered that she had been worshipping Ganapathi, giving as offerings flowers, fruits and eatables. Baba told her that all those offerings had come to him and since her childhood he had been seeing her. Thus he identified himself with Ganapathi.

Sometime in May 1914 when Mrs. Tendulkar, a Bandra lady, came to Shirdi with her son, Baba told her that he had to go to her house in Bandra thrice a day. A local lady who was present was astonished since she had never seen Baba leaving Shirdi at any time. Baba said, "I never speak falsehood. I am Mahalakshmi. I come to your house and you offer me things to eat, is that not true?" This shows that Baba was referring to the puja done by the Bandra lady at her house thrice a day.

Similarly Baba had shown to different devotees that he was Krishna, Siva, Maruti, Dattatreya and other forms of God. A true devotee of Sri Sai gets convinced that when he had Baba's darshan he had the darshan of his own Ishtadevata.

Baba called the mosque he was dwelling in as Mother Dwaraka (Dwarakamayi). Sri Krishna was born in Mathura, brought up in Brindavan (Gokula) and created Dwaraka as His abode. Sri Sai is said to have been born in Patri village, was moulded by his Guru Venkusa in Selu and chose Shirdi village as his abode. In Shri Sai Satcharitra a view is taken that Shirdi itself could be part of Dwaraka. "Mr. B. V. Dev, retired Mamlatdar of Thana has proved by his researches that Shirdi comes in the limits of Pandharpur which was the southernmost centre of Dwaraka and therefore, Shirdi was Dwaraka itself." Baba had appeared as Vittal to some devotees.

To the devotee Uddhavesa Bua, Baba gave advice to follow what instructions he had given (as Krishna) to Uddhava, that is in the Ekadasa Skanda of Srimad Bhagavata. By meditating on Baba's form and by offering Puja to Baba, a devotee can please Sri Krishna.

It is worth contemplating on what is narrated with conviction in Shri Sai Satcharitra.

"Lord Shri Krishna has said to Uddhava in the Bhagavat that the saints are His living forms; and see what Baba has said for the welfare of his devotees; "Those who are fortunate and whose demerits have vanished, take you over the seven seas; believe in these words and you will be certainly benefited. I do not need any paraphernalia of worship – either eight-fold or sixteen-fold. I rest there where there is full devotion".

SAI KRISHNA

(Sai Sudha – September 1999)

How Sri Sai gave his unique interpretation to one of the verses in Srimad Bhagavad Gita to his devotee Nana Chandorkar is well known. When Nana requested Baba to help him in understanding the entire Gita, Baba advised him to do Gita parayana in his presence. The mere presence of Baba had the power to transmit the right knowledge to the devotee. Baba is hailed as *gitapoornopadesakah, gitacharya* and *gita-adbhuta varaha* in Sri Sai Sahsranamavali.

From time to time Baba exhorted many of his devotees to take to the study of Gita. He advised some devotees to do parayana of Ekadasa Skanda (eleventh canto) of Srimad Bhagavata which enshrines the famous Uddhava Gita, Sri Krishna's exposition to His devotee Uddhava. When asking his devotee Uddhavesa Bua to study Ekadasa Skanda, Baba said, "Read what I had spoken to Uddhava". This reveals the identity between Sri Krishna and Baba.

Baba's advice to some devotees to do Bhagavata Saptaha Parayana is very significant. Srimad Bhagavata is considered to be the most sacred among all the works of Sage Vyasa. Parayana of this sacred grantha stimulates deep devotion to Sri Krishna. Baba is *bhaktimargapradarsakah* (one who expounds the path of devotion).

Bhishma Pitamah who had realised that Sri Krishna was the Supreme Divinity, from his death-bed revealed the greatness of Sri Krishna to Pandavas in the form of Vishnu Sahasranama. Baba attached utmost importance to Vishnu Sahasranama parayana.

It is said that when Baba first came to Shirdi he appeared like a lad of seventeen. His earlier life is shrouded in mystery and could only be inferred from his utterances on various occasions. Baba's life in Shirdi is known fairly authentically. After coming to Shirdi, Baba did not engage himself in any scriptural studies. Then how did he gain mastery over Gita, Bhagavata and other scriptures? Baba himself answered this question. He served his Guru with steadfast devotion to Guru for twelve years. His Guru did not blow any mantra into his ears. He meditated upon nothing but the Guru and had no goal or object other than the Guru. To Baba Guru was the only God. He did not differentiate between Guru and God. His unalloyed, pure and bargainless love to his Guru-God made him realise his divine nature. Once he reached this stage, he became the embodiment of all knowledge, the storehouse of all knowledge. He could explain in a very simple and practical manner, in a way that everyone could easily comprehend, the truths contained in Vedas, Upanishads and scriptures. The Guru transformed his chosen disciple into a Samartha for the upliftment and emancipation of mankind. Baba became *gitagnana-mayah* (identified with the wisdom enshrined in Gita).

Sri Sai proclaimed that He was not the body, "Does Baba mean to you only this visible body of 3.½ cubits height?" he asked Nana. Baba has been appearing in different forms and assuming different bodies continuously for the welfare of humanity. The form of Baba which we see and are familiar with is one such body. Baba told some devotees that they were associated with him in earlier births.

Sri Krishna is the Supreme God and also the Jagadguru. He is two-in-one. Guru and God. Baba's nature is also identical. To his devotees he was *chalthe-bolthe* god (walking and talking God) and also Samartha Sadguru. Devotion to Baba amounts to devotion to Sri Krishna.

KRISHNA JAYANTHI

(Sai Sudha – August 2001)

Following Vyasa Puja or Guru Poornima Day, the first of the series of major festivals in Dakshinayana is Krishna Jayanthi. This year this festival is celebrated both in August and September, as Janmashtami or Gokulashtami in August by one set of devotees and as Sri Jayanthi in September by another set of devotees. On this day Sri Krishna is worshipped with a variety of flowers, fruits and sweets and the Jayanthi is celebrated with gaiety and ecstasy.

Of all the incarnations of the Supreme Lord, Krishnavatara is unique. The Lord appeared with all His insignia, in full splendour, a Purnavatara, not as a normal human baby. Srimad Bhagavata describes how Vasudeva saw the child when Devaki gave birth to Him in Kamsa's prison:

Tamadbhutam balakam ambujekshanam
chaturbhujam sankhagadaryudhayaudam I

Srivatsalakshmam galasobhikaustubham
peethambaram sandrapayoda sowbhagam II

Mahavaidoorya Kireetakundalatvisha
parishvaktasahsrakuntalam I

Uddhama Kanchyangada Kankanadibhir
Virochamanam Vasudeva aikshata II

A Child with four arms holding the conch and weapons like the mace, Srivatsa adorning the chest, bedecked with Kaustuba jewel, attired in peethambara, with the crown having Vaidoorya stone ornaments like bracelets, ear rings, etc, curly knots of hair dancing on the forehead! This was the child which Vasudeva, the father, saw.

Right from the night He was born, His divinity shone forth through His various lilas. When Vasudeva was asked to take Him to Gokula, the prison gates opened up, Lord Ananta, Sesha, gave protection from rain by spreading His hoods as an umbrella; the unfathomable river Yamuna roaring with waves gave passage to Vasudeva to cross easily. In Gokula various demons deputed by Kamsa to kill Krishna were slain effortlessly by the Lord. Who else other than the Supreme Lord could hold aloft the Govardhana Hill with His little finger for seven days to protect the Vrajavasis and their cattle and other possessions from torrential downpour of rain! Who else other than the Supreme Lord could subdue the terrible serpent Kaliya residing in the River Yamuna frightening the Vrajavasis, by dancing on his hoods!

At the same time child Krishna gave Nanda and Yasoda the greatest pleasure by His playful pastimes and sports. One moment He made mother Yasodha see all the worlds in His mouth and the next moment He made her forget that experience through His Maya! Even today it is the blissful experience of many devotees that it is sweet to think of His wonderful sports and it is sweet to sing His glorious lilas!

The purpose of the Lord's manifestation was annihilation of the wicked and protection of the sadhus, and thus the establishment of dharma, righteousness.

Paritranya sadhoonam vinasaya cha dhushkrutam I
Dharmasamsthapanarthaya sambhavami yuge yuge II

Sri Krishna is acclaimed to be the Jagadguru, the foremost of all Gurus. On Guru Poornima Day - Vyasa Puja is concluded with Sri Krishna Ashtotrasata Nama archana. *Vyasaya Vishnuroopaya Vyasaroopaya Vishnave*. Sri Krishna, through Sage Vyasa, left as legacy to humanity Srimad Bhagavad Gita and Uddhava Gita containing valuable codes of conduct to be followed by human beings.

Sri Krishna left the Earth for Sri Vaikunta in the beginning of Kali Yuga. If He were to annihilate all the wicked people to establish dharma now as proclaimed by Him in Gita, the world will have only very limited inhabitants. Therefore, out of infinite mercy and consideration for people, He decided to annihilate only the wickedness in people. For this purpose, He manifests Himself in the form of saints and sages to lead the people on the right path.

Sri Ramakrishna Paramahamsa and Sri Sai Baba appeared in the Nineteenth Century and by precept and practice led, and even today are leading in their apantaratma rupa, millions of people all over the world in the path of dharma.

Sri Sai Baba who is hailed as Samartha Sadguru advised devotees who were earnest in getting atmajnana or sakshatkara, i.e, God-realisation, to read repeatedly Bhagavad Gita and Uddhava Gita (Ekadasa Skanda of Srimad Bhagavata) propounded by Sri Krishna as Jagadguru, Baba taught His devotees that by pure Love, intense devotion, Bhakti, one can attain dharma, artha, kama and moksha. What is needed is Shraddha –absolute Faith (nishta) and unswerving perseverance (saburi).

Shraddhavan labhate jnanam tatparah samyatendriyah I
jnanam labdhva param shantim achirena adhigachchati II

(Gita IV -39)

"One who has faith obtains jnana and one who has subdued his senses and is dedicated to its practice obtains it; having obtained jnana ere long he attains shanti or peace", said Sri Krishna. Baba's emphasis is also on bhakti with shraddha, nishta and saburi.

Sri Krishnam vande jagadgurum!
Namameeswaram Sadgurum Sainatham!

YOGA SAMPOORNA AVATAR

(Sai Sudha – June 2001)

In compiling Sri Sai Sahasranamavali, H. H. Sri Narasimhaswamiji starts by invoking the Master as *Om Akhanda Satchidanandaya Namah* i.e. "I bow to Him who is perfect Sat Chit Ananda".

Majority of us cannot say exactly what it is like to be Sat Chit Ananda. From various religious texts and scriptures and by reading the lives of great Saints and Avatarapurushas like Sri Sai Baba, we understand that Sat Chit Ananda is a state of *Paramananda*, Supreme Pure Bliss, the highest goal any spiritual aspirant, sadhaka can hope to reach. Sri Sai is *Ananda-paramanandah*. Bliss and Supreme Bliss. Not only that, He is armed with the power or siddhi to confer that *Paramananda* to others also at his will. He gave this *Paramananda* to a South African Doctor *Africagata vaidyaya paramananda Dayakah*.

A South African Doctor happened to come to Shirdi. He was a staunch devotee of Sri Rama and he was always conscious of his high birth as a Brahmin, A Mamlatdar friend of his was proceeding to the Dwarakamayee, the mosque where Baba was staying, to have darshan of Baba. At his request, the South African Doctor accompanied him but on condition that he would not enter the mosque for fear of being polluted, himself being a Brahmin.

When both the friends came to the mosque, the Mamlatdar friend went inside to have Baba's darshan leaving the South African Doctor Outside. From outside the Doctor had a look at Baba. Forgetting all about his resolve, he suddenly rushed inside and fell at Baba's feet. When asked about the reason for this sudden change, he answered, "This Baba is a *Yoga Sampoorna Avatar.* I am a Rama Bhakta having spent years with Rama Bhakti, but I have had no sakshatkara or darshan of Rama. Now for the first time I see Sri Rama with all His attributes or Chinnas in this mosque in the figure of Sai Baba. When I looked on Sai, I found he was Neelamegha Shyama Sareera Rama, my *Ishta Devata*. Hence I bowed to him".

The South African Doctor was one of the small number of devotees who realised that he had come to One who can confer the highest gift that God or a Godman alone was capable of giving. He wanted to have from Baba *Satchidananda, Paramananda*, Bliss Supreme. The Doctor realised that Baba knew everything in his heart. So he made up his mind that he would not go to the mosque again till Baba granted the desire of his heart. This way three days went on, thought of Baba, whom the devotee identified with Rama, completely gripping his mind. For three days the Doctor, though away from the mosque, was totally Baba conscious. On the third day, an old friend of the Doctor came. Both of them engaged themselves in conversation and forgetting about his resolve the Doctor accompanied his friend to Baba. He fell at the feet of Baba who with kindness asked him, "Did anyone send for you?" The Doctor felt ashamed, seeing that Baba knew the secrets of his heart and prayed that Baba would grant his highest desire. And Baba did grant! During his succeeding days of his stay at Shirdi, Baba filled him with a strange feeling of Bliss which the Doctor termed as "*Paramananda*". This *Paramananda* is a feeling of bliss not caused by external or internal contact with any object of the senses, but which filled the heart completely and gave its highest possible satisfaction, according to Sri Narasimhaswamiji.

Sri Swamiji writes, "The doctor called Baba a Yoga Sampoorna Avatar, because he could at will display the Rama form over himself and show that he was having Godhead, *Satchidananda*. Others who have practised Yoga and who live up to *Satchidananda* and are competent to talk about it, have described Baba as 'A Yoga Sampoorna Avatar", that is one who had the fullness of the derived by Yoga and that this Ananda came out from him at will".

"The proof of the pudding is in the eating. If a person could grant another *Paramananda*, he must have *Paramananda* in himself. That must be his nature".

SRI SAI, A MAHABHAGAVATA

(Sai Sudha – September 2001)

Sai Sahasranamavali hails Sai as *bhagavata-sahayah* (One who helps bhagavatas), *bhagavata-pradhanah* (the First among bhagavatas) *bhagavatottamah* (the best among bhagavatas). Since he is the foremost and the best among bhagavatas, he is able to help bhagavatas. Therefore he is Mahabhagavatah.

The word bhagavata is commonly being used to denote a good musician. A person who carries on bhajans is also being called a bhagavata. But a bhagavata in reality is one whose mind and intellect are ever fixed at the Lotus feet of Bhagavan. As Sri Gopalakrishna Bhagavataswami used to sing every day both in the morning and evening, for a bhagavata only the Name of Sri Hari is the source of life and nothing else.

Harer namaiva namaiva namaiva mama jeevanam
Kalou nastyeva nastyeva nastyeva gatiranyata

'Hari's Name only, Name only, Name only is my livelihood; In the age of Kali any other means is not there, is not there, is not there' The words *namaiva* (only the Name) and *nastyeva* (nothing else) have been repeated thrice to provide emphasis to the statement A bhagavata who firmly believes that only bhagavan-nama is his livelihood and nothing else is identified with Bhagavan Himself. Coming into contact with such a bhagavata or being privileged to be in the company of such a bhagavata is satsang which will help one to taste real bliss and lead in bhakti or prema marga.

The five namas immediately following the nama "*Mahabhagavataya Namah*" in Sai Sahasranamavali amply illustrate the nature of a Mahabhagavata. *Mahanubhava Tejasvine namah, Mahabhayaparitratre namah, Mahatmane namah, Mahabalaya namah, Maha Yogeswaraya namah.* A maha-bhagavata is: One from whom his great experience of tasting Divinity or having merged in Divinity shines forth; One who saves (is capable of saving) His strength and a great Yogeswara. Not many can be called Yogeswara. Sri Krishna is hailed as *Yogeswara - Yatra Yogeswara Krishno yatra partho dhanurdarah.*

Let us see how and why Sri Narasimhaswamiji invokes his Master Sri Sai as a Mahabhagavata. In Chapter IV of Life of Sai Baba, Vol. I, Swamiji substantiates his claim that Baba is Mahabhagavata by referring to the norms laid down for a sage, a Mahabhagavata, in Ekadasa Skanda of Srimad Bhagavata.

The sage should be content to get just what would keep body and soul together and see that his powers of knowing, speech and wisdom may not perish. [SB XI (7) 9]

The sage sometimes concealing (his nature and attainments) and sometimes revealing them, is approached and worshipped by those desirous of achieving their (highest) well-being and eats everywhere the food given by donors and (thereby) burns up their past evil karma and subsequent evil karma also. [SB XI (1) 46]

Whether food be tasty or tasteless, plenty or scant, the sage, following the python's example, should just take what comes of itself without any exertion on his part. [SB XI (8) 2]

Whether he has plenty of comforts or none, as his heart is set on Narayana alone, he neither overflows or shrinks, just as the ocean does not overflow when the river throw their floods into it, nor shrink when the rivers do not. [SB XI (8) 6]

Sri Narasimhaswamiji affirms that these verses from Srimad Bhagavata aptly describe Sai Baba's condition and mentality and thus people could see in him a Parama Bhagavata or Maha Bhagavata.

In the early days of his stay at Shirdi, Baba's nomadic habits of running hither and thither as per his whims showed that he did not care for his bodily comforts nor did he mind the opinion of the society around him.

Sri Krishna tells Uddhava (Srimad Bhagavata, XI Canto, Ch. II, Verse 17) *atmarama anayaa vruttyaa vicharen jadavat munih* i.e absorbed in God (within himself), the sage rambles like an idiot. Baba, a Mahabhagavata, fully absorbed in God-consciousness, was behaving exactly like that.

He did not care for food for days together and Bayyaji Bai had to trace him in woods to feed him. "He knew full well that many people thought him to be mad or foolish and insulted him calling him pagal, i.e. mad, or treated him as a totally negligible factor, But he had no vanity or *amor propre* to be wounded by such lack of regard. He was like the Bhikshu in the Bhikshu Gita (Srimad Bhagavata XI-23-33 to 41) who was subjected in indignities or insults and bore up with all silently as part of his Karma", writes Sri Narasimhaswamiji. Baba lived as a true sanyasi upto the end of his life on bhiksha food. The bhiksha food collected by him was not entirely consumed by him but was shared with others, even animals like dogs. Sri Narasimhaswamiji writes:

"Baba followed the direction of the sastras for hermits and fakirs that a hermit should not put by anything for the morrow. Verse II, Chapter VIII, of Ekadasa Skanada of Srimad Bhagavata says, "The sage should not store what he obtains by begging for the evening or keep it for the next day. His vessel for receiving alms must be either the hand or the stomach. He should hoard nothing like the bee'. 'If he does, like the bee he will be killed'. Spiritually persons who store develop attachment or moha, which means death of the soul". Baba was a perfect *jitendriya*.

Let us bow to Sri Sai, the Mahabhagavata, the Bhagavatapradanah, Bhagavatottamah with whom Bhagavan Himself had identified.

KRODHAJIT

(Sai Sudha – December, 2009)

Sage Valmiki asks Narada who in this world is endowed with all qualities of excellence, perfect in all respects; one of those qualities is *jitakrodha*, i.e. one who has conquered anger. Narada replies that such a man is Sri Rama.

We say *Satrujit*, conqueror of enemies. This does not mean that one who has no enemies. Every person will have enemies. A person who conquers the enemies and keeps them under his control as a master does his slaves, he is Satrujit. Man's six inherent enemies (Shadripus) are said to be Kama, Krodha, Moha, Lobha, Mada, Matsarya. A Gnani or a Yogi is one who has total control over them.

Normally an ordinary human when overcome by anger loses self-control, does not exactly know what he or she does in a fit of rage and loses the thinking faculty. Sri Krishna says:

"Anger generates delusion, and delusion results in loss of memory. Loss of memory brings about the destruction of discriminative intelligence, and loss of discriminative intelligence spells ruin to a man." (B.Gita II – 63)

Sri Krishna here talks about anger that seizes a man as a result of his desires. But what about anger which manifests in a person who has conquered desires?

Mother Sita was abducted by Ravana. Sri Rama along with Lakshmana moves from place to place from Panchavati in search of Devi enquiring hills, rivers, trees, animals etc., whether they know about Sita's whereabouts. On the way he sees the chariot, flag, etc. of Ravana lying in a damaged state. He thinks that Sita has been killed by Rakshasas, gets very angry and says that he would destroy the whole world. When angry his personality undergoes a change; it becomes like that of Rudra who is known for peak of anger. Lakshmana pacifies Rama reminding him of his nature which is Satva. Rama's nature is patient as Mother Earth. Always with a pleasing countenance (*Sadaiva Priyadarsanah, Sarvalokapriyah, Sadhu*). Sri Rama spontaneously cools down. He was able to get rid of the anger as fast as he got it; that is 'conquering anger'.

On the shores of the ocean Sri Rama prays to Samudra Raja (King of Oceans) for three nights to allow passage for him to cross the ocean along with the Vanara Army. There was no response from Samudra Raja. Rama gets angry and vows to dry up the ocean with his astras. Then the King of Oceans appears before him with folded hands and prays for pardon. Rama was able to shed his anger immediately. Here we see Sri Rama's control over anger.

On the final day of the war with Rakshasas, while engaged in fierce combat with Ravana, Rama was at the peak of anger, and he was like Rudra. Immediately after Ravana was killed, Vibhishana was filled with remorse at his brother's death. Instantaneously Rama became his normal self, Santa-murthi, calm and composed, extolled the good qualities of Ravana and advised Vibhishana to perform the last rites for the departed warrior. Here again Rama shows that he is *Jitakrodha*.

In Sai Sahasranamavali, Sri Sai is hailed as:

1. *Kaalaagni Sadhrusca Krodhah:* One whose anger is as terrible as the Fire of Destruction.
2. *Kopavyaaja subha pradah:* One who by showing anger bestows blessings.
3. *Krodhajitah*: One who conquered anger.
4. *Jitakrodhah*: One who had subdued anger.

Sri Sai is also *jitendriyah* (one who had conquered the senses) and *Jitashadripuh* (one who had conquered the six internal enemies - Kama, Krodha, Moha, Lobha, Mada, Matsarya).

When we read the Life of Sri Sai Baba, we come across several incidents where Baba suddenly flew into fits of terrible anger for no apparent reason. This explains the first of the above epithets. In all such instances, the anger resulted in conferring benefits individually or collectively. This earned him the second praise. Always Baba became normal affable self as fast as he grew angry and showed his mercy and kindness to devotees present. Hence, the third and fourth stuthis.

Since Baba's anger was not caused by any desire but was for the good of others, it did not result in loss of memory, destruction of discriminative faculty, etc. Though outwardly he seemed to be angry, he always retained his self-composure, he remained in his self-realised state. He was thus able to be as omniscient as ever, to be the antaryami of one and all and to know and reveal what was passing on in the minds of others even while he appeared to be in a fit of anger.

On one of his earlier days in Shirdi, Prof. G.G. Narke went to the masjid to attend arati. Baba was seen in a towering passion. He was fuming, cursing and threatening; whom and what for, nobody could say. 'Is Baba mad?' – This was a passing thought in Narke's mind. When later Narke went to Baba and massaged his feet and legs, Baba stroked the devotee's head and said, 'Arre, Narke, I am not mad!' This showed that Baba was in full control of his faculties even when he was seen in towering passion.

Baba wanted his ankita devotee Purandhare to own a house. Building a house was beyond the means of a poor wage-earner like Purandhare. Until Purandhare started making efforts to acquire a piece of land and start construction, Baba made the devotee's life miserable by show of anger in the form of violent abuse and threats, which was considered unreasonable. By use of anger Baba blessed his devotee to have his own house to live in.

Gadge Bua's construction of a dharmasala at Nasik stopped for want of funds. Gadge Bua thought that this was due to some misfortune or evil effect. He went to Shirdi to see Baba. As soon as he came before Baba, Baba became angry and shouted using foul and obscene language. Immediately Gadge Bua laughed and Baba also laughed. Baba's abuse was directed to the forces that were hindering the construction process. Bua went back to Nasik, the obstacles were removed by Baba's abuse and the dharmasala construction was completed.

B.V. Dev could not make any progress in carrying on with Jnaneswari Parayana. Baba grew angry with him and accused him of stealing his old

rags; he threatened Dev that he would kill him with a hatchet. It turned out that Baba's anger and abuse were directed towards the negative influence which was hitherto hindering the parayana process. Dev was able to carry on with his parayana with Baba's blessings.

Baba never got angry with any individual. Whenever he exhibited anger it was invariably to ward off calamities or troubles approaching his devotees. His anger also was a means to shower his blessings on his chosen devotees. He wanted his devotees to give up anger totally. He himself declared, "I get angry with none. Will a mother harm her little ones? Will the ocean send back the waters of the streams?"

Baba knew that it is not possible for all people who are caught in the whirl of Samsara to conquer the 'Six enemies'. So he advises the devotees to exercise control over them. He says:

"Desires must be controlled. You must master them and not be their slave. Yet you can (and must) use them, the inner enemies, within limits, e.g., (Besides *Kama* for the wife) have

- *Krodha* (anger) against unrighteousness
- *Lobha* (greed) for Hari Nama – uttering God's name
- *Moha* (fondness) for mukti (salvation), and
- *Matsarya* (hatred) towards evil action.
- Have no *Mada* (pride)

THE EMBODIMENT OF LOVE - I

(Sai Sudha – December 1999)

Generally when one tries to learn about the life and mission of an avatarapurusha like Sri Sai Baba and reads his life and teachings, the questions to which answers are sought are –

What is the religion the avatarapurusha belongs to?

What is his school of philosophy?

Has he established a new cult and if so, what is it?

What is the specific sadhana he followed and he advocated to his devotees?

What is the essence of his teachings?

Last but not the least, what are the miracles performed by him?

Baba's birth and parentage are shrouded in mystery. That he was born of brahmin parents in a village called Patri in the erstwhile Nizam State is only an inference and is not backed by authenticity. Therefore, the religion or sect to which Baba belonged cannot be established absolutely. A study of his life and teachings reveals that he belongs to all religions and all sects. His was a universal religion; it was not exclusive, but all-inclusive. Both by precept and practice, he demonstrated that he belonged to humanity as a whole and the essence of his religion is love.

Baba did not profound any abstract philosophical maxims. He did not owe allegiance to any specific school of philosophy. His advices to devotees are practical. The essence can be summed up in one word-LOVE.

Shun hatred and love ye each other.

The Mission of Baba is to confirm each one in his own faith. He was very specific that each one should follow his own dharma. *Sreyan swadharmaithyuktva svesvedharmaniyojakah* – He is one who said that it is safer for each person to remain in his own dharma (be it Hinduism, Vaishnavism, Saivism, Islam or Christianity) and made his devotees to stick to their own faith. Baba did not establish any new cult. His was the essence of all cults, all religions – LOVE.

Baba did not undertake any detailed sadhana. He said, LOVE, LOVE to one's Guru, pure, unalloyed, bargainless Love to Guru, is the only sadhana. He is *premamargaika sadhanah* (his sole marga or prescribed path is LOVE. What he gave is also Love, *premadayakah* (he confers prema or Love); he can be influenced, he will be pleased, by Love-*premavasyam*, because he is *gurupremasamalabdhaparipoorna swarupavat* (he attained perfection by simply loving his Guru) and *gurupasanasamsiddhah* (achieved success, became a siddha, by serving his Guru).

The essence of Baba's teaching is again LOVE. He exhorted his devotees to break the walls that differentiated one from the other and learn to love each other. As the first step, he advised his devotees to shun hatred.

Did Baba perform any miracle? Any act that is out of ordinary, that does not happen in the normal course, is called a miracle. Baba's lighting the lamps with water was called a miracle. Sri Swamiji calls this a chamatkar. All siddhis were at Baba's command and lights burning with water as fuel is the manifestation of one such siddhi. Baba was against performance of miracles. Devotees of Baba did get, nay, even now get, benefits from Baba which they would not have got in the normal course. A devotee is cured of a fatal disease and he proclaims he had a miraculous escape. A devotee is involved in an accident but escapes unscathed; he calls this a miracle. These are all the benefits conferred by Baba on his devotees out of his LOVE for them. The greatest miracle is that the simple fakir who in physical frame did not transcend the limits of the remote hamlet Shirdi is now worshipped by millions of people throughout the world. Eight decades after Baba passed from the finite to the infinite, the presence of Baba, the Embodiment of Love, is felt everywhere.

THE EMBODIMENT OF LOVE - II

(February 2000 edition of Sai Sudha)

Pure love, bargainless love, brings with it a sense of tyaga, sacrifice. Nothing is considered to be too valuable to be sacrificed at the altar of Love. A mother is prepared to sacrifice anything for the welfare of her child. Similar is the case of a true lover for the sake of the beloved. One is prepared to sacrifice his or her own life, which is considered to be most precious, for his or her loved ones. True love is itself a state of bliss; sacrifice or tyaga propelled by this love makes one realise that blissful state.

Baba is an Embodiment of this Supreme Love. Baba's love for his devotees is unfathomable. A study of the Life of Baba reveals how he always kept a vigilant eye on the welfare of all his devotees wherever they were. For the sake of some devotees Baba sacrificed his own health. By his yogic powers he transferred to himself some unbearable maladies from his devotees and endured the suffering himself. Baba whose sole sadhana or marga is Prema or Love, (*premamargaika sadhanah*) is compared to Lord Mahadeva in tyaga (*Girisasadhrusa tyagin*).

It is said that Baba gave up his own life to avert the death of Tatya Patil. Baba knew and predicted that Tatya Patil's life would come to an end on Vijayadasami on 1918. By the end of Bhadrapad of that year Tatya fell sick and was so bedridden that he could not even move to go and have Baba's darshan. Gradually his condition grew worse and at the dawn of Vijayadasami day his pulse began to beat very slow. Perhaps Baba did not want his devotee to precede him in giving up life. Tatya had immense faith in Baba. Curiously in the afternoon Baba who was also having fever gave up his life and entered into Mahasamadhi leaving Tatya to recover and remain alive.

In the early years at Shirdi, Baba used to wander and get lost in the nearby woods. Though he was a fully realized Godman, he appeared externally to be a dull-headed madcap or an obsessed person, *jadonmaththa pisachabhopyantah satchitsukhasthithah.* In those days one of the few residents of Shirdi who recognized the divinity of the young fakir Baba, Bayaji Bai, mother of Tatya Patil, out of immense love used to go to the woods every noon carrying on her head a basket containing bread and vegetables and roam hither and thither in search of the young fakir. Once she found him, she used to place a leaf before him, spread the bread and vegetables and feed him with the love of a mother. Baba always remembered this pure love and devoted service of Bayaji Bai. According to him Bayaji Bai was his sister in earlier births. No wonder her son Tatya considered Baba to be his maternal uncle and Baba is hailed as *Patil Tatyaji Matulah*.

Whatever material wealth one accumulates in his life time is inherited after his death by his heirs or descendants. Similarly the fruits of the meritorious deeds of a person are also inherited and enjoyed by the heirs or descendants. For the services rendered by Mother Bayaji Bai, the son Tatya enjoyed the fruits by the loving care Baba bestowed on him throughout.

VENKATESA SAI

(Sai Sudha – March 2013)

As far back as 1950, when the name of Sri Sai Baba was not so widely known and the orthodox Hindus were still hesitant to accept a 'Muslim' fakir as a divine person and scoffed at worshippers and followers of Baba, Sri Narasimha Swamiji, a *deergadarsi*, wrote prophetically.

"Abdulla Jan in his statement of 1936 says, 'All that glory of Sai Maharaj was then grand, but in 1936 there is no relic of the crowd". The halls of Dwarakamayee and the puja rooms were visited only by a few people on ordinary days. And Abdulla Jan thought that Baba's, like all human glory, rose to the zenith at one time and afterwards went down to the nadir. But Abdulla Jan did not know Baba's ways, Even as Jan was giving his statement, the movement was progressing and within a very few years, the number of visitors to Shirdi increased and went on increasing in arithmetical or geometrical progression.

"At present it is difficult to say whether we are anywhere near the zenith of Baba's popularity. Perhaps it is only just now that Baba is getting to be recognized in various parts of India. The more he is known, the most assuredly will he draw groups to his feet. One index of his growing popularity is the large number of children we name after Him in so many families, Hindu and Muhammadan, and the large number of temples and bhajan salas named after Him. So he is sure to equal Tirupati Venkatesa in the matter of attraction of people. Incidentally it may be noted that Tirupathi Venkatesa and Sai are not different, Sainatha Manana says:

Venkatesastu sayeesah tayor bhedam na vidyate
Tayor aikyam smaran nityam tat sthanam labhate narah

This means: "Venkatesa is indeed Sayeesa or vice versa. Sayeesa is the same as Venkatesa. There is no difference between the two. Perpetually remembering this identity one reaches that position (the position of Venkatesa or Sayeesa)." As may be seen from the historical sketch of Sai Baba's growth and development in his last birth, he attained his present position, as stated by himself several times, by the grace of Venkatesa, his Guru. His Guru was originally named Gopal Rao, but had become identified with Venkatesa. And to Baba Venkatesa is only one of the names of God, Allah, Hari, Khandoba, etc., all denoting the same God. Therefore, his Guru having become identified with God (Venkatesa), divine powers permeated and saturated his nature and these flowed on to Baba especially at the time of initiation or diksha and dwelling his mind upon his Guru. So no wonder that Shirdi began to resemble Tirupati."

How prophetic! Today it is acknowledged that Shirdi is next only to Tirupati in attracting huge crowds. Even in receipts of donations and other contributions including Hundi collections Shirdi Sai Sansthan is just behind Tirupathi. Lord Venkatesa, hailed as Govinda and Balaji, is known as bestower of the boons desired by devotees; people believe that by making vows and praying to Sri Venkatesa they could get their desires fulfilled. A vast majority of people do get the coveted benefits and rush to Tirupathi to fulfil their vows. This is exactly what we now see happening in the case of Sri Sai Baba. Millions and millions of people all over the world are of the firm conviction that by praying to and worshipping Sri Sai Baba they could get their wishes fulfilled. Today not only at Shirdi but in all places, towns villages and cities, where Baba's shrines have come up, one sees large number of devotees gathering to offer worship and prayers. As in the case of Sri Venkatesa, one sees in circulation pictures and calendars of Baba everywhere. How does this happen?

Swamiji has written that Baba's Guru Venkusa was a staunch devotee of Lord Venkatesa. Because of this though his actual name was Gopal Rao, he came to be known as Venkatesa or Venkusa. In chapter 26 of Bhakti Saramrita (Harikathas) Das Ganu Maharaj has given a detailed account of the greatness of Guru Venkusa. As a very staunch devotee and worshipper of Lord Venkatesa, he derived all powers and siddhis at the command of Lord Venkatesa. In Chapter 15 of Eleventh Skanda of Srimad Bhagavatam, the Lord Himself tells His devotee Uddhava that a devotee who has fully surrendered to Him and who has unflinching devotion to Him, always thinking of Him only, will be vested with all the powers that are at His command.

Before attaining samadhi, Guru Venkusa transferred all the powers that he possessed, the powers of Lord Venkatesa, to his foremost disciple Sri Sai Baba. The Guru effected the transfer of his powers by making the sishya drink three seers of milk milched from a 'barren' cow. When the sishya drank the milk, through Gurukrupa everything surrounding him appeared as God (Narayana). Immediately after this benediction, the young fakir boy, later to be known as Sai Baba, was able to bring back to life a dead man who offended him and his Guru.

Thus we can see that since Baba is endowed with the powers of Lord Venkatesa, through his Guru Venkusa, people in large numbers are attracted to him also as to Sri Balaji of Tirupathi.

Sri Narasimhaswamiji has narrated an interesting incident. "A staunch Vaishnavite Brahmin was worshipping God as Tirupati Venkatesa and refused to pay any regard to any other form. He was ailing from very acute and painful sciatica and rheumatism. His son-in-law gave him Baba's udhi and asked him to repeat Sai Baba's name with faith. At first he resisted this attempt to subvert his faith in Venkatesa, as he termed it. But necessity is the mother of faith. One night when the pain in his body could not be endured any further, he suddenly took Baba's udhi and applied it to his legs thrice, calling on Sai Baba to remove his pain. The effect was instantaneous. The pain was off. Sleep that he could never obtain instantly supervened. He woke up in the morning freed from sciatica and was able to walk. He first thought that Venkatesa had led him into faith in Baba. He finally discovered that Baba was Venkatesa, Baba's Guru being Venkatesa, or one that had merged his self in Venkatesa. (Glimpses of Sai Baba, Ch XXVII).

A recent development in Madurai reveals the divine link between Lord Venkatesa and Sri Sai Baba. A temple of Sri Vinayaka came up in TVS Nagar, Madurai in 1994 and gradually Sri Vinayaka inspired the team of enthusiastic sevaks to surround Him with other Murtis – Sri Andal, Sri Sudarsana, Sri Anjaneya, Sri Hayagriva and Sri Lakshmi Narasimha, Vishnu Durga, Saraswati, Meenakshi Sundaresa and Subrahmanya,

Navagraha, and to crown all these installations a life-size murti of Lord Venkateswara, who is fondly christened 'Nalampuri Srinivasa Perumal'. In 2009 construction of Gopurams and other renovation work were taken up and the people managing the temple wanted to perform a grand Kumbabhisheka. At that time an ardent desire arose in the mind of one of the sevaks that a Murti of Sri Sai Baba should also be installed here. Events followed miraculously. A devotee offered to sponsor the procurement of a suitable marble statue of Sri Sai Baba. An unimaginable incident happened. An electric transformer which was occupying considerable space to the right of Sri Srinivasa Perumal's shrine was caused to be shifted in a very short span of time with the help of some unexpected influential quarters. Funds required for construction of Baba's quarters also came without any effort. Another notable feature was that the beautiful statue of Baba acquired in Chennai in May 2009 spent a Wednesday night in the sanctum sanctorum of Baba's shrine in Mylapore Sai Samaj and after abhisheka and puja in the early hours of Thursday, left for Madurai and Baba was given an enthusiastic send off by the office bearers of All India Sai Samaj and other devotees. Sri Sai Baba occupied the spacious portion next to Lord Venkatesa. In temples of Sri Sai Baba, other Murtis are generally installed; here is the unique instance where murti of Sri Sai Baba has been installed among a galaxy of Hindu forms of God.

Om Sri Venkatesaramanaya namah!

GANGADHARA SAI

(February 2013 edition of Sai Sudha)

Jaya mani jaisa bhava, Taya taisa anubhava,
Davisi dayaghana

With whatever faith and expectation one approaches you, you grant him/her experience accordingly.

This is what millions of devotees sing every day in the famous Arati song composed by Madhav Adkar and sent by Baba to Nana Chandorkar at Jamner for perusal.

There are staunch Vaishnavities and they wouldn't accept any form of God other than that of Mahavishnu. Even here there are some who meditate on worship of a particular form of Vishnu, like Sri Rama. Let us take the case of the South African doctor; he wouldn't care for any form of God other than Sri Rama. When he came to Dwarakamai with his friend with a determination not to bow before Sai Baba, Baba gave him darshan as Sri Rama and the doctor spontaneously ran inside the mosque and prostrated before Baba. According to his bhava was his anubhava, experience. For the sake of South African doctor, Baba assumed the form of Rama.

Sri Ramakrishna says: "There is a thing called nishtha, single-minded devotion. When the gopis went to Mathura they saw Krishna with a turban on His head. At this they pulled down their veils and said: "Who is this man? Where is our Krishna with the peacock feather on His crest and the yellow cloth on His body?" Hanuman also had that unswerving devotion.

He came to Dwaraka in the cycle of Dwapara. Krishna said to Rukmini, His queen, 'Hanuman will not be satisfied unless he sees the form of Rama.' So, to please Hanuman, Krishna assumed the form of Rama."

People who are devoted to Datta saw Baba as the latest manifestation of Lord Dattattreya, after Akkalkot Maharaj. People who are devotees of Lord Vittal of Pandaripuram saw the form of Sri Vithala in Baba which made Das Ganu Maharaj sing "*Shirdi Maje Pandharipura, Sai Baba Ramavara*". Persons who are staunch followers of a particular Guru witnessed the form of their Guru in the person of Baba.

For some ardent Siva bhaktas Baba was Gangadhara. Mahlsapathy's ishta devata, kula devata was Khandoba, a manifestation of Siva. When Baba decided to make Shirdi his place of stay, he desired to stay in the Khandoba Temple, but Mahlsapathy, an orthodox Hindu, could not allow a Muslim fakir into Khandoba's Temple. Nevertheless it was Mahlsapathy who spotted the divinity in the Muslim fakir, addressed him 'Baba Sayee' and started worshipping him also in the mosque. Mahlsapathy went to Pandharpur and in the temple the crowd was so huge that he found it difficult to march in. But when he thought of Baba at that moment, by Baba's grace people in the shrine including the priests saw the form of Khandoba in the person of Mahlsapathy and they rushed forward, took Mahlsapathy near the Murthy of Vithala. Thus Mahlsapathy, a Siva devotee, was blessed to have an inspiring darshan of Lord Vithala.

Megha, a rustic Brahmin, was a staunch devotee of Siva. Rao Bahadur Sathe sent him to Shirdi to see Baba, stay at Shirdi and undertake Baba's worship. Megha felt a repulsion to bow before a Muslim but persuaded by his master Sathe, he came to Shirdi. But Baba did not allow him to enter the mosque and severely scolded him. Megha went to Triambak but be became restless. After a few months he came back to Shirdi and this time Baba did not prevent him to come near him. Megha began to see Siva in the form of Baba. One night Megha dreamt that Baba entered his room, drew a Trident on the wall and scattered akshatas all round. When he woke up he was surprised to see the Trident and akshatas. But how could Baba enter his room when he had bolted the door from inside? When he went to Baba, Baba told him that he did come into his room and closed doors and walls could not prevent his entry. Baba gave Megha a linga for worship. Meghashyamasya pujartham sivalingam upaharate – thus hails

Sai Sahasranamavali. After doing Puja at Khandoba's temple, Megha used to come to Dwarakamayee every day to offer worship to Baba. One day in the noon, Khandoba's temple doors were closed and Megha proceeded to Dwarakamayee for Baba's worship. But Baba told Megha that the doors of Khandoba temple would be open then and sent him back to Khandoba temple so that Megha might not swerve from his routine of worshipping Khandoba first. On a Sankaranthi day Megha wanted to do abhishekam with Ganga-jal (water of Godavari river) to Baba who, he was sure, was none other than his Ishta Daiva Lord Shiva. But when Megha poured the pot of water on Baba's head, not a drop flowed down and Baba's dress was as dry as before. Baba is hailed as 'sirasthambita gangambharah'. Baba thus confirmed Megha in his faith. When Megha breathed his last in Shirdi, Baba shed tears and it was only in the case of this wonderful devotee Baba accompanied his body to the cremation ground and undertook all expenses for his obsequies.

. *Om Sri Krishnaramasivatreyamarutyadhi swarupadhrute namah*

Salutations to Sri Sai who appeared in the forms of Krishna, Rama, Siva, Datta and Maruti (to his devotees).

RAGHAVA SAI

(April 2013 edition of Sai Sudha)

"*Sairupadhara Raghavottamam bhakta kama Vibudhadreemam prabhum*" hails Sri Upasani Baba in his Sai Mahimna Stotra. Sri Raghava Himself has taken the form of Sri Sai to fulfill the desires of His devotees. Earlier also in the eighth sloka Sri Upasani extols Sai as '*Ramamevavatharinam*' Sri Rama himself has incarnated as Sai.

It was the firm belief of many contemporary devotees of Baba that Baba was not different from Sri Rama. That Baba encouraged devotees like Gopal Rao Gundu and Rasane to celebrate an Urs on the Ramanavami Day may be a reason for this. The Urs that commenced on Sri Ramanavami under Baba's instruction later developed into a grand Jayanthi celebration of Sri Rama and this continues to be so not only in Shirdi but also in all places where Sai worship is carried on.

In the wonderful Arati song (The first Arati Song in praise of Sai) composed by Madhav Adkar, which was sent by Baba to Nana Chandorkar through Ramgir Gosavi for approval, the bhakta proclaims '*avatarasi to yeta dharmate glani nastika nai the lavisi nijabhajani*' "Whenever righteousness declines you take birth and even the non-believers begin to have faith in you".

Sri Rama was the abode of all auspicious qualities one can think of. He was *saranagatavatsalah* (protector of all those who surrender to Him.) More than that was '*ripunam api vatsalah*' (He was kind and considerate even to His enemies). Sri Rama let off Jayanta, the crow, who committed a most heinous crime to Mother Sita, with a light punishment even though he deserved to be killed, just because he surrendered to Sri Rama. Before being killed, even Rakshasa enemies including Ravana were given ample opportunity by Sri Rama to mend and surrender unto Him.

When we read Baba's life we come across many instances where Baba converted those who scoffed at him, jeered at him and talked ill about him, into ardent admirers and followers. This characteristic of Baba was similar to that of Sri Rama and this has been highlighted by Madhav Adkar in the arati song as mentioned above. Megha felt repulsive to serve a Muslim; he became the first one to do regular puja to Baba and became very endearing to Sai. All of us would have read about Bhate, Mamlatdar at Kopergaon, who was spilling venom about Sai when he met people who were going to have darshan of Sri Sai Baba at Shirdi. Once Baba's eyes fell upon him during his chance visit to Shirdi on official duty there was total metamorphosis in his outlook. Bhate became a permanent resident of Shirdi, he never wanted to be away from Baba and he even gave up his prestigious career and his family. Sri Sai Sahasranamavali hails Baba "*Bhateh devesham samakrishya bhaktim tasmai pradattavat*". One who removed from the mind of Bhate the hatred he had and endowed him with devotion. The doctor devotee from South Africa, a staunch Rama bhakta, did not want to enter the mosque nor to bow before Baba. But Baba appeared to him as Rama and the doctor prayed to Baba to get paramananda and Baba did bestow that on him. *Africagata vaidyaya paramananda dayakah* was Sri Sai. The doctor considered Baba to be a *yoga Sampurna Avatar*.

The orthodox Brahmin priest, Bhatt in Pradhan's house felt that it was sacrilegious to worship a muslim fakir and equate him to Datta. Baba kindly condescended to give him the conviction that he was an avatar of Datta and made him a devotee of his.

There have been several people who had absolutely no faith in or devotion to Baba, but later became ardent Sai devotees. This writer himself, in the last five decades, came across a number of people who were initially against Sai worship but later miraculously became ardent followers of Baba.

According to one version Sai's Guru Venkusa was Ramananda and Sai was Kabir in previous birth. Sai himself proclaimed occasionally that in an earlier birth he was Kabir (*Kabirdasavatarakah* – Sai Sahasranamavali).

Baba once said that he was even revered by Emperor Akbar. This should be in reference to his earlier advent as Kabir (*Akbarajnabthivanditah*). In the arati song '*Jayadeva Jayadeva Datta Avadhuta*', in the second verse, Sri Krishna Bhishma says '*momina vamsee janmuni lokan thariyale*' (born in the family of weavers as Kabir – you had uplifted many people). In Bhakti Saramrit, Chapter 53, Das Ganu Maharaj has mentioned how Kabir's tomb found a place in Shirdi also; it was a thrilling account. That Samadhi was under the neem tree and that was the reason why Baba chose the shade of the neem tree as his place of abode. Kabirdas was the musician saint who sang '*antare Rama, bahare Rama. Yahan dekhom vaha Rajahirama*'. Sri Rama was inside him, outside him, wherever he turned his sight he saw only Rama. As Sai, this characteristic of Kabir should have continued; Sai was always Rama-conscious; he was *Ramabhaktiprapurnah* (Sahasranama).

The name 'Rama' is said to have the potency of a powerful mantra. In fact it is called 'Taraka Mantra', a mantra that will enable the chanter to cross the ocean of samsara, that is to get released from the cycle of births and deaths. Since Lord Siva himself initiated Parvati Devi into chanting of this mantra, saint Purandaradasa in his song praising Lord Siva hails Him as '*Taraka-upadesi*'. Sri Sai who never undertook initiation of anyone gave this mantra for japa to a few devotees – *Ramamantropadesakah* (Sahasranama). Sri Sai had attained the stature of Sri Rama Himself by constant japa and was therefore *Ramasarupyalabdha* (Sahasranama). Since he had attained Rama's stature his name 'Sairama' also became an effective mantra for chanting. Being an absolute novice in spiritual matters, this writer cannot say with certainty whether anyone had crossed the ocean of samsara by chanting 'Sairama'. But he can say with certainty, through his contacts with several Sai devotees in the last six decades, the nama 'Sairama' has enabled and is enabling the chanter to cross various hurdles the devotee comes across in the mundane life. This gives the devotee the much required faith and puts him or her on the path of spiritual sadhana required to cross the bhavasagara or ocean of samsara.

Saint Tyagaraja extols Sri Rama as '*Jagadanandakaraka*', the one who makes the whole world joyous. Sri Sai also makes all those who come in contact with him joyous. He showers bliss on those who surrender to him. He is *Anandapradha* (Sahasranama). He is himself, 'Ananda' and he gives Ananda to all – *anandadayakaha* (Sai Ashtotram).

The intent of this writer in penning this article is to share his thoughts on Sri Sai and Sri Rama on the occasion of Sri Rama Navami and pray to Sri Sairama to enable us cross the *bhavasagara* besides making the present life joyous and purposeful.

URS

(Sai Sudha – March 2007)

To all Sai devotees the word 'Urs' would mean Sri Ram Navami celebration in Shirdi and Sai Mandirs and temples everywhere. Urs is a festival. About *Urs* it is stated, "once a year *urs* festivals are held all over Maharashtra to honour the great *Sufi* saints of the past at their *dargahs*, which are still preserved by the saint's family or *pirzada*. Both Hindus and Muslims flock to these festivals for the blessing of the saint and for his curative power which is said to be still active even from the tomb"*. In the case of Sri Sai Baba, an *Urs* festival was introduced even when he was very much alive, not by his family but by devotees.

According to Sri Sai Satcharitra, one devotee by the name of Gopal Gund, Circle Inspector of the Revenue Department at Kopergaon, who had no children got a son with Baba's blessings and this devotee wanted to give expression to his gratitude; with the consent of Baba he was instrumental in introducing a *Yatra* or *Urus* in Shirdi, at the time of Sri Ramanavami. Nana Saheb Nimonkar and Damodar Rasne (another grateful devotee who got children with Sai's blessings) provided one new flag each and the two new flags were ceremoniously carried in procession and tied to the dome of the Masjid and permanently fixed there. This was in 1895 or 1896.

The Muslim devotees did not lag behind in making this *urs* unique. As was their custom to honour great Muslim saints, at the instance

---

* UNRAVELLING THE ENIGMA: SHIRDI SAI BABA IN THE LIGHT OF SUFISM BY Dr. Marianne Warren

of a Muslim bhakta, Amir Shakkar Dalal, a sandal procession was simultaneously introduced. Thalis (plates) containing sandal paste and scrappings are carried with all grandeur through all streets and lanes of the village and on reaching the masjid, the sandal paste is thrown on the 'Nimbar' and walls of the masjid with hands. Thus came into vogue a glorious festival in honour of Sri Sai Baba in which the procession of the 'flags' by the Hindu devotees and the 'sandal' by Muslim devotees went on side by side. Baba's mission is essentially unification of people of different faiths and this urs is one major step taken in that direction. In the statement given to Sri Narasimha-swamiji (*Devotees' Experiences of Sri Sai Baba*) Bayyaji Apaji Patel reminisces as follows about the introduction of Sri Ram Navami Urs.

"In 1896, i.e. my seventh year, the Ramanavami Urus Celebration began. It was then that Baba began to allow Hindus to affix sandal or to do puja to him and Moslems to read Koran before him at the masjid.... Baba finding that Hindus and Moslems would have differences as to the way and manner of celebrating the Urus allowed Sandal Panja to be put on all – Hindus and Moslems alike".

Later on, around 1912 at the instance of K.G. Bhishma and a few other staunch devotees, the urs was transformed into Sri Rama Navami celebrations, celebration of the birthday of Sri Rama.

According to Shri Sai Satcharitra (adaptation by N.V. Gunaji), Sri Sai Baba came to bridge the enlarging gulf between the two major communities, the Hindus and Moslems. "His constant advice to all was to this effect. "Rama (the God of the Hindus) and Rahim (the God of the Mohammedans were one and the same; there was not the slightest difference between them; then why should their devotees quarrel among themselves? You ignorant folk, children, join hands and bring both the communities together, act sanely and thus you will gain your object of national unity. It is not good to dispute and argue. So don't argue, don't emulate others. Always consider your interest and welfare. The Lord will protect you. Yoga, sacrifice, penance, knowledge are the means to attain God. If you do not succeed in this by any means, vain is your birth. If any one does any evil unto you, do not retaliate. If you can do anything, do some good unto others".

On Sri Rama Navami Day, all Sai devotees should go through the above message of Sri Sai Baba again and again and try to follow his advice, which will help gain the object of national unity. At this hour, when vested interests are working overtime to widen the gulf between people of one State and another, people of one caste and another, people of one community and another, the only course open to all to achieve peaceful co-existence, a wonderful unity in diversity, to go nearer the dream of Mahatma Gandhi to establish Ramarajya, is to follow the advice of Sri Sai Baba, "Love one and all" and "Give up hatred totally". Just celebrating Sri Ramanavami as Sri Sai Jayanthi pompously, spending lavishly on puja materials, decorations and the like, can only help bloat the ego and cannot take one even one step in the spiritual Sadhana.

SAI RAMA - I

(Sai Sudha – March 1998)

That Sai appeared as Rama, Krishna, Vittal, Siva, Datta, Maruti and other manifestations of God to various devotees is well known. He is hailed as *Krishnaramasivatreyamaruthyadiswarupah*. However, Sai is identified more with Rama than any other form of God. Ramanavami Urs which originated in Shirdi with the blessings of Sai Himself if being celebrated in a grand manner as Sai Jayanthi. Millions of devotees are seen chanting the name 'Sairama' and having taken this nama for japa.

In Sri Saimahimna Stotra, Sri Upasani Baba extols Sai as "*ajanmadhyamekham parambrahma sakshat swayam sambhavam Ramamevavathirnam*" and "*Sairupadhara Raghavottamam*". Here again it is the conviction of Sri Upasani Baba that Sri Rama Himself has appeared as Sai again and Raghava has taken the form of Sai.

A study of the life of Sri Sai Baba reveals the significance in people seeing Rama in Sai.

Sri Rama is *saranagatavatsala*. His magna carta is that it is His Vrata (vow) that He will always protect from fears from all quarters the devotees who surrender to Him as their sole refuge. (*sakrudeva prapannaya tavasmeethi yachate abhayam sarvabhutebhyo dadamyetat vratam mama*). Sri Sai also gives the same assurance to His devotees. "If any one casts his burden on me and thinks of me, I look after all his concerns". "If one perpetually thinks of me and makes me his sole refuge, I am his debtor and will give my head to save him".

Baba advised Sri N.R. Sahasrabhude, Mrs. G.S. Khaparde, Sri M.W. Pradhan and many others to always do Rama Nama japa. Several devotees were asked to do parayana of Adhyatma Ramayana.

Vishnusahasranama parayana was very dear to Baba. In presenting this book to Shama, Baba said, "Oh Shama! This book is very valuable and efficacious, so I present it to you, you read it. Once I suffered intensely, my heart began to palpitate and my life was in danger. At that critical time, I hugged this book to my heart and then, what a relief it gave me! I thought that Allah Himself came down and saved me. So I give this book to you. Read it slowly, little by little; read daily one Nama at least and it will do you good". There is significance in Baba asking Shama to read daily 'one Nama at least'. Most of us, caught in the whirl of exacting mundane activities, may not find time to do Vishnusahasranama parayana every day. Not that there is no hope for them. An easy and simple alternative is prescribed – 'Chant at least one nama'. But what could be that one Nama? On behalf of such helpless children, the Gracious Mother asks Easwara, "By what means the thousand names of Vishnu can be easily read?" Easwara assures that it can be done by the repetition of one Nama 'Sri Rama' which is as potent as the entire thousand Namas. Ramanama is acclaimed as tarakanama, i.e. the name that enables us to cross the ocean of samsara easily. Easwara who prescribed this tarakanama for repetition is hailed as '*taraka upadesi*' by Saint Purandaradasa. Perhaps this could be the reason why Sai gave so much weight to the chanting of Rama Nama.

On some occasions Baba claimed that He was Kabir in a previous birth and His Guru Venkusa was Kabir's Guru Ramananda. The Rama-consciousness, therefore, should have continued in this advent as Sai also. That consciousness should have revealed itself in the person of Sai.

Sai Satcharita narrates how the lady devotee, chief of the Madrasi Bhajana Mela (Bhajan Party), who ecstatically did Rama bhajan in the presence of Sai, had the darshan of her Ishtadeva, Sita Rama, in the person of Sai. A doctor from South Africa, a staunch Rama bhakta, was not willing to bow before Sai whom he thought to be a Mohammadan. Standing outside the Dwarakamayee, the Doctor had a vision of Sri Rama in Sai, rushed and prostrated at His feet.

It was a unique experience to hear directly from Sri Rege that once when he went to Nasik (before Baba's Mahasamadhi) to have darshan of

Kala Rama, he could not see Rama but only Sai. In 1967 when Sri Rege visited Nasik again with the pilgrimage party from All India Sai Samaj, he said that he got the same experience again.

In 1960 once when Sri Gopalakrishna Bhagavataswami was conducting divyanama sankirtan in the sannadhi of Sai at Chennai, chanting the name of his Ishtadaiva Rama, he went into ecstasy and lost consciousness. When he regained consciousness, his lips were still muttering Rama, Rama. Later it was a thrilling experience to hear from him that while chanting Rama nama he had a vision in which Krishna, Rama and Maruti descended from the portrait of Baba displayed on top in the hall. (This portrait is now seen under the Aswatta tree behind the main Mandir.)

In Krishnavatara, the Lord's divinity in all its splendour was manifest throughout. Yet people in general did not recognize His divinity and considered Him to be human. "Foolish people do not recognize Me as the Supreme Lord, but take me to be a human" laments Sri Krishna in Bhagavad Gita. In Ramavatara, the Lord skillfully and meticulously played His role as a human being. His divinity was veiled. Still people, awed and attracted by His majesty, approached Him with all respect for succour. Sri Narasimhaswamiji attributes this to the blend of human and divine. He says that as in the case of Rama, in Sai also this blend was total so as to attract devotees. "The divine portion within the human frame has so powerfully radiated its light as to throw out or drown out the human side and impress on us that we are dealing with Sai Baba as with the other great names. The divine and the human blend together and are both necessary to make up the entity that gives human beings their impression of God. Without the human element no approach is possible, and without the divine element the approach is worthless, for we do not wish to approach mere finite entities like human beings but rather wish to approach the divine, though the divine may be enshrouded for the time being in a human casing."

Chanting the nama "Sairama" is bound to purify our minds and serve as the powerful taraka mantra to safely ferry us through this ocean of samsara.

SAI RAMA - II

(Sai Sudha – March 2000)

Of all the avatars of the Lord to establish dharma, Ramavatara is unique. Born as a human being the Lord concealed his divinity totally and showed to the world by practice how a human being should conduct himself, as an ideal son, ideal brother, ideal husband, ideal friend and ideal ruler. Rama was the only human being who possessed all the rare good qualities that any human being can possess. In the very first chapter of Balakanda, sage Narada tells Valmiki that Rama was the repository of all good qualities. He was *sarvalokapriyah* (dear to the whole universe), *sarvasamah* (impartial and equal to all). His love flowed to everyone without any discrimination regardless of caste, creed, community or social status. Not only humans, all living beings enjoyed his love.

The hunter-chief Guha was Rama's very intimate friend – atmasamah Sakha. What respect Jatayu, the king of birds, commanded from Rama! Rama placed him in the same pedestal with his father Dasaratha. Says Rama:-

Raja Dasarathah Sriman yatha mama mahayasah l
Poojaneeyascha manyascha thathayam pathageswarah ll

Dasaratha at the time of death did not have Rama by his side to perform his funeral rites, but Jatayu was privileged to have Rama lit his funeral pyre and attain moksha.

Similarly Rama showed his love to the old woman Sabari who by virtue of her devoted service to the Rishis in Mathangavana became siddha and siddhasammatha. Her intense tapasya, service to Gurus enabled her to see the Supreme Lord in Rama and by His grace attain moksha. Exclaims Sabari at the sight of Rama:-

Adhya praptha tapah siddhih tava sandarsananmaya l
Adhya me' sapalam janma guravascha supoojitah l
Adhya me' sapalam taptam swargaschaiva bhavishyati ll

We see people greet each other with affection shaking hands. This practice of friends shaking hands was there even in Rama's time. Rama and the Vanara King Sugriva became friends by shaking hands and taking the oath of friendship with Agni, the Fire-God, as sakshi, witness. Sugriva offers his hand to Rama with the words '*gruhyatam panina panih maryada badhyatham dhruva*'.

Even against the counsel of Sugriva and other Vanara leaders, Rama gave refuge to Ravana's brother Vibhishana when he surrendered to him. "It is my vow to give protection to anybody who takes refuge in me". He says, 'even if Ravana himself seeks refuge, he will get it". That is why Rama is extolled as *saranagatavatsalah.* When being harassed by Ravana in Asokavana, the compassionate Mother Sita advises him to make friendship with Rama if he wants to save his life, as Rama is *sarvadharmajnah* and *saranagatavatsalah*. Rama is so compassionate that even the worst sinner will be forgiven and given protection when surrendered to him. Sugriva rightly calls him *ripoonam api vatsalah* – compassionate even to enemies.

The name "Rama" is called taraka mantra. This one name is equivalent to the thousand names of Vishnu.

Baba wanted his devotees to celebrate Rama Navami with devotion. Baba advised his devotees to take "Rama" nama for japa. Baba himself was steeped in Rama-consciousness and identified himself with Rama. He is thus dearly addressed as Sairama by his devotees. Like Dasaratha Rama of Ayodhya, Sri Sai Rama of Shirdi also proclaimed that he will take care of his devotees wherever they are when surrendered to him.

SRI SAI RAMA - III

(Sai Sudha – April 2001)

The first major religious function of the Hindus after the advent of New Year (according to Chandramana) is Sri Rama Navami. Whenever we enter a New Year we pray for prosperity and happiness. We pray to our Ishta Daiva that the New Year brings with it all the happy tidings.

The Lord's incarnation as Rama is the most ideally suited one to be appealed to by people for redressal of their grievances and for protection from all evil forces and tendencies. The one Supreme Lord, Parabrahman, is known by several names. Of all His namas, Rama Nama is considered to be the most potent one. It is called Taraka Mantra – the mantra that ferries people easily across the ocean of samsara, the ocean of miseries. Eswara tells Parvati that this one nama "Rama" is as powerful as chanting the thousand namas, Sri Vishnu Sahasranama.

Though the Lord took birth as Rama, the son of Dasaratha, as a human being, to protect the sadhus and punish the wicked, the purpose of the avatar seems to be more to show people how an ideal man should conduct himself. His main aim was to establish dharma.

Rama is hailed as *dharmatma, satyasandhah, saranagatavatsalah, sarvabhuta hite ratha, bhutadhayaparah.* Rama is known as '*apannanam para gatih*- the only refuge for people in difficulties, He is very *saulabhya* –easily accessible, though He is *sarvanbhouma*, the Lord of the entire Universe. His love knew no barriers. All living beings, not only human, enjoyed His Love. He was the first to bring about harmony among all people, nay, all living beings.

The advent of Sri Sai Baba is also similar to that of Sri Rama. The main aim of Baba was to make people to stick to dharma. By precept and practice he showed to people the potency of vairagya, tyaga, born out of Love. All living beings enjoyed his Love, He offered protection to all. He is also *sarva bhuta hite ratah and bhuta dhayaparah*. He worked very hard to bring about national unity, unity among various communities. He demonstrated to some devotees that He was the indwelling Paramatma in all living beings. He had shown that he could appear as a dog, a cat, an ant and also as a low caste man. He wanted his devotees to see him in all and love all.

Sri Sai exhorted many devotees to chant Rama Nama. He appeared as Rama to some Rama bhaktas and gave them bliss. Like Rama Sai offered protection to devotees who surrendered to him. Sri Sai is hailed as *Ramabhaktiprapoornah, Ramarupapradarsakah, Ramasaroopyalabdah, Ramamantropadesakah and Ramamoorthyaadhisankartre*.

It will please Sri Sai and Sai Rama – Sri Sairam, if all Sai devotees vow to work for bringing about total unity and harmony in the country. Whenever people love each other and live in total harmony there Sri Sai manifests spontaneously. Mere worship of Sai, mere Sai bhajan, will not bear any fruit unless it is fortified by the nectar of Love.

SRI RAMA AND SAI

(Sai Sudha – April 2005)

The very first celebration in honour of Sri Sai Baba commenced on Sri Rama Navami day around 1896. Gopal Gundu and Damodar Rasne, who were not destined to have any progeny as per the grahaphala were blessed with children by the grace of Sri Sai Baba. To show their love born out of gratitude they mooted the idea of holding an Urs, procession, and this found favour with all other devotees like Nimonkar, Madhav Rao Deshpande and Tatya-Kote Patil. As directed by Baba, the urs was first started to be celebrated on Sri Rama Navami Day. Since then the celebration is continued with great fervour. Due to the efforts of renowned poet Krishna Yogeshwar Bhishma, author of Shirdi artis, on Rama Navami Day Rama Janana utsav was also introduced as per tradition from 1911.

The multitude of people who took refuge in Baba comprise devotees of various forms of God – nay people of different faiths – devotees of Siva, Vishnu, Rama, Krishna, Vittal, Khandoba, Vinayaka, Devi, Lakshmi, Dattatreya etc. Each one was enabled to see his or her ishtamurthi in Baba and was given an onward push in their spiritual Sadhana conforming to each person's mental disposition. However, to a large extent Sai Baba was identified with Sri Rama; the nama 'Sairam' is preferred for japa by many. That is because both Sri Rama and Sri Sai appeared on the Earth essentially to show the path of dharma.

The term 'dharma' is unique in connotation and does not have a suitable equivalent in any other language. According to Oxford dictionary, dharma is 'the eternal law of the universe with Sanskrit origin, decree or custom'. So, dharma is something eternal, changeless and immutable with universal applicability. Dharma connotes leading a virtuous life in the world, stipulating inexorable moral and ethical codes to be adhered to.

Srimad Valmiki Ramayana commences with an enquiry by Sage Valmiki and the reply of Sage Narada. Valmiki wants to know about a person who is perfect in every respect. The question is raised in three slokas; Narada answers in twelve slokas. Rama was *dharmajna* (knower of dharma) and *satyasandha* (strict adherer to Truth); not only was he the protector of all living beings, but also the upholder of dharma. He was sarvagunopetah – endowed with all auspicious qualities. He was like Lord of Dharma in upholding satya (just not Truth but includes righteousness, ahimsa, etc.). In the whole of the epic Valmiki very frequently extols Rama as *dharmatma*. Even the wicked rakshasa Mareecha could not resist calling Rama as '*Vigrahavan dharmah*' – Embodiment of Dharma. By meticulously following the path of dharma, Rama was an exemplar of an ideal man, ideal son, ideal sishya, ideal brother, ideal husband, ideal friend, ideal king, an ideal warrior. No wonder the very name of such a supremely meritorious person becomes highly potent and is acclaimed as 'Taraka' nama by saints and sages, i.e. the name that is capable of ferrying one across the ocean of samsara. No other divine name is recommended for japa and chanting as much as Rama nama. It is equivalent to *sahasranama*, thousand names of the Lord.

"Pray to Rama. Meditate on Him. He will certainly provide you with everything". Advising one devotee thus, Sri Ramakrishna Paramahamsa says: "All cannot recognize an Incarnation. When Narada visited Rama, Rama prostrated Himself before Narada and said, 'We are worldly creatures. How can we be sanctified unless holy men like you visit us?" Further, Rama went into exile in the forest to redeem His father's pledges. He saw that, since hearing of His exile, the rishis of the forest had been fasting. Many of them did not know that Rama was none other than the Supreme Brahman". (*The Gospel of Sri Ramakrishna*).

Baba instructed a few devotees to take to Rama nama japa. Some devotees were advised to do parayana of Adhyatma Ramayana which presents Rama as none other than the Supreme Being. Sometimes he identified himself with the foremost among Rama bhaktas, Sri Hanuman. According to Somanath Shankar Deshpande, son of Nan Saheb Nimonkar,

"Sai Baba and Sri Ram are not different. I was privileged to serve Sai Baba during his life for four days … During those days, I had a blessed vision. I was at the Mosque. Baba was in his usual place and Madhav Rao near the steps. Suddenly Baba appeared to me in the form of Maruti. There was the Maruti body. Only I did not see if there was a tail. Seeing that form I told Madhav Rao at once 'Take his dharshan. See he is Maruti'. Baba was undoubtedly a Rama bhakta".

Of course, Baba had given darshan as Rama to a few devotees, e.g. South African Doctor, the lady devotee of Madrasi bhajan party, Sri Rege, etc.

Baba wanted his devotees to tread the path of Dharma; he told people to shun hatred, to love all, see him in all living beings, to be honest. According to Purandhare, Baba told him, "You should have truth always with you. Then I will always be with you, wherever you are and at all times". "He often insisted on my adherence to Truth". Mrs. Tarkhad says, "Purity, strength, regularity and self-denial one noticed about him always". When we read the Experiences of Devotees, we see that Baba invariably exhorted all his devotees to lead a virtuous life and laid great stress on following dharma. If only we hearken to Baba's teachings, our lives here and hereafter are bound to be better.

RAMA SAI

(Sai Sudha – April 1968)

Sri Sai is invoked as *Ramabhaktiprapoornah* (One who had full faith in and devotion to Rama), *Ramarupapradarscakah* (One who revealed himself as Rama) *Ramasaroopyalabdah* (One who had attained the nature of Rama), *Ramasayeethi-viscrutah* (One who is well-known as Rama Sai or Sai Rama), *Ramadutamayah* (one who had identified himself with the Messenger of Rama – Sri Hanuman), *Ramamantropadescakah* (One who gave Rama Nama as an effective Mantra, *Ramamoortyadiscankatre* (One who gave primal bliss in the form of Rama) and so on in Sri Sai Sahasranamavali.

Sri Sai revealed himself to many devotees as Krishna (Vittal), Rama, Siva, Maruti, Dattatreya and in various other forms of God. But Sai as Rama appealed and appeal to a large number of devotees. It is said that the great Rama bhakta Kabirdas reappeared in the form of Sai and Sri Ramananda, Guru of Kabir, as Venkusa, Guru of Sri Sai.

The obstinate South Indian Doctor who would not bow before anyone other than the image of his *ishtamurti* Sri Ramachandra, came to Shirdi just to keep company with his friend, a Sai Devotee. But when he came in the Master's presence, he prostrated himself at full length before the Master whose benign grace made the doctor realise his *ishtamurti* Sri Rama in Sri Sai himself. In Sri Sai Sahasranamavali, *africagatavaidyaya paramanandadayakah* refers to this lila of the Master.

Conversely, an intimate child of the Master, the Sai-minded devotee, Sri Rege, could see only his *ishtamurti*, Sri Sai, in the image of Kala Rama at Nashik-Panchavati!

Pleased with the services rendered by Mrs. Khaparde in the previous as well as the present births, the Master who never gave any oral instruction to anyone, broke the rule in her case and initiated her into Rama Mantra.

Rama proclaimed that it was His solemn vow that he should save from all harm, from all beings, any person that took complete refuge in Him, saying even once 'I am Yours, Save Me!', vide *Sakrudeva prapannaya tavasmeeti cha yachate, abhayam sarvabhutebhyo dadameeti vratam mama.* Look at Sai's proclamations: "If one perpetually thinks of me and makes me his sole refuge, I am his debtor and will give my head to save him". "If anyone casts his burden on me and thinks of me, I look after all his concerns". "I will not allow my devotees to come to harm. I have to take thought for my devotees. And if a devotee is about to fall, I stretch out my hands, and thus with four outstretched hands at a time support him. I will not let him fall". Baba's charters to his devotees in this spirit are countless. That is why Sahasranamavali hails Baba as *scaranagatavatsalah and samascritajanatranavrata palanatatparah*.

Revenue Circle Inspector Gopal Rao Gundu who was issueless for many years got a son by the grace of the Master. His gratitude and love knew no bounds. He wanted to commence a celebration in honour of the Master. When approached, the Master advised him to celebrate Rama Navami inn a grand manner in his honour. How significant is this! That was how Sri Rama Navami Urs was started at Shirdi about 20 years before the Master's Mahasamadhi, attracting thousands of his devotees. No one knew or knows when the Master was born. Since the Master himself advised his devotees to celebrate Ram Navami in his honour, that day is considered to be Sai Jayanthi day also.

Rama means one who makes (his devotees) happy. Sai is God. So Sairama (the auspicious combination) is that form of God which makes the devotees happy by blessing them with what is best for the life here and hereafter. So, in this season of Ramanavami, the advent of Rama the Most Auspicious One, Rama who reappeared as Sri Sai of Shirdi, let us repeat the sacred mantra "Sairama" as many times as possible and invoke His blessings thus:

Premabhiramam pranatharibhimam rajeevanetram sukrutaih sulabhyam

Karyartharupam karunakaram tam srisayeenatham scaranam prapadhye.

"I seek refuge with Sri Sainatha, whose prema or love makes him so charming, who is so terrible to the enemies of his devotees, whose eyes are like the lotus, who is easily won and reached by punyas, whose very form spells success and who is a mine of mercy". (Sri Sainatha Mananam – verse 269)

TYAGA SAI

(Sai Sudha – December 1969)

"What is the significance of Gita? It is what you find by repeating the word ten times. It is then reversed into 'tagi', which means a person who renounced everything for God. And the lesson of the Gita is: 'O man, renounce everything and seek God alone'. "Whether a man is a monk or a householder, he has to shake off all attachment from his mind". Thus spake Sri Ramakrishna Paramahamsadeva (The Gospel of Sri Ramakrishna).

Sri Krishna, the Gitacharya, was Himself this Tyaga personified. He showered bounties on His devotees. He shaped the destinies of the empires of His time. He did not Himself became a king, but preferred to remain the Cowherd, Blue Boy of Brindavan, the darling of the Gopis!

As Sri Rama, the Lord showed the world by practice what perfect detachment was. Chosen as the Crown Prince and with all arrangements ahead for the Yuvarajya Pattabhisheka, he was summoned by His stepmother Kaikeyi to convey the command of His father, - to leave the country and live in the woods as hermit for fourteen long years, giving up the kingdom to His younger brother Bharata. Without the least demur, He took the command cheerfully. The Lord, Who could proclaim that it was His solemn vow that He would protect all those who surrender unto Him, renounced everything.

Early October this year, I had the good fortune of being present at the 78th Birthday celebrations of Sri Gopalakrishna Bhagavataswami, a living example of total renunciation and abject humility combined with unparalleled devotion to the Lord, at Kodavasal, a small town in Tanjore District. The function was unique. During the bhajan, a devotee requested that the kriti "Lekhana…." by Saint Tyagaraja might be sung. Sri Bhagavataswami, in his inimitable way, expounded to the audience the meaning of the song and presented before the mental eye of everyone an unforgettable picture of Sri Rama, the Sarvabhauma, seated on the throne, Sri Sita Devi drinking in the Lord's beautiful form, Lakshmana concentrating on the Lord's eye awaiting therefrom His commands, Bharata enjoying the Lord's profile, Satrugna meditating on the Lord's form and Anjaneya at His feet. This is the scene which Saint Tyagaraja visualized and presented to posterity in the aforesaid song. When Sri Bhagavataswami spoke, he became Tyagaraja himself. "*Tyagaraja means* the Lord of Tyaga, Sri Parameswara, Who did not hesitate even to give away His Consort Sri Parvati Devi when asked for as boon by His devotee Ravana" said Sri Bhagavataswami. So, the Lord of Kailas, *Girisha*, is the foremost of Tyagis! The Lord Who can confer anything and everything to His devotees, even His Consort, simply for the asking – this All-Merciful Lord – prefers to remain a *Bhikshadanar*, clad in tiger skin, with matter hair, ashes smeared all over the body, venomous snakes as ornaments! Oh! Where else can we find a better definition for perfect tyaga, renunciation!

And what about Maruti who sits at the feet of Sri Ramachandra? He represents the ideal sevant. We find in Sri Anjaneya another example of Tyaga, having sacrificed everything for the service of the Master.

As Sri Bhagavataswami presented the above picture and spoke, certain *namavalis* in Sai Sahasranamavali flashed across my mind. Verily, Sai represents all the above forms of the Lord - Krishna, Rama, Siva and Maruti. Sri Sai Baba, like Sri Parameswara, gave everything to everyone. Nay, he went a step further in that he drew his devotees from far and near voluntarily and conferred on them bountiful benefits, material and spiritual. But it pleased him to remain a Fakir in rag, in the dilapidated mosque in the obscure village of Shirdi, begging his food every day, till he gave up his body. No wonder, therefore, the Sahasranamavali hails Sai

as *"Girisa-sadrusa-tyagi"* (One who equals the Lord of Kailas in renunciation).

The very next namavali is "*Gitacharya*" (Propounder of Gita), followed by another namavali "*Gita gnanamaya*" (One who is identified with the wisdom enshrined in Bhagavat Gita). According to Sri Ramakrishna Paramahamsadev, who is himself another example of complete renunciation, the essence, - the wisdom – of Gita is "renunciation supreme". Thus, the Sage Narasimhaswamiji, the compiler of Sai Sahasranamavali, has conceived his Master as a Tyaga-Raja.

When I heard Sri Bhagavataswami that day, the Master set my mind to think on the above lines.

That is the effect of being in Satsangh!

SETHU BUILT BY RAMA - FICTION?

(Sai Sudha – April 2008)

Sri Sai Baba of Shirdi was a great saint who lived in a remote hamlet in Ahmednagar District of Maharashtra in the Nineteenth and Twentieth centuries. The birth, parentage and ancestry of this saint is shrouded in mystery. He was neither a Hindu nor Moslem, but, all the same, he was a rare gem of a Hindu saint and also a Moslem fakir, avlia; he was a wonderful Hindu Mahabhagavata and at the same time an illustrious Sufi mystic.

Recently this writer came across a book written by Dr. Vinny Chitluri – Baba's Rinanubandh – narrating some very interesting anecdotes from the life of Sri Sai Baba. One such anecdote, a very illuminative one, is as follows:

Baba's trusted attendant Madhava Rao Deshpande, Shama, once got a doubt. He wanted Baba to clarify.

Shama: Deva, it is stated in Ramayan that Lord Rama got a bridge constructed across the sea by one crore of monkeys, so that Rama with his army could cross the sea and reach Lanka. There he vanquished Ravana. Is this true?

Baba: Yes it is true. The sea is real and Lord Rama was also really there.

Shama: Deva, where did so many monkeys sit? And how did they sit?

Baba: They sat on the trees and clung to the branches. They looked like myriads of ants.

Shama: Did you see this with your own eyes?

Baba: Yes, I saw it with my own eyes, Shama

Shama: When I first saw you here, you had no semblance of even a moustache. How could you see the Vanara Sena?

Baba: You and I have been together for many generations. I remember them but you do not.

Shama: (In wonder) How old were you then?

Baba: Just as you see me now!

Shama: Is this really true?

Baba: Have I ever lied sitting here in the Dwarakamayi? What I say is true. I swear by you.

Rama declared in unequivocal terms that he would not speak at any time that which is not true. So also, Sri Sai declared on more than an occasion that, sitting in the mosque – a holy place, he would never speak what is not true. Baba stuck to the maxim '*Satyam Vada*' (speak the truth) and exhorted his devotees to do likewise. Therefore, Baba's affirmation that the existence of Sri Rama was real and the construction of the bridge across the sea through the vanaras was also real is true.

Today, next to Lord Venkateswara of Tirupati if any form of God is resorted to and worshipped in such a massive scale, it can be only of Sri Sai Baba. Unless Baba is a manifestation of the supreme God, how could this happen? In deposing before a Commission, Baba declared that his caste or race was 'God (*parvardigar*)' and that his age was lakhs of years. He had given ample indications that he is the one who is eternally present albeit in different forms. Therefore, if Baba said that Rama did build the Sethu across the sea with the help of the vanaras, millions of his devotees of various hues, communities and religious faiths will not have the least trace of disbelief.

In the last millennium a galaxy of mystics and saints, like Tulsidas, Kabirdas, Tyagaraja, Purandara Das, Samartha Ramadas, Swami Ramadas of Bhadrachalam and a host of Maharashtra saints, have all experienced the living presence of Sri Rama and have sung extolling the feat of Sri Rama in building the Sethu across the sea.

Besides Sri Sai Baba, in the last two centuries India witnessed the advent of two great Divine personalities, Sri Ramakrishna Paramahamsa Deva in th East and Bhagavan Sri Ramana Maharishi in the South, both of whom attracted vast number of earnest spiritual sadhakas not only from India but from all over the world, people of different faiths. All of them frequently gave quotations from Srimad Ramayana to make the path of virtuous life and spiritual Sadhana easy to tread for their followers. Mahatma Gandhi literally breathed 'Ram', to be honoured as 'Mahatma' universally.

A man's whole life revolves around faith. Even a person calling himself an atheist has immense faith in his leader and literally worships him. It is the faith of crores and crores of people professing the Hindu faith, the *sanatana dharma*, that Rama and Krishna did exist, Rama did build the Sethu and Krishna did expound the Gita. Over the last thousands of years, generation after generation this faith has percolated. Even while blossoming into a foetus in the mother's womb, this faith is ingrained. As a child while suckling the mother's breast, it draws this faith too with the milk. The faith is so mixed in the blood that it cannot be separated. This faith is very powerful and sometime or other it will rise, assert itself and revolt against all blasphemous talk questioning about the veracity of the life of Sri Rama and other forms of God, and their accomplishment like the building of a sethu. All sincere devotees should distance themselves from such diatribe which hurts more than physical assault. Let us abide by Baba's prescription – *Nishta and Saburi* – unassailable faith and steadfast perseverance. The latter is termed as 'manliness' in man by Baba.

SRIMAD RAMAYANA

(Sai Sudha – April 2000)

For ages Srimad Ramayana parayana is done by millions of people throughout the country. Discourses and lectures by eminent scholars are arranged at several places incessantly. People never get tired of hearing the glorious story of Rama time and again. People are always thrilled to hear Rama's Charita. Or is it the great charita of Mother Sita?

Kavyam Ramayanam Kritsnam Sitayascharitam mahat
Poulastyavadhamityevam chakara Charitavratah

(Fourth Sarga, Valmiki Ramayana)

We now see that when a new book is written a function is being arranged for release of the book by an eminent person. As soon as Valmiki created this wonderful epic, Rama's own sons Kusa and Lava were chosen to render the Kavya in front of great Rishis and scholars. They then sung this Kavya in important road junctions and main royal roads enchanting the hearers. Sri Rama Himself was enthralled hearing this great epic rendered by Lava and Kusa and brought them to the palace and expressed His appreciation.

Valmiki first heard the story of Rama from Devarishi Narada himself. Narada concludes his narration saying

Idam pavitram papagnam punyam vedaischa sammitham l
Yah patheth Ramacharitam sarvapapaih pramuchyate ll

"One who studies this holy meritorious story of Rama which enshrines the essence of Vedas, will get absolved of all sins." There is no sin too powerful to be destroyed by studying or hearing Ramayana.

Sage Valmiki created this monumental epic at the command of Brahma Himself. Brahma advised Valmiki to produce this Kavya as heard by him from Sage Narada. "In this great Kavya being produced by you there will not be a single word which is devoid of truth", *na the vaganruta kavyo kachidatra bhavishyathi.* Brahma further tells that as long as there are mountains and oceans in the world Ramayana Kavya will also exist. *Yavat sthasyanthi girayah saritascha maheethale, thavad ramayanakatha lokeshu pracharishyathi.* The word used is '*pracharishyathi*'. That is why thousands of scholars give discourses and lectures on Ramayana and millions of people enjoy hearing them eternally.

On return from Vanavasa, Bharata gives back the Kingdom to Rama and requests him to be the Lord of the Earth as long as the Sun moves, as long as the Earth exits. *Yavadavarthathe chakram yavathi cha vasundhara, Thavath thvam iha sarvasya swamitvam anuvarthaya;* Rama takes back the Kingdom saying "let it be so". *Thathethi prathijagrah.* Rama Himself declared earlier "*Ramo dwirnabhi bhashathe*". Rama is dharmatma and satyasandha. Therefore Ramayana is eternal and Ramanama is eternal. Rama pervades the whole universe ready to grant the prayers of those who hear this great Kavya created by Valmiki. *Srunvanthi ya idam kavyam pura valmikina krutham, the' prarthithan varan sarvan prapnuvantheeha Raghavath.*

Vedavedye' pare' pumpsi jathe' Dasarathatmaje'
Vedah prachethadasaeeth sakshat Ramayanatmana.

The Lord of Vedas was born as human being, as the son of Dasaratha; Veda through Valmiki became Ramayana.

SRI SAI BABA AND SRI RAMA NAVAMI

(Sai Sudha – March 2012)

Sri Sai Baba's essential advice to his devotees is to shun hatred totally and develop love towards each other. All the troubles in life are caused by allowing a sense of differentiation in our minds; Baba wanted this differentiation to go. 'Remove the Teli's wall, that separates you from me, and then we see each other clearly face to face'. To serve me, give up differentiation', said Baba. Baba's aim was to remove the antagonism that had developed between the two major communities in India, the Hindus and the Muslims, and make them join together in adoring or worshipping or following a unique saint, Mahatma or Avalia who did, and even continues to do after his Mahasamadhi, everything in his power to promote the welfare of his followers, here and hereafter. Baba started this mission far back as 1897 at Shirdi. Let us see how.

The issue-less Circle Inspector of Kopergaon, Gopalrao Gundu, got a son by the blessings of Sri Sai and his devotion to the Master became greater. To express his gratitude, he felt that celebration of an 'Urs' or festival in honour of Sri Sai should be introduced at Shirdi. He held consultations with the other earlier devotees at Shirdi like Nanasaheb Nimonkar, Tatya Patel, and others who were all unanimous in giving effect to such a proposal. When they approached Baba, he gave them his approval and he advised them to have it on Rama Navami day.

Hurdles like difficulty in getting the permission of the Collector, ensuring adequate water supply in the village, etc., were got over by the earnest devotees with the unseen divine help of Sri Sai. Damodar Sawalram Rasne (Damu Anna) was another great devotee of Baba, who joyously joined this band of devotees and agreed to prepare and supply a nice flag for the procession of the fair, while Nana Saheb Nimonkar came forward to supply the second flag.

While the Hindu devotees of Baba started celebration of this urs in this manner, the Moslem devotees did not lag behind. A 'sandal' procession, with the idea mooted by a Moslem devotee called Amir Shakkar of Korahla, was also introduced. The 'Sandal' procession is held by Moslems in honour of great Moslem saints; sandal paste and scrappings are put in Thalis (plates) and are carried with burning incense in procession to the accompaniment of band and music through the streets of the village and after reaching the mosque, the contents of the thalis are thrown on the 'Nimbar' or niche and walls of the masjid. The Moslem devotees who recognized Baba as a great Moslem saint conducted this programme. Thus, on one and the same day, Ram Navami urus of the Hindus and the 'Sandal' procession of the Moslems began to be celebrated at Shirdi with great enthusiasm and fervour in a unique and harmonious atmosphere created by the presence of the wondrous saint Sri Sai Baba. Thus Baba successfully began his mission of unification of two major communities who had divergent customs and views in following their respective religions.

Devotees of Baba were very enthusiastic in making arrangements for this festival as they considered Rama Navami an important day. While Tatya Kote Patil and others actively involved themselves in the service, special mention has to be made about the jewel among women devotees of Baba, Radhakrishna Mai. While she accommodated several outstation devotees as guests at her residence, she tirelessly worked in managing the paraphernalia of the fair. She undertook to clean and whitewash Baba's masjid, its walls and floor; this she did on alternate nights when Baba slept at the Chavadi. Feeding the poor, which was dear to Baba, was undertaken in a grand scale. Preparation of various items of food for this purpose was also undertaken by this mother-devotee.

In the following years the celebration assumed greater importance and significance drawing larger number of devotees to Shirdi from Mumbai, Pune and other places. In 1912 a thought arose in the mind of Krishnarao Jogeshwar Bhishma; since the urus is being celebrated in honour of Baba on Sri Rama Navami Day, why not celebrate the birthday of Sri Rama also simultaneously and make the event more glorious? He discussed this with other devotees like Kaka Mahajani and they got Baba's consent also for this. Radhakrishna Mai supplied a cradle, and a Kirtan (Harikatha) programme was also arranged. While the Rama Navami festival was going on, the procession of the two flags (supplied by Rasane and Nimonkar) went on by the day and the 'Sandal' procession by the night with all pomp and chat. From then, the Urus of Baba was transformed into the Rama Navami festival.

Next year, i.e., in 1913, Radhakrishna Mai started a 'Nama-Saptah' – singing of the glory of the Lord for seven days continuously from the first day of Chaitra. Several devotees participated in this programme in turn. Gradually, in the years that followed, the festival grew in grandeur attracting thousands of devotees.

In Sri Sai Mahimna Stotra, Sri Upasani Baba hails Baba as *ajanmadyamekam* and *Ramamevavatirnam*, i.e., Birthless and the Absolute being, and Rama Himself reborn. Yes, details of birth of Sri Sai continue to be shrouded in mystery. Baba did and continues to do what Sri Rama did, giving succour, abhaya, to all who surrendered to him wholeheartedly. Baba is '*Sairupadhara Raghavottma*'. Sri Raghava Himself in the form of Sai, according to Upasani Baba.

We have all read how Sri Sai gave darshan as Sri Rama to the South African doctor, and the lady of the Madrasi bhajan group.

As no one knows the day of birth of Sri Sai, it is very appropriate the birthday of Sri Rama – Sri Ramanavami – is celebrated by Sai devotees as the birthday of Sri Sai also, Sai Jayanthi. The Japa of the nama 'Sairam' is very efficacious and potent and chanting of this 'nama' – Sairam – on Sri Rama Navami / Sri Sai Jayanthi Day will give lasting joy and peace.

NISHKAMYA BHAKTI

(Sai Sudha – January 2001)

God is worshipped by a vast majority of people with a view to get some material benefits. Prayers are offered to get relief from illness, to attain success in examinations, to secure a job, to flourish in business endeavours and so on. But there are some exceptionally few devotees whose devotion is bargainless. They do not even crave for moksha. They are content with the bliss they get in meditating on the wonderful form and leelas of the Lord. They consider nothing more precious than the pleasure they derive in serving the Lord and His devotees.

In Srimad Ramayana we come across one such devotee, Sabari. Though born in the clan of a hunter, she had the good fortune of serving in the ashram of Sage Matanga where many Rishis frequently gathered. The satsang instilled in the mind of the simple servant-maid pure, unalloyed devotion to the Lord. She learnt from the discussions the sages had, that the Lord has taken birth as Rama in Ayodhya to save the Devas, Rishis and all good people from the tyranny of the wicked Asura Ravana. She also heard that Sri Rama would pass through Matanga Ashrama on the way to Rishyamooka Parvatha. A firm determination to have the Lord's darshan gripped her mind. In course of time the sages after intense tapasya were on their way to heaven. Pleased with the devout service rendered to them by Sabari, they offered to take her also along with them to heaven. But Sabari who was determined to have the darshan of Sri Rama declined their offer and stayed back in the ashrama awaiting the arrival of the Lord. Now at her advanced age her sole aim was Sri Rama's darshan. This is pure nishkamya bhakti.

Sri Rama finally came with brother Lakshmana. Sabari was overwhelmed with joy on seeing the Lord. Sabari offered him various fruits which were first tested by her. The Lord relished them very much. Sri Rama who all along concealed his divinity and played the role of a human had to reveal His divinity to this simple-minded old devotee and grant her moksha, an eternal place in Sri Vaikunta as a reward for her nishkamya bhakti. Nothing pleases the Lord more than such nishkamya bhakti.

When thousands of devotees were going to Shirdi during Ramanavami time to have Baba's darshan, one year, one old lady who had strong conviction that the Lord Himself has come in the form of Baba, wanted to have his darshan. She set out on pilgrimage to Shirdi by foot from her remote village. She carried with her one loaf of bread and some onions to be offered as naivedya to Baba. On the way she got very tired and she felt hungry and thirsty with her mind fully resting on Baba, on the banks of a river she bit half the loaf of bread and the onion to appease her hunger and drank some water. The bread loaf had become very dry. With the remnants she reached Shirdi. Because of the huge crowd she could not make her way to Dwarakamayee where Baba was seated. The omnipresent and omniscient Lord, Baba, asked Shama to go out and lead the old lady-devotee to His presence. The old lady, the Sabari of this age, was overwhelmed by the tender Love and affectionate grace showered on her by Baba and forgot about her offering. Baba told her, "Mother! How long am I to wait for you! Give me the bread and onion to eat!" Baba took the piece of dry bread loaf and onion once tasted by the devotee and relished eating the same. What a blissful experience the old woman-devotee got as recognition of her nishkamya bhakti!

BHAKTI

(Sai Sudha – May 2001)

Of all the incarnations of the Lord, Sri Narasimhavatara is unique. In Ramavatara and Krishnavatara saints and sages knew in advance that the Lord would appear on Earth as Rama and Krishna to establish Dharma. They also knew as to where, when and as whose child the Lord would appear. But in Sri Narasimhavatara, there was total suspense.

Devas, Rishis and others, oppressed and harassed by Hiranyakasipu realised that only the Lord could save them from the Asura. In answer to their prayers, they heard a voice from above, with no form, which said "Do not fear! I am aware of the evil deeds of the Asura and I shall kill him at the appropriate time. Wait patiently till then!" The Lord also gave a hint as to when He will kill the Asura.

nirvairaya prasantaya svasutaya Mahatmane
Prahladaya yada druhyet hanishye api varorjitam

The Lord only hinted that He would appear when summoned by His child devotee Prahlada, the Mahatma.

Through very hard tapasya, Hiranyakasipu obtained a boon from Brahma that he should not face death by any being created by him (Brahma): he should not be killed inside or outside, below or above, by any weapon whatsoever; not on the Earth or above, not at the hands of human or animals; not by Devas, Vasus, and so on. He covered every aspect that could cause him death. Brahma granted the boon.

Hiranyakasipu became arrogant, thought he was invincible and considered himself to be the Lord of Lords. He thought that he was very intelligent in having obtained a boon from Brahma by which he could avoid death for ever.

Having heard about the Lord Sri Hari from Sage Narada even when in the mother's womb, Hiranyakasipu's son Prahlada was born as a devotee of Sri Hari. The cruel father who hated Hari was appalled at his son's devotion to his enemy. Once seating child Prahlada on his lap the Asura asked him what he considered best in life. Prahlada without fear told his father that the nine modes of bhakti to Vishnu are the best panacea for all ills. Having failed in his efforts to kill Prahlada who enjoyed the constant protection of the Lord, Hiranyakasipu asked Prahlada that if his Lord Hari is all-pervasive would He be in a pillar which he pointed. When Prahlada answered in the affirmative, the Asura hit the pillar forcefully with his maze. The pillar broke into two and the Lord appeared in a very terrible form. Not as a man nor as an animal, but as a Man-Animal, Nrisimha, Man-Lion combination! Not one created by Brahma because He is the creator of Brahma Himself! Hiranyakasipu was not to be killed on earth or above, inside or outside, by day or by night, by any weapon. The Lord took him to the doorstep and placed him on His lap and tore him with the sharp nails. It was evening – sandhya kala – neither day nor night!

The Lord seemed to be keeping Himself ever alert to appear in whatever place His dear devoteechild and his cruel father decided! In killing the Asura the Lord had to ensure that the boon he got from Brahma was also honoured!

This is one Avatara where the Lord was keeping Himself ever alert waiting for the call of His devotee. That is why He is hailed as bhaktaparadeena. Nothing pleases the Lord as pure devotion, Bhakti.

Sri Sai Baba laid great stress on bhakti. He prescribed Prahlada's navavidha bhakti to His devotees.

In the month of May falls Sri Narasimha Jayanthi. Let us pray to Lord Narasimha and Samartha Sadguru Sainath to endow us with bhakti.

PRAHLADA VARADA SRI NARASIMHA

(Sai Sudha – May 1998)

In May falls Sri Narasimha Jayanthi. Out of the ten main avatara of the Lord, Sri Narasimhavatara is the fourth. This avatar is very significant since the Lord spontaneously sprang up from a pillar to establish that He is bhakta-paradeena.

The child devotee Prahlada had absolute and total faith in Lord Hari and he had the unassailable conviction that the Lord was the indweller of all animate and inanimate beings. When his father Hiranyakasipu, who considered Hari as his bitter enemy, asked him where Hari was, Prahlada declared emphatically that the Lord was manifest in a particle as also a pillar. Hiranyakasipu pointed to a particular pillar and asked Prahlada whether Hari was in that pillar too. When Prahlada replied in the affirmative, Hiranyakasipu hit the pillar with his mace. Out of the broken pillar Hari manifested in the form of Narasimha and proved what His devotee Prahlada was saying was true. The devotee's faith in His allpervading nature was confirmed.

If Valmiki's Ramayana extolled as *sitayascharitam mahat* (the great story of Sita), the seventh Skanda of Srimad Bhagavata which narrates the advent of the Lord as Narasimha is *Prahladacharitam mahat*, (the great story of Prahlada), the foremost among devotees. Mother Sita's unflinching devotion to and implicit faith in Sri Rama even in the most adverse circumstances can be seen repeated in Prahlada.

The tortures inflicted by Hiranyakasipu on Prahlada aimed to kill him for praising Hari could not harm the devotee in the least. Hiranyakasipu's vindictive attitude towards His dear devotee made the Lord extremely angry. Even after killing the Asura, the Lord's anger did not subdue. Prayers of Brahma, Siva and other Devas that the Lord may be pleased to give up His anger were of no avail. Once Bhakta Prahlada prayed to Him to give up His anger and restore His usual Sattwic form, the Lord responded at once by becoming santaswarupa and loving. The Lord is thus hailed as "Prahlada Varada Narasimha".

Prahlada's bhakti to Lord Hari was so unique and absolute that it earned him the first place in the hierarchy of Paramabhagavatas. One of the invocative stotras daily recited by Sri Gopalakrishna Bhagavataswami, one of the greatest Bhagavatas of this century, during his bhajans is:

Prahlada Narada Parasara Pundarika Vyasa Ambarisha
Suka Sounaka Bhishma Dhalbhyan

Rukmangadarjuna Vashishta Vibhishanadheen
Punyanimaan paramabhagavatan smarami

Even the name of Narada who initiated Prahlada in Hari bhakti is mentioned after Prahlada!

It was Prahlada who laid stress on navavidha bhakti (nine modes of devotion) or attaining the goal of life, God-realisation. Therefore, when some devotees prayed to Baba to give them sakshatkara or to show them the path of moksha, Baba exhorted them to follow the navavidha bhakti which is described as follows:

Sravanam kirtanam vishnoh smaranam padasevanam
Archanam vandanam dasyam sakhyam atmanivedanam

The nine steps of devotion are: (1) listening to sacred works or accounts of God and Godmen; (2) reciting the Names of God; (3) remembrance and meditation; (4) prostration at the Feet of God and Godmen; (5) worship of all forms representing God; (6) paying respects to God and Godmen; (7) service to the Lord and His devotees; (8) cultivating a feeling of friendship towards the Lord and (9) surrender of the Self to the Lord.

Baba essentially preached bhakthi as the best of sadhanas. He was a great Bhagavata like Prahlada. The nine modes of devotion were prescribed by Baba to His devotees depending upon their mental receptivity. It has to be noted that since Sri Narasimhaswamiji by nature was more receptive to the path of devotion (bhakti marga), he was directed to go northwards first by Sri Ramana Maharishi and later towards Shirdi by Sri Narayana Maharaj of Khedgaonpet. Sri Swamiji's quest had its fruition at the Feet of Sri Sai Baba at Shirdi. Swamiji fully realized that Baba is still active and fully alive from His Samadhi and dedicated himself to the mission of spreading the message of Sri Sai, the message of Love, the message of bhakti.

The best manner in which devotees can pay obeisance to Lord Lakshminarasimha is to think of Him as Prahladavarada and contemplate on Prahlada's unique bhakti and prapatti (absolute surrender to the Lord) which will please the Master Sri Sai.

SRI NARASIMHA JAYANTHI

(Sai Sudha – May 2005)

In the month of May, the Jayanthi or advent of the Supreme Lord as Sri Narasimha – the Man- Lion form – is celebrated with great devotion. In so doing, we pay our respectful homage to the foremost among the devotees of the Lord, Prahlada. It is Prahlada who propounded the efficacy of nava-vidha bhakti (nine modes of devotion) which was relied upon by many of the devotees and saints and sages who have been appearing on the earth from time to time, including Sri Sai Baba. When a devotee who was well versed in all scriptures and sastras but had no peace of mind approached Sri Sai Baba for his grace, Baba advised him to take recourse to Navavidha bhakti.

Prahlada learnt the glory of devotion to the Lord, Hari bhakti, even when he was growing from the embryo stage in his mother's womb. Prahlada was born as a Hari bhakta. Even at birth Hari bhakti had taken unshakeable, unassailable root in his heart. Nay, the Supreme Lord Himself took abode in the child devotee's heart. "Among Daityas (demon race) I am Prahlada" proclaims the Lord; "Among Devarishis I am Narada". Therefore, the preceptor and the disciple – Narada and Prahlada – are embodiments of the Lord Himself.

Prahlada says that by unalloyed devotion alone the Lord is pleased – not by being a Brahmin, deva (god), sage (rishi), nor by character, versatility, charity and austerity, nor by performance of sacrifices nor by purity, nor sacred vows – all are empty show. Prahlada exhorts other Asura children, "Practise devotion to the Almighty Lord Sri Hari, the Indweller of all created beings, by treating every creature as though it were your very self...... Exclusive devotion to Lord Govinda, which is the same as beholding Him in every creature, alone has been declared to be the highest goal of a human being in this world". Sri Krishna says, "Betaking themselves unto Me, even if they be lowly-born, women, Vysyas or Sudras, they shall attain the Goal Supreme" (Bhagavad Gita, Ch.IX-32). Saint Jnanadev in his commentary on Gita, Jnaneshwari says:

"Born in the demon race, My devotee Prahlada won his eternal glory by making Me incarnate as Nrisimha. That great Prahlada suffered the worst tortures in God's name, and therefore, did by his mere word command all that I would give. Born though he was of the demon family, the very Indra could not equal him in rank and glory. The one crucible here, therefore, is devotion and passionate love to God; all else like race or caste is the merest trash".

Let us see what is recorded in "The Gospel of Sri Ramakrishna".

"While listening to the story of Prahlada's love for God, Sri Ramakrishna went into an ecstatic mood".

"Hiranyakasipu, the King of the demons and father of Prahlada, had put his son to endless torture to divert the boy's mind from the love of God. But through divine grace all the King's attempts to kill Prahlada were ineffective. At last God appeared, assuming the form of Nrisimha, the Man-lion, and killed Hiranyakasipu. The gods were frightened at the rage and roaring of the Man-lion and thought that the destruction of the world was imminent. They sent Prahlada to pacify the Deity. The boy sang a hymn to Him in words of Love, and the Man-lion, moved by affection, licked Prahlada's body".

"Still in an ecstatic mood, the Master said, "Ah! Ah! What love for the devotee!" The Master went into deep Samadhi. He sat there motionless. A tear-drop could be seen at the corner of each of his eyes".

Sri Sai Baba says: "Jnana Marga is like Ramphal, Bhakti Marga is like Seethaphal (custard apple), easy to deal with and very sweet. The pulp of the Ramphal is inside and difficult to get at. Ramphal should ripen on the tree and be plucked ripe. If it falls down, it is spoiled. So if a jnani falls, he is ruined; even for a jnani there is the danger of a fall, e.g. by a little negligence or carelessness". Baba preached bhakti to vast number of his devotees.

Prahlada is the ideal for those who want to follow the path of devotion, *nishkamya bhakti*; for such devotees, bhakti is not only the means and end, it is their very 'self', prana. When the Lord wanted Prahlada to accept some boon from Him, the boon sought by the devotee is unique: "If at all You desire to bestow a boon on me, I solicit from You this boon alone that no desire should sprout in my heart". The Lord assured Prahlada, "Those who follow the path tread by you shall become My devotees. Indeed you will serve as a model for all my devotees". In concluding the narrative, Prahlada Charitra, the Avatar of the Lord as Nrisimha, Sage Narada concludes:

"Whosoever reads with a concentrated mind the story of the pastime of Lord Vishnu, the Primordial Purusha, assuming the form of a lion, and annihilating the Demon King Hiranyakasipu and the glory of Prahlada, the foremost among virtuous souls, shall reach the realm of the Lord where there is no fear from any quarter".

As Sri Sai Baba showed to the Valambi Station Master, unlike the pots with mouths down, one should tread the bhakti marga with a receptive heart. Sri Ramana Maharshi says, "The Lord's grace is always flowing. There is no time at which it is not flowing, and there is no person towards whom it is not flowing. But only those can receive it who have developed the capacity. Devotion is a condition precedent, not for the flowing of grace from the Lord, but for your being able to receive and assimilate the grace which is there always flowing".

FESTIVAL OF LIGHTS

(Sai Sudha – November 2012)

In the month of Ashwin – Tamil month Aippasi – i.e. October – November, Deepavali or Diwali is being celebrated as festival of lights with great eclat and joy by all Hindus. It is believed that this festival is to celebrate the annihilation of darkness in the form of Naraka by Sri Krishna. Naraka was the son of Mother Earth (Bhooma Devi) and was known as Bhaumasura and Bhagadatta. It is learnt from Vishnu Purana that this cruel demon Bhaumasura was born of Mother Earth through her touch with the Lord when He manifested as the Boar (Varaha) at the time of His lifting Her up from the depths of the ocean after killing the demon Hiranyaksha.

Though privileged to be born of Mother Earth Herself through none other than the Supreme Lord, Bhaumasura excelled in evil ways harassing the demigods, snatching away their properties, nay even the earrings of Aditi, the mother of Devas. Not only that, he brought to his city Pragjyotishapura sixteen thousand one hundred maidens, princesses from various kingdoms, daughters of Siddhas, Gandharvas, etc. Unable to stand the atrocities of this Asura any longer, the Devas headed by their king Indra prayed to Sri Krishna to give them protection. Sri Krishna, accompanied by His Queen Satyabhama and mounted on Garuda went to Pragjyotishapura to slay the ferocious demon Naraka. Why did the Lord take His queen when He was going to fight with a great giant? The Puranas reveal: The Lord has conferred a boon on Mother Earth saying that He would not take the life of her son Naraka without Her consent.

And Satyabhama being an incarnation of Mother Earth (Bhooma Devi), the Lord took Her with Him in order to secure Her consent before killing the demon. Again it is mentioned in the scriptures that Indra complained to the Lord about the behaviour of Bhaumasura while the Lord was in the place of Satyabhama and hence he took her just for her diversion.

The Lord killed Bhaumasura, and all the valuable things snatched away by him were retrieved and returned to the respective owners. All the sixteen thousand maidens mentally chose Sri Krishna, their saviour, as their spouse. And the Lord acceded to their prayer and they were all taken to Dwaraka.

We can see here that the Lord never hesitates to punish even the son of Mother Earth if he chooses to go on evil ways. Likewise if even one happens to be born in the family of an Asura, if he happens to be His bhakta he and his descendants are always recipients of the Lord's favour. This we see from the story of Prahlada, who is shown as the foremost among devotees, even ahead of his Guru Narada. *Prahlada Narada Parasara Pundalika Vyasa Ambarisha...*

Mahabali was the grandson of Prahlada. Though very much devoted to Sri Hari, Bali conquered the kingdom of Devas and made Indra and others to go into exile. As usual, the Devas represented to Sri Hari. Bali was not only His devotee, but happened to be the grandson of Bhakta Prahlada who was the foremost among His devotees. Therefore, the Lord appeared as Vamana and by begging for three feet of land from Bali and taking the form of Trivikrama took away from Bali all his kingdom. When Bali Chakravarthi lost all his possessions he was bound. Even then his bhakti, devotion to the Lord, did not waver and he was very firm. Therefore the Lord Himself said that Bali had become the most famous among the asuras for in spite of being bereft of all material opulances, he is fixed and firm in his devotion. 'Therefore', the Lord declared, 'I have given him (Bali) a place not obtainable even by the Devas. He will become king of the heavenly planets during Savarni Manvantra. Till then he shall live on the planet Sutala, which was designed by Visvakarma as per My order. Because it is specially protected by Me, it is free from mental and bodily miseries, fatigue, dizziness, defeat and all other disturbances'. The Lord told Bali, "You may go to Sutala which is desired even by Devas. Live there peacefully, surrounded by your kith and Kin.

“All good fortune to you. In Sutala, not even the predominating deities of other planets, what to speak of ordinary people, will be able to conquer you. As far as the asuras are concerned, if they transgress your rule, My disc will kill them. O great warrior, I shall always be with you and give you protection in all respects along with your associates and paraphernalia. Further, you will always be able to see me there”.

What a great benediction!

In Karnataka the day next to Deepavali Amavasya day (Prathama, first day of shukla paksha) is observed as Balipadyami, a very important festival, to honour the great devotee of the Lord, Mahabali, though he happened to be born in the family of Asuras.

It is also said that King Mahabali visits the people of Kerala once every year and his visit is celebrated as the festival of Onam.

It is learnt from some sources that it was on the occasion of Deepavali, Festival of lights, that Sri Sai Baba lit the earthen lamps in his mosque with water as fuel when he was refused it by the vanis. The advent of Sri Sai is to bring light and love in all quarters dispelling darkness and hatred. The lighting of the lamps by Baba was not just to provide light for people visiting the mosque, a place of worship, but mainly to light the hearts of people who not only refused to give oil but also wanted to enjoy the sight of Baba suffering in darkness. Baba’s lila was to remove the darkness of viciousness in the minds of the vanis.

Salutations to Sri Sai Krishna!

NARAKA CHATURDASI

(Sai Sudha – October 1998)

Naraka Chaturdasi or Deepavali is perhaps the premier festival that is celebrated with great eclat and joy all over India. How this festival came into vogue is known to all. The celestials and human beings were all oppressed by the tyrant Narakasura. In response to their prayers Sri Krishna chose to kill the Asura and save the world from his tyranny. But just before death, Narakasura realised his follies, repented for his evil deeds and prayed to the Lord that the time and day of his deliverance by Him should be remembered by all and celebrated. In the early hours of Krishna-chaturdasi in the month of Aswin (Aippasi in Tamil) corresponding to October-November of the English calendar, people celebrate Naraka Chaturdasi by having bath in mild hot water (a bath then is considered to be as good as a dip in the Holy Ganges and hence called Ganga snana), wearing new clothes, exchanging sweets and greetings and rejoicing.

When festivals are generally associated with the various forms of God, like Ramanavami, Vinayaka Chaturthi, Sri Krishna Jayanthi, Durga Puja, Skandasashti, Shivaratri, etc., Naraka Chaturdasi is perhaps the only festival named after an Asura who inflicted harm for ages on heaven and earth. That is because the Asura repented his evil doings and prayed to the Lord for mercy. The All-Merciful Lord also readily condescended to grant his prayer.

In Karnataka the day next to Deepavali Amavasya, i.e. the Sukla Prathama, is celebrated as Balipadyami. This day is considered to be the day on which the Lord took the form of Trivikrama and blessed the Asura King Mahabali by placing His foot on his head. Here again we see the festival being named after an Asura because of his devotion to the Lord.

Sri Krishna proclaimed in the Gita that "for the protection of the virtuous, for the extirpation of evil-doers and establishing dharma (righteousness), I take birth from age to age".

Paritranaya sadhunam vinasayacha dushkrutam
Dharmasamsthapanarthaya sambhavami yuge yuge

The Lord's message is very clear. The main purpose of His advent from time to time is protecting the virtuous by establishing dharma. The Lord does not want to destroy the evil-doers but only their evil deeds. Celebration of Naraka Chaturdasi as Deepavali for ages clearly establishes this. In today's context, if the Lord were to destroy all evil-doers, it will amount to near annihilation of half the human race since we see evil is more prevalent than virtue.

Abusing the Lord was the second nature of Sisupala. It is said that in response to the prayer of Sisupala's mother, Sri Krishna agreed to bear with Sisupala's invectives for hundred times. Actually the Lord bore with him several hundred times. When Sisupala hurled abuses on the Lord with all venom in the Rajasuya Yaga Mantap, the Lord was calm. Srimad Bhagavata says '*novahca kinchit Bhagawan yatha simha sivarutham*'. But the Lord's devotees, especially the Pandavas, could not tolerate Sisupala's Bhagavanninda. When Sisupala turned to attack the Pandavas, the Lord was forced to kill him. It can be seen that the Lord resorts to *vinasa of dushkrutam* only when the evildoer does not mend his ways, even after he is given several opportunities to do so, and persists in his evil acts. *Dharmasamsthapana* is the sole object of the Lord's advent.

In the Age of Kali, Kali Yuga, the Lord appears in the form of saints with the sole aim of redeeming the fallen souls and showing them the path of dharma. By contact with such saints, satpurushas, mahapurushas, mahatmas, sadgurus or samarthas, - called by any of these epithets – millions of people derive benefit both materially and spiritually. These great ones remove from the minds of people who come in contact with them all traces of evil tendencies and create a fertile field for cultivation of bhakti.

It is Sri Krishna Himself who appears in the form of such saints. This is what He meant in saying *tadatmanam srujamyaham* (I body Myself forth).

Our Master Sri Sai Baba, the great Samartha, is one such advent of the Lord. That is why he is hailed as Sai Krishna. Sai could make Nana understand easily the correct meaning of Gita; Baba could give Uddhavesa Bua and other devotees an insight into the Eleventh Canto (Ekadasa Skanda) of Srimad Bhagavata which contains the exposition of Sri Krishna to Uddhava. Just like Krishna, Sai proclaimed Yogakshemam *vahamyaham*. He could assure all devotees who surrender to him that he will bear all their burdens and protect them always, wherever they are. He is verily *bhayanasana* for his devotees who wholly surrender to him.

Let us, therefore, bow before Sai Krishna and place ourselves in his care and lead a life of Peace.

BLISS

(Sai Sudha - November 1998)

When someone derives immense pleasure out of something in the world, he exclaims "What a blissful experience!" But actually what is bliss? Bliss is a state which cannot be defined in words; it is an experience beyond words. It can only be experienced, but cannot be explained. That is the aim of all religious sadhanas, pursuits. A perfect Guru who has experienced the bliss, who always remains in that blissful state at the same time attending to earthly functions, can make his sincere and ardent disciple also experience such bliss. Pleasure of any magnitude cannot be compared to bliss. Worldly pleasures are transient and are bound to be followed by the opposites – pain. A man who had a sumptuous feast of most delicious food says "it was brahmananda". Whereas the sumptuous feast can bring indigestion and stomachache in its wake, perfect peace, santi, follows brahmananda.

Generally, except a miniscule percentage of people, the vast majority take to religion only as a means for obtaining worldly benefits. Prayers are offered for getting material benefits like jobs, success in examination, marriages, relief from illness, etc. Someone talks about a Sakthi upasaka or upasaki or Anjaneya or Narasimha upasaka who is believed to have vast powers and can give relief. People rush to them and stand in long queues. They may or may not get the relief sought for. Once their purpose is served, they do not think of that upasaka any more, till they have another problem to be solved. We can see people endlessly going from one upasaka to another. Problems always come in quick succession with no end till death. It should also be noted that for a majority of such upasakas, such offer of reliefs is only a profession, a means to livelihood, to amass wealth.

The role of a Mahapurusha like Sri Sai Baba is totally different. Ever remaining in satchidananda state or state of bliss, his aim is only redemption of mankind. Most of the people approach Baba also only for material benefits. Baba does give benefits prayed for. The benefits are conferred unconditionally, purely out of love. When one gets the object prayed for from Baba, he also gets a taste of Baba's Love. Consciously or unconsciously he always think of Baba. In stages he is converted into a true sadhaka whose bhakti to Baba becomes pure, expecting nothing in particular, which is bargainless Love, *nishkamya* bhakti. He develops absolute faith in Baba. He becomes Sai-conscious and no problem can worry him. This itself is the first stage in experiencing bliss.

In Bhagawad Gita, Sri Krishna says: "Four types of devotees of noble deeds worship me, the seeker after worldly possessions, the afflicted, the seeker of knowledge and the man of wisdom. Of these the best is man of wisdom, ever established in identity with Me and possessed of exclusive devotion; I am extremely dear to the wise man and he is extremely dear to Me."

Chaturvidha bhajante mam janah sukritino Arjuna
aartha jijnasah artharthee jnani cha bharatarshabha
tesham jnani nityayukta ekabhaktirvisishyate
priyo he jnanino atyarthamaham sa cha mama priyah II

The special characteristic of getting prayed for benefits from Baba is that the beneficiary is taken up the rung. The *artharthee* (seeker after worldly benefits) is elevated gradually to the position of a man of wisdom when he will be able to experience the state of bliss. When a devotee objected to people going to Baba for temporal benefits, Baba said: "Do not do that. My men first come to me on account of that only. They get their hearts desires fulfilled; and comfortably placed in life, they then follow me and progress further. I bring my men to me from long distance under many pleas. I seek them and bring them to me. They do not come of their own accord".

There is nothing wrong in approaching God or Godmen for temporal benefits. In fact, most of the sacred granthas like Vishnu Sahasranama, conclude with *phalastuthi*, describing the temporal benefits that will accrue if they are recited with devotion. But our quest should be to reach the level of a 'wise man' as stated by Sri Krishna, when the hankerings after worldly pleasures will fall off and blissful experience can be tasted.

Every cause has an effect. Everyone in the world has to face the pairs of opposites. One cannot hope to get only what is pleasant to the exclusion of the unpleasant. Our actions in life are like running a bank account. When we go on making deposits into the bank, our credit balance increases; when we over-draw, we have to pay interest charges. Systematic prayers and good deeds are like deposits whereas overindulgence in worldly pleasures and engaging in the unbecoming acts amount to excess withdrawals. When we approach a Samartha like Sai, our credit balance multiplies.

NEED OF THE HOUR

(Sai Sudha – February 1998)

If some things are frequently spoken of, it is certain that they are rare and difficult to find. For example, people make so much noise about 'secularism' and 'transparency'. These are two commodities which are scarce; in fact one cannot be sure that people who utter these words understand their real meaning at all.

According to the Oxford Dictionary, 'Secular' means 'concerned with the affairs of this world or to things not spiritual, not bound by monastic rules, and 'skeptical of religious truth or opposed to religious education'. People talk about a Secular State. Does it then mean a State governed by worldly people, skeptical of religious truth? Should that be so, there will be a State governed by people having no faith in Dharma.

According to votaries of secularism, it means 'not inclined towards religion'. This is a misnomer since all normal human beings are inclined towards some religion or other.

Transparency means that all actions by individuals or institutions should be strictly conforming, visibly, to set norms and principle without giving any room for suspicion or doubt of any unfair or questionable intent. This is treading the path of satya or dharma.

All religions essentially preach Love as the unifying force. Long before the advent of Buddhism, Christianity and Islam, a religion has been in existence in Bharat, which was called "Sanatana Dharma", with stress more on moral values, right conduct, tolerance and harmony than on rituals or doctrines. It taught people to see divinity in all living beings, to see unity in diversity. This Sanatana Dharma is universal in its appeal in that it does not propagate any exclusive religious practice or any exclusive God. Just like all rivers reach the ocean, all religious paths lead to God, by whatever name one may call that God. This God is equally present in all beings, not only humans but also animals and plants. He is not only without form but is also manifest in all forms. He bestows His benevolence on all impartially.

Samoham sarvabhuteshu na me dveshyosthi na priyah
Ye bhajanthi thu mam bhaktya mayi the theshu chapyaham

"I am equally present in all beings; there is none hateful or dear to me. However, they who devoutly worship Me abide in Me and I too stand revealed in them", says Sri Krishna.

A country governed by people who have no faith in dharma can only lead to anarchy. A welfare state, in a true sense, has to be ruled by people, to whatever faith or dharma or religion they owe their allegiance to, who have an equal vision, who can look upon all communities with equal respect (*sama dhrushti*), who are keen in the welfare of all the people of the country without any discrimination, whose sole aim is service to people and not being the lord of the people. People say that the State should not be allowed to be ruled by communal forces. But are they not motivated by communal, caste or class prejudices? All the same, they seek power by whipping up communal passions only. Power is sought in the name of community, caste, sub-caste, linguistic divisions. 'Secular Secular', they cry at the top of their voices. Is this secularism? These votaries take the gullible people for a ride in their craze for power. A welfare society, where there is total harmony, total peace, is not at all in their agenda. So, where is transparency?

Let us, therefore, use our discrimination and choose what is best in the overall interests of the society. Let us heed to the advice of our Great Master Sri Sai Baba:

"Rama (the God of the Hindus) and Rahim (the God of the Mohamadans) were one and the same; there was not the slightest difference between them; then why should their devotees quarrel among themselves? You ignorant folk, children, join hands and bring both the communities together, act sanely and thus you will gain your object of national unity. It is not good to dispute and argue. So don't argue, don't emulate others. Always consider your interest and welfare. The Lord will protect you. Yoga, sacrifice, penance, knowledge are the means to attain God. If you do not succeed in this by any means, vain is your birth. If anyone does any evil unto you, do not retaliate. If you can do anything, do some good unto others". – Sri Sai Satcharitra, Chapter X

The Master has exhorted all His devotees to join hands and bring all people together, thus act sanely, for gaining the object of national unity. One has to be sincere in his thoughts and deeds. That is real transparency. In the name of our Master Sri Sai Baba, let us take a pledge to harness all our resources to the promotion of universal love, harmony and peace!

DID BABA KNOW SANSKRIT?

(Sai Sudha – June 2008)

Such a question did not arise till one day Sai Baba questioned Narayana Govind Chandorkar on the real meaning of Sloka 24 of Chapter IV of Srimad Bhagavad Gita. This incident created the impression that Sri Sai Baba knew Sanskrit and was familiar with the Bhagavad Gita. Dr. Mariane Warren who had to her credit an exhaustive research on the life and teachings of Sri Sai Baba observes in her book "Now it was assumed by everyone that Sai Baba was illiterate, and as a Muslim would have no knowledge of Sanskrit, but if he 'knew' the Bhagavad Gita then perforce he must be a Hindu dressed in Muslim garb".

Sri Sai Baba gave a unique interpretation to this sloka, totally different from the interpretations given earlier by great Acharyas like Sri Sankara. The traditional meaning of this sloka is that perceivers of Truth impart 'jnana' or Knowledge when approached. But Baba says they impart 'ajnana' or ignorance! Their instruction is simply a piece of ignorance used to remove the disciple's ignorance just as a thorn is used to remove another thorn from the foot. Jnana is already there, but is covered by the veil of 'ajnana' or ignorance, and what is required is to remove this veil when the ever existing jnana is revealed – not imparted.

Dr. Mariane Warren assumes that this is in line with a Sufi notion, "that every soul before birth passes through seventy thousand veils which separate him from Allah, the One Reality, before he enters the world of matter and sense objects, according to his own merit. The passage through the veils brings forgetfulness of one's true divine source ….. The goal of Sufism and the role of the Sufi Master therefore is to help the aspirant escape from this prison and recover his original unity with God while still in the body. Sai Baba's unique interpretation of the Bhagavad Gita verse was thus very much in line with Sufi understanding that removing layers or veils of ignorance, was the task of the Master, *to reveal what was inherently there all along, rather than teach wisdom*".

Whether Baba was a Sufi Master or a Hindu Sage is a question which will be debated eternally, with absolutely no chance of coming to any definite conclusion. Whether Baba knew Sanskrit or not is irrelevant. There can be no doubt about Baba being one of the "Perceivers of Truth" ("*Tatvadarsinah*") referred to by Sri Krishna in the Gita verse. Language is only a means of communication, a means to gain knowledge. Jnana or knowledge is not confined to any particular language. Baba says that 'Jnana' is something which is already there and revealed, not something which is imparted anew.

Whether Baba knew Sanskrit or not, Baba was able to confer the benefit of learning Sanskrit on a chosen devotee. Nana Saheb Nimonkar wanted to take up Srimad Bhagavata Parayana but was not able to do so because he had not learnt Sanskrit. Baba told him, 'Masjid Ayi will teach you Sanskrit, and gradually you will learn. Begin'. Nana Saheb soon attained enough proficiency in that language and he was even able to clear doubts of other people.

Whether Baba knew Sanskrit or not, he was in a position (1) to make Das Ganu Maharaj understand the meaning of Isavasya Upanishad, (2) to make Dixit benefit by the study of Adhyatma Ramayana (3) to advise Uddhavesa Bua on Ekadasa Skanda of Srimad Bhagavata – Krishna-Uddhava Samvada and to enable B.V. Dev to proceed with Parayana of Jnaneswari without interruption and Baba persuaded some devotees to take up Sri Vishnu Sahasranama Parayanam.

It is the experience of several devotees that Baba knew their inner most thoughts wherever they may be. Thoughts would generally arise in the mind only in the language with which the particular person is familiar. A Maharashtrian will think in Marathi, a Tamilian in Tamil, a Telugu man in Telugu and so on. But Baba was aware of all the thoughts of devotees whatever may be the language the devotees are familiar with. Language is not a barrier for his omniscience.

Sri Ramakrishna Paramahamsa Deva did not attach any importance to formal education and did not attain mastery over any literature or language. But he was able to reveal the truths hidden in all the scriptures, Srimad Bhagavad Gita, etc., with perfect ease.

Before coming to Tiruvannamalai in search of his 'Father' at the age of 16, Bhagavan Ramana did not have any knowledge of Sanskrit. The great Sanskrit scholar Kavyakantha Ganapati Sastri visited Bhagavan Ramana for the first time in 1903. The erudite Sastri fell at the feet of Sri Ramana and with a voice trembling with emotion cried "All that has to be read, I have read. Even Vedanta Sastra, I have fully understood. I have performed japa to my heart's content. Yet still, up to this time I have not understood what tapas is. Hence I have sought refuge at thy feet. Pray enlighten me about the nature of tapas". And he got enlightened as prayed for.

"By his thorough mastery of Sanskrit language, and the ease and excellence of his Sanskrit poetry, he (sastri) must, to some extent, have influenced Maharishi who was always receiving ideas and language from persons and books, almost unconsciously. The Swami (Sri Ramana) who began to learn Sanskrit from his perusal of Vivekachudamani with its Tamil verse translation made very rapid progress and was able to compose a stanza in 1915, his Arunachala Panchaka in 1917, and upadesa-sara in 1927. The contact with Sastri was perhaps one of the elements in developing Maharishi's command of Sanskrit". (SELF REALISATION by Sri B.V.N.Swami). Bhagavan Ramana composed the Upadesa Sara not only in Tamil, his mother-tongue, but also in Telugu, Sanskrit and Malayalam. Sri Ramana had explained the meaning of certain slokas in The Bhagavad Gita as and when he was approached by devotees. He actually selected 42 verses from the Gita and translated them into Tamil and Malayalam.

Language is determined by the spoken words, the source of which is the mind. Bhagavan Ramana says, "We must bear in mind that the jnani's state being one which transcends the mind cannot be described with the help merely of the mind and that all description therefore must be defective. Only silence can correctly describe their state or characteristics. But silence is more effective than speech. From silence came thought, from thought the ego and from the ego speech. So if speech is effective, how much more effective must its original source be?"

With the communication of an idea the role of the language ends. Then it is for the mind to formulate thoughts and proceed towards the source, i.e. silence. The tattvadarshins or jnanis referred to by Sri Krishna, like Sri Sai Baba and Bhagavan Ramana, help earnest devotees to proceed towards the source, 'Silence', by removing the veils of ignorance created by speech and thoughts. In this context the instruction of Baba to Upasani to keep quiet doing absolutely nothing is very significant.

MUSIC

(Sai Sudha – November, 2008)

In Tamil, music is described by the word "Isai". Isai means 'to merge' or blend. Because music helps the enraptured individual soul to merge with the Personal God of one's choice or with the Cosmic Soul, it gets the name 'Isai'.

In the nine modes of bhakti expounded by the foremost among bhaktas, Prahlad, Kirtan takes the second place, the first being *sravanam* (hearing). *Sravanam* is hearing the praises of the Lord. All those who have ears, not born deaf, can easily resort to this mode. All are not endowed with the gift of a sweet melodious voice to sing in praise of the Lord. But all can hear and enjoy sweet music. Music is the conduit through which gushes forth the unsaturated love of the devotee for his or her Ishtadevata. *Kirtan* thus follows *sravanam*. Sage Narada is always engaged in Hari Kirtana. Prahlada's mother Kayatu was staying in Sage Narada's ashram when she was pregnant. The child in the womb had the good fortune of constantly hearing Hari Kirtana from Sage Narada himself. Through *sravana*, hearing, Prahlada was born as a Hari bhakta and his unparalleled devotion to Sri Hari earned him the reputation of being the foremost among Hari bhaktas.

In Srimad Bhagavata, acclaimed as the bhakti-sastra, in the Tenth Canto dealing with the advent and lilas of Sri Krishna, we see Krishna drawing the devoted souls to Him through His flute – Venugita. Unable to bear the separation from the Beloved Lord Sri Krishna, the simple unlettered Gopis, the village maidens, pour out their heart in the nectarine Gopika-Gita. They say:-

"Munificent are those who extensively recite on earth your nectarine story which is life-giving to the afflicted, has been celebrated by the wise, eradicates all sins, auspicious to hear and is most soothing to the heart".

Mahaprabhu Chaitanyadeva appeared on earth to propagate the efficacy of namasankirtan in this Kali Age. His message is that by chanting Hari Kirtan with intense longing one can lose the body consciousness, enabling the soul, the jivatma, to merge with the Paramatma, the Lord. Through kirtan one is enabled to enjoy bliss right here.

Sri Ramakrishna Paramahamsa used to go into Samadhi both by himself singing (*kirtan*) and hearing others sing (*sravana*) the glories of the Lord as also the Mother of the Universe. Sri Ramakrishna says: "All the sins of the body fly away if one chants the name of God and sings His glories. The birds of sin dwell in the tree of the body. Singing the name of God is like clapping your hands. As, at a clap of the hands, the birds in the tree fly away, so do our sins disappear at the chanting of God's name and glories". (The Gospel of Sri Ramakrishna).

Sri Ramakrishna also says: "Higher than worship is japa, higher than japa is meditation, higher than meditation is bhava, and higher than bhava are mahabhava and prema. Chaitanyadeva had prema. When one attains prema one has the rope to tie God."

During the last century a great Mahabhagavata with mahabhava and prema appeared in our land, in the South. He was acclaimed as a 'musician par excellence among saints' and a 'saint par excellence among musicians'. Travelling throughout the country he carried on nama-prachar. For him namasankirtan was both the means and end, nay it was his vital 'prana'. At times one could feel the vibrations of his heart-pouring in the very atmosphere. Sri Sai Baba and Sri Narasimhaswamiji, both of them, loved bhajan. Perhaps on account of this only this great Bhagavataswami's soul elevating namasankirtan was a frequent feature in the durbar of Sri Sai Baba at the All India Sai Samaj, Mylapore, for nearly twelve years. He was the illustrious Bhagavatottama, Sri Gopalakrishna Bhagavataswami of Pudukottai. In referring to him, Sri Rege said, "He is the Tower of Bhakti. Even if you subject him to the severest test of microscopic scrutiny, you cannot find the least trace of ego in him." That is, with the name of Sri Rama being his very breath, ego could find no place in him.

"In his earliest days (even upto 1980), Baba had a youthful love of art and music, and at night he went often to the Takia, the resting place of visiting Muslims. There he would, with his very sweet and appealing voice, sing songs mostly of Kabir or songs in Persian or Arabic, which the local people could not understand. He tied tinklets (gunguru or salangai) and danced about in joy while he was singing his songs with rapt devotion. (Life of Sai Baba, Ch.III, Part I).

Sri Rege loved music and bhajans; when he met Sri Bhagavataswami at Chennai in May, 1965 for the first time, he was captivated by the Bhagavataswami's serene appearance and then by his soul stirring bhajans. Bhagavataswami saw Baba Himself in Rege. Both of them left their mortal sheaths in 1971 and till then they had excellent rapport on the spiritual level. Sri Rege writes: "As for religious exercise, Ayi was an excellent singer with a divinely charming voice and a good knowledge of music. I had a good ear for music and I easily attained manolaya." He also stated that Baba had musical gifts and musical appreciation – especially of bhajana kirtans – that Baba sent for him at midnight, and made him sing and corrected mistakes in 'Ragas' and gave him some tips and that Baba himself sang with a charming voice. (*Devotees Experiences of Sri Sai Baba*). In 1914 Sri Rege was proceeding from Indore to Shirdi along with Sri P.R. Awasthi. All night in the train Sri Rege went on with bhajans, with prayers to Baba. When he stood before Baba, Baba said "He gave me no sleep at night. All night 'Baba, Baba' was the cry round my bedside".

Once in Shirdi, the whole night there was music. Next day when Abdul Rangari came, Baba told him, "If you had come yesterday, it would have been better ….. There was music. I wept all night. They abused me". By the word "abused" what Baba meant, Abdul Rangari understood, i.e., "One who loves God would weep, laugh and dance as the songs in praise of God go on". Baba told him that he was able to understand since his Guru was Baba Baleeshah Chishti Nizami. This Chishti Guru was accompanied by music whenever he travelled. The Chishti sec use music as an aid for attaining trance. (*Charters and Sayings – 202*).

For great saints like Purandaradasa, Sri Tyagaraja and Bhadrachala Ramadas and a host of Maharashtra saints music was a sadhana for realizing God or Self. Sri Ramana Maharshi says: "Just as a child is lulled to sleep by lullabies, so *nada* soothes one to the state of Samadhi; again just as a king sends his state musicians to welcome his son on his return from journey, so also *nada* takes the devotee into the Lord's Abode in a pleasing manner. *Nada* helps concentration."

Sri Narasimhaswamiji writes: "Baba is a Perfect Sufi and a Parama Bhagavata". In his book "*Shirdi Sai Baba – In the Light of Sufism*", Dr. Marianne Warren writes: "Love of music was a shared passion between Sufis and followers of the Bhakti Movement. The Sufis, especially the Chishtiyya, regarded music (sama) as the food of the soul. They extolled God through the singing of *qawwalis*. The poet-saints sang of the glories of God through abhangas, bhajans and kirtans, and most became renowned kirtankars, extolling God through music, dance and song. Khwaja Gesudaraz was very fond of music and it was through his influence the music festivals became very popular in Deccan, to the chagrin of the more orthodox Muslims. Music was said to influence a state of ecstasy which is permissible for those with discretion."

In the South the twelve Vaishnavite Saints (Alwars) and the sixtythree Saivite saints (Nayanmars) have bequeathed to posterity their soul-stirring musical compositions (*Divya prabandham and Thevaram*). In the North, Meerabai, Tulsidas, Kabirdas, Surdas and a galaxy of musician-saints have left behind an inexhaustible treasure.

Music is proved to be an effective means for attaining laya, to become one with God.

KRISHNA AND DURGA

(Sai Sudha – December 2012)

The month of Margazhi (December – January) reverberates with bhakti all round. Traditionally this month is considered to be most suited to engage in devotional activities and spiritual sadhana. The Supreme Lord Sri Krishna tells Arjuna (Bhagavad Gita) and later Sri Uddhava (Srimad Bhagavatam, Eleventh Canto, Discourse 16) that He is month Margasirsha among months. This may be due to the fact that saints and sages of yore and the great Bhagavata bhaktas starting from the Gopis chose this month to commune with the Lord.

A study of Srimad Bhagavata reveals that the ultimate aim of all spiritual sadhanas is to reach the Eternal Abode of Sri Krishna, having been released from the cycle of births and deaths. It is found that with the Grace of Sri Durga Devi one can easily attain the spiritual aim. Before the advent of Krishnavatara, before entering into the womb of Devaki as her eighth child Bhagavan deputes Durga Devi – Yogamaya (His transcendental creative energy) to (1) transport from the womb of Devaki the embryo (seventh child) who is none other than Lord Sankarshana to the womb of Rohini in Vraja and (2) enter the womb of Yasodha and take birth as a female child. The Lord tells Her, "People will always worship you as the bestower of all desired boons, they will erect temples for you at various places and worship you with a number of appellations such as Durga, Bhadrakali, Vijaya, Vaishnavi, Kumuda, Chandika, Krishna, Madhavi, Kanyaka, Maya, Narayani, Isani, Sarada and Ambika". As pronounced by the Lord, we see Devi being worshipped in a number of temples all over Bharat, from Kashmir to Kanyakumari under different Names and devotees easily having their material desires fulfilled prompting them to take to spiritual Sadhana.

The maids of Vraja, the Gopis, whose sole aim was to be always in the company of their darling Sri Krishna, chose the month of Margasirsha, the first month of Hemanta Rithu or season to observe a Vrata of worshipping Durga Devi in the form of Goddess Katyayani. Their prayer to Devi was –

Katyayani Mahamaye Mahayoginyadhiswari
Nandagopasutam Devi Patim me 'Kuru te' namah

"O Goddess Katyayani, the great deluding potency of the Lord" possessed of infinite yogic powers, O Supreme Ruler of the Universe, pray make Sri Krishna the son of Nandagopa my husband! Hail to you!"

The whole month of Margasirsha the maids of Vraja meticulously observed the vow with proper ceremonies worshipping Goddess Bhadrakali entreating Her to grant their prayer of making Sri Krishna as their husband. From subsequent events, Sri Krishna sporting the glorious Rasa Lila dance with the maids of Vraja resulting in their enjoying Supreme Bliss, it can be seen that Mother Durga answered their prayers.

Again we see that mother Rukmini who wanted to be the spouse of only Sri Krishna approaching Ambika, Devi Bhavani in Her Shrine and earnestly praying to Her, "I repeatedly bow to you, the consort of Lord Siva with Thy children (Ganesha and Karthikeya). Let Lord Krishna be my husband, let that be ordained by Thee". It is also stated that the elderly Brahmana ladies assembled in the shrine of Goddess Ambika gave Rukmini a part of offerings made to the Goddess and added their own blessings. By the Grace of Goddess Durga, Rukmini Devi was lifted to His chariot by Sri Krishna on the way from Devi's shrine, taken to Dwaraka and married.

Satyabhama's father Satrajit had a glowing gem called syamantaka, bestowed on him by the Sun- God. Once Satrajit visited Dwaraka wearing this valuable gem which was capable of yielding every day eight bharas of gold, besides warding off all evils like famine, pestilence, other calamities, etc. Sri Krishna felt that this gem should be in possession of a great king like Ugrasena, His grandfather. But Satrajit refused to part with the gem. Once Satrajit's brother Prasena went on a hunting spree wearing this jewel. In the forest, a lion killed Prasena and took away the glittering gem. The mighty Jambhavan, King of bears, killed the lion and carried away the gem to his cave. When Prasena did not return after hunting, a rumour was spread by some malicious people that Sri Krishna who once asked for the gem should have killed Prasena and taken away the gem. When Sri Krishna learnt about this, He went to the forest, saw Prasena dead and following the footmarks of the lion He came to Jambhavan's cave. He saw the gem and a fight, duel, wrestling bout, ensued between Sri Krishna and the mighty Jambhavan. The fight lasted for 28 days till Jambhavan's strength depleted and he realised that it was the Supreme Lord with whom he was fighting. Sri Krishna's followers and well-wishers grew anxious when Sri Krishna who entered Jambhavan's cave did not return for several days and people in Dwaraka were worried and grieved for Him. All the people, cursing Satrajit and stricken with grief prayed to Goddess Durga (known by the name Chandrabhaga), the Supreme Energy of the Lord, for the safe return of Sri Krishna. In response to their prayer, with the benedictions of Goddess Durga, Sri Krishna appeared in their midst not only retrieving the hitherto missing gem Syamantaka, but also with a bride, the daughter of Jambhavan - Jambhavati.

Baba identified himself with Sri Krishna. He called the mosque he was staying "Dwarkamayi". He laid emphasis on Sri Vishnu Sahasrananama parayana and his teachings are those contained in Bhagavad Gita. He advised some of his devotees to study Gita, Jnanadev's Jnaneshwari.

In a temple at village Vani in Nasik district the presiding deity Durga Devi is called Saptashringi. The pujari in a disturbed mind was advised by Devi to go to Shirdi and have Baba's darshan for relief. Shyama, Baba's close aide, was advised by Baba to go to Vani and fulfil the vow undertaken by his mother to make offerings to Goddess Saptashringi. The pujari of Saptashringi Devi's temple did not know how to go to Shirdi and Shyama's arrival there to fulfil the vow made them to meet and enabled the pujari to come to Shrdi with Shyama.

In the month of Margazhi, the period ideally suited for bhakti marga doing namasankirtan, during which period we will be entering a New Year, let us all offer our heartfelt prayers to Sri Krishna, Goddess Durga Devi and Samartha Sadguru Sainath for universal peace and prosperity.

BABA: UNPARALLELED CONTRIBUTION TO NATIONAL ECONOMY

(Sai Sudha – May 2008)

Special Economic Zones are now talked about by various Government bodies to ensure rapid growth of economy which is already on its wings. But, many may not be aware that Sri Sai Baba started serving as a nucleus for an ever expanding economic boom over a century back.

Sri Narasimha Swamiji has vividly portrayed in Chapter XXII of Part I of Life of Sai Baba, "Shirdi Village Life", how the Shirdi Village was before or at the time of arrival of Sri Sai Baba there. "It was in those days a mere group of about 80 to 100 mud houses interspersed with narrow lanes between them and surrounded on all sides by an abundance of babul, prickly pear, and other wild growth.... . There were no roads, no street lighting and no public comforts such as public privies, etc. If once a tonga (jutka) came into the village, the village children and elders would stare at it as a rarity.

Swamiji wrote in1955, "Today Shirdi looks exactly like a township with numerous buildings of brick and stone and concrete with number of storeyed structures. Now in 1955 it daily presents the appearance of Tirupati Venkateswara Temple and its approaches." Swamiji rightly foretold, "At present it is difficult to say whether we are anywhere near the zenith of Baba's popularity". Sri Swamiji is not physically present today, after five decades of his having written as above, to see the thorough metamorphosis it has undergone, all due to the relentless prachar work done by him for over two decades, making the name of Sri Sai Baba as familiar as that of Ganapati, Siva, Rama and Krishna.

In attracting pilgrims, it is not an exaggeration if we say that Shirdi is next only to Tirupati. In terms of revenue also Shirdi Sai Samsthan stands next to Tirumalai Tirupati Devasthanam. The village which was once "so wretchedly poor that with a very little income or none one could pull on with his life there", today abounds in affluence. It has become a boon to Tourism and Hospitality Industries. All sorts of traders thrive; a haven for beggars. Railways, road transport, buses and cars, even airways all are making hay. With more and more VVIPs and VIPs, down from the President of India, and other people of importance, visiting Shirdi, the infrastructure at Shirdi, its surroundings and the roads leading to Shirdi are being constantly developed and improved.

"Perhaps it is only just now that Baba is getting to be recognized in various parts of India" observed Sri Swamiji in 1955. Even the Mandir built by Sri Swamiji, as part of All India Sai Samaj, in Mylapore, Chennai had to be run with a very low income as the devotees then visiting the Mandir were only in hundreds. It was an uphill task to generate income enough to complete construction of the permanent structure of the main hall in 1966. Today we see the monumental growth in the number of devotees visiting the temple. The seeds sown by Sri Swamiji have begun to give a rich harvest. Sai Mandirs are sprouting in every nook and corner of our country; even beyond the seas Sai's glory is shining bright.

The total number of Sai Mandirs in the country will be several thousands. Let us see how this has promoted economic growth.

1. Increase in the construction materials used in building the mandirs, bhajan halls, etc., in the name of Sri Sai Baba.

2. Construction workers employed.

3. Baba's lifelike statues are made mostly in Jaipur and transported to various parts of the country by road. The sculptors are benefited; transporters are benefited.

4. Each Sai Mandir employs priests, cooks and other staff depending upon the locality, size of the mandir and number of devotees visiting. The

priests employed in temples in strategic locations like that in Mylapore derive income monthly running into five figures. Four decades ago the priests had only a hand-to-mouth existence.

5. Vendors: Around each temple, there is a cluster of vendors dealing in puja articles like plantains, coconuts, flowers, camphor, agarbathi etc.; those dealing in pictures, marble and other idols of Baba in different sizes, books on Sai, shawls, etc.

6. Annadanam: Thousands are fed in the Sai Mandirs as Baba laid great stress in feeding the poor and hungry.

7. Books on Sri Sai are being published in various languages voluminously; pictures of Baba in different poses are being printed massively. The printing industry and the persons employed by them thrive on account of the constant need for such books and pictures.

8. Social Activities : Big institutions like All India Sai Samaj, Chennai, Sri Sai Samaj, Bangalore, Sri Sai Spiritual Centre, Bangalore and many others run hospitals/dispensaries to cater to the poor, schools, libraries etc; they organize periodical medical camps also.

9. Thousands of beggars are seen around Sai Temples. It is learnt that the cash received by some from devotees is so large that they have investments in deposits, etc.

10. In various localities of Chennai and some other cities and towns, hundreds of families derive sustenance by taking the picture of Sri Sai Baba in cycle-carts to the accompaniment of bhajans and songs on Baba (recorded music) around residential localities.

11. There are people who profess to heal ailments, to solve domestic problems, etc., acting as 'agents' of Baba; these people also derive adequate income and live comfortably using the name of 'Sai'.

12. The amount of collections in cash and kind in some Sai temples is so large as to attract many people to contest for a position in the managing committee or Board of Trustees and even resort to litigations, in the process enriching people engaged in legal profession.

The advent of Sri Sai Baba was mainly to make people lead a normal life, to eschew hatred altogether, to love all living beings, to make people see unity in diversity, to bringing people of different religious faiths and communities into one common fold with him as the binding force and to turn as many as possible on the spiritual path, towards self-realisation or God-realisation. Baba conferred material benefits on devotees so that out of gratitude they can think of him, meditate on him and gradually strive to become one with him. Even after eight decades since he attained Mahasamadhi we see millions of people deriving material benefits by resorting to Sri Sai, and the number of such beneficiaries is swelling every day.

From time to time saints and sages are appearing in our land to make people tread a virtuous path and realise the evanescence of material prosperity. But the advent of Sri Sai Baba is unique in that he grants material benefits to his devotees and thus turn them Godward. Swamiji writes in Life of Sai Baba (Part I Chapter XVII):

"Baba's great purpose in life was to benefit humanity. Many a person who for some reason or other is unable to treat Baba as God is still able enough to perceive some of the highest elements in Baba, e.g. his miraculous power and beneficence and approach him either for aid or for any other purpose, and will undoubtedly derive benefit all round – temporal and spiritual alike".

"Just as in the mango season, mangoes go round the country, similarly this is the Baba season, and everyone can benefit by Baba. This season is provided by providence for greater knowledge about Baba so that all people may approach him for benefit, either individuals, political, social, spiritual or of other sorts".

SPREAD BABA'S MESSAGE: MESSAGE OF LOVE

(Sai Sudha – April 1998)

All peace-loving people are appalled at the manner in which innocent human lives were extinguished by bomb blasts in many places. Fanaticism has made people forget the value of human lives. Acts of violence are found to be spreading.

It is said that religious fundamentalists were responsible for such violent acts. But there can be no such person as 'religious fundamentalist'. If a person is religious, he cannot be a fundamentalist. A truly religious person, to whichever faith he owes allegiance to, would have realized that love is the essence of all religions and would never indulge in acts of violence that harm others. One cannot be a fundamentalist and religious person too.

Fanaticism leads to violence. What makes people fanatics? It is only the propaganda that is being carried on by many political parties, setting one community against the other, one caste against the other, that make people fanatics. If Babri Masjid was pulled down, it was definitely an act to be condemned. But observance of that particular day, year after year, as a Black Day and talking frequently about same to appease one community just to gain political mileage are bound to arouse the emotions of a large section of people. Fanatics do not land from somewhere. A section of our own people, with their subtle emotions driven to a frenzy, become fanatics. Thus fanaticism is a creation of political propaganda. Nearly five decades back, Sri Narasimhaswamiji observed, "political propaganda is another name for lying, deliberate lying, unjustifiable lying, and selfish lying of the worst sort in order to delude and ruin others". In the past temples were looted, damaged and destroyed. But were our forefathers making noise about same incessantly and observing any Black Day? Wise as they were, they chose to bury the past and build a harmonious future.

Now is the time for all religious-minded public, devotees of Sri Sai Baba in particular, to instill in the minds of people the efficacy of Love which will drive away fanaticism. Nothing of consequence can be expected from our politicians to cure this malady, their aim being only to grab power by any means. The new Government will do well to concentrate not only building a Ram Mandir but on establishing a Rama-rajya where people, irrespective of caste, creed and community, can live peacefully and amicably, loving each other and eschewing hatred.

In Sri Swamiji's words, "Love is one force which upholds the Universe, and love is that force which can overcome the innumerable obstructions to the manifestation of love which arise in our imperfect civilization, between individual and individual, group and group, and nation and nation. All bitterness, hatred, rivalries and antagonism will melt into thin air at the contact of powerful love, and such love has to be directed to the world in increasing measure to enable it to cast aside the darkening clouds that cover it and restore to it the blissful light of love. The ultimate future of humanity cannot be and should not be mere ruin and wreck. It must be an integrated whole, integrated by the force of Love. For that, the proper dynamo that can work upon the world is the dynamo that we call Sai Baba".

"Baba had both Hindu and Muslim features in his body and in his actions and practice, and his mission in life was to unify Hindus and Muslims into one compact mass with common religious, spiritual and worldly interests," says Swamiji.

By propagating the wonderful life, mission and teachings of Baba, the dynamo of Love can certainly be recharged. Baba's mission was essentially to bring about a fusion among all sections of humanity through Love. Frequently he admonished people against harbouring hatred towards others and talking ill of others. He compared people indulging in scandals

to pigs gulping excreta with gusto. Mahatma Gandhiji's precept of Ahimsa is a logical extension of the dictum of Baba.

Let each and every Sai devotee spend some time in a day in spreading the Message of Love. Thus every person termed as a fanatic can be brought back into the main stream as a decent peace-loving normal being.

BABA AND SAMSARA

(Sai Sudha – February 2003)

Everyone is caught in the whirl of births and deaths. How one is born again, whether as a human being, that too in a respectable family or otherwise, or as a mute animal, is determined by the effects of Karma. Again how a man is placed in life is the result of karma, present or past. Says Baba, "What you can account for as the result of your present effort is the result of present karma. What you cannot thus trace is due to your past karma. Results accrue differently to two persons doing the same acts; that difference may be put down to the difference in their poorva karma". Baba emphatically exhorts, "Recognise the existence of the Moral Law as governing results. Therefore unswervingly follow the Moral Law. If you do not get the fruits or results of your actions now, they will come in latter births. As for the vasanas, the Moral Law is inexorable and evident. So, by following and observing the Moral Law, you reach your goal – God, the perfection of the Moral Law".

Baba says that the jiva takes birth in body to work out former karma. Once Baba said that by the action of karma he got embroiled and came to a body. Baba on many occasions told that he had taken births several times in the past, that he had been with one particular devotee for 72 janmas. But there is a difference between Baba's being born again and again and ordinary human beings being reborn. Repeated births and deaths of ordinary beings are conditioned by prarabdha karma. But Great Ones like Sri Sai Baba are not bound by karma and hence their taking birth on the earth is of their own sweet will. They appear on earth to guide and show ordinary human beings how they can escape from the effects of karma and ultimately from the cycle of births and deaths. This can be called mukti, God–realization or self–realization. If we read the Life of Sai Baba we can find that several ankita or intimate devotees of Baba like Chandorkar, Upasani Baba, Kaka Dikshit, Rege, Khaparde and a host of others had been privileged to be guided by Baba in their previous births, and that Baba had drawn them to him in this birth also. Baba's charter is that he would account to God for every pie that has been given to him. Baba once declared to Mr. Khaparde, "In a former birth, I, you, Jog, Kaka (Dixit), Shama and Dada Kelkar were all living together with our Guru in a blind alley. I have now therefore brought all these again together".

Baba's taking birth and subjecting himself to samsaric influence is purely out of compassion for the living beings. "Baba's sacrifice for the masses and for the public, has been characterizing him, janma after janma, as we see from an account of his recitals of his own past janmas. In every janma we find that he was self-sacrificing and working wonders, and always helping all people, especially those who put their trust in him and were attached to him", writes Pujyasri Narasimhaswamiji. He further writes:

"Baba's body had previous existence in previous states and lives, and Baba has given various accounts of himself in previous times and his connections with his bhaktas in previous janmas, with some even for 72 janmas or 10000 years. So Baba declared that samsara was binding him also. Now, in a sense, that is obviously true. But still there is the counsel which Baba himself gives that one must behave properly in Samsara and thus escape the effects of samsara, that is, samsara need not be painful if one acts properly. One may escape trouble, sorrow and difficulties, and thus lead a life of asanga which is prescribed by the sastras for escaping samsara".

In 1886 Baba resolved upon entering into mahasamadhi; at the same time he was wondering whether he should live for some more years to carry on his mission, mission of serving humanity. Therefore, before entering into mahasamadhi, he asked his foremost devotee Mahlsapathy to take care of his body, for all practical purposes a lifeless body, for three days. After three days, Baba reentered the body, as a result of which today millions reap the benefit of his loving care and grace both materially and spiritually.

On several occasions Baba impressed on devotees that the three-and-a-half cubit of body which they saw and recognized as Sai Baba, was not actually the real Baba. He said that his Guru had already pulled him out of the body, that is, he was never body–conscious. Thus, upto October 1918, Baba was there both as a walking–talking Deva and an unseen Divinity; today. Baba continues his mission both from his Samadhi and as *apantaratma* – unseen Divine. Will Baba appear again in a new body as he did in the past? Pujyasri Narasimhaswamiji writes further:

"It is the duty of the Guru to follow the sishya birth after birth, and Baba says, 'I will account to God for every pie he has given to me'. He said that it was his duty to take his disciple to God and not to leave him in the middle. When Baba makes a promise, he keeps it up, just as Rama said,

Apyaham jivitam jahyam tvam va Site salakshmanam
Nata prascrutya me vak yam brahmanebhyo visceshatah

Rama said to Sita, "Once I made a promise, I will keep up that promise. I would rather give up my life, yourself and Lakshmana than give up my plighted word, especially the word plighted to Brahmins'. That is why Baba's rebirth is looked for by several people. That would be samsara of Baba to fulfil his promises of rebirth. Baba is not one who is afraid of rebirth. It is only one that has attachment to earthly objects that is to be afraid of rebirths. If one wishes to carry out his promises with detachment, keeping himself in the '*aham brahmosmi*' state, that is, without detriment to his soul–realization, there is nothing to regret. That is not samsara to regret. (See Srimad Bhagavata, Eleventh Canto, XI – 10 to 12 and Srimad Bhagavad Gita IV – 7 & IV)".

1. Baba told the elderly lady Radhabai Deshmukh who was adamant that Baba should give her upadesa, that his Sadhana was only total devotion, love and service to his Guru for twelve years. His Guru took from him as Dakshina two pice, nishta (Shraddha or firm faith) and Saburi (perseverance).

2. Baba loved namasankirtan, bhajan, Sri Narasimhaswamiji writes: "Baba himself in his early days used to dance with anklets tied to his feet singing rapturously songs of Kabir, some of which undoubtedly referred to the beauty and blissfulness of infinite Godhead. Baba must have enjoyed what Tyagaraja says is enjoyed by the devout bhakta in moments

of musical laya". Once Baba told Abdul Rangari that on the night previous to his coming there was bhajan and music and all night he was in rapture.

3. Baba prescribed Prahlada's navavidha bhakti (nine modes of bhakti) to devotees on spiritual quest. The nine modes include sravanam (listening) keerthanam (recitation) smaranam (meditation) archanam (worship) and atmanivedanam (surrendering oneself absolutely). These are not difficult to follow for a man in the thick of worldly activities. We can easily spend a few moments in listening to namasankirtan or religious discourses. Even while engaged in our day-to-day activities we can mentally repeat Bhagavan-nama of our choice. As regards recitation, one can do sahasranama or other stotra parayana. By repeating the Ashtotra or sahasranamavali we do archana and worship. All these are steps to Atmanivedana.

4. Baba laid special emphasis on Sahasranama parayana. Sahasranama implies generally Vishnu Sahasranama only. Sage Vyasa, who is none other than Lord Vishnu, has given this to the world. This was expounded to Yudhishtira and other Pandavas by no less a person than Bhishma Pitamah, grandsire, a Parama Bhagavata, in the presence of the Lord Himself lying on death bed – bed of arrows specially prepared for him by Arjuna. Baba says that once when he was having chest pain, he kept this book on his chest and Sri Hari descended into his heart therefrom. From then onwards, he became one with Sri Hari and he was able to cure various maladies by simply giving udhi, without the help of any herbs which he had till then been giving. Vishnu Sahasranama is highly potent. Baba is invoked as Sahasranama Viswasah, Sahasranama Lakshitah.

5. The foremost among Sri Sai's Apostles, Pujyasri Narasimhaswamiji, did yeomen service to the devotee world by bequeathing to them Sai Ashtotra Satha namavali and Sai Sahasranama Stotra. While Ashtotra Archana is done every day by several devotees, Sai Sahasranama Parayana has not been given much thought.

6. We can see that recently several people have taken to the parayana of Shri Sai Satcharitra mostly to derive material benefits. The Satcharitra which was originally composed in Mahratti verse form by Anna Saheb Dabholkar is now available in English and other Indian languages rendering it easy for people of different

areas to do the parayana in their respective languages and derive immense benefit therefrom.

7. What Anna Saheb Dabholkar has endeavoured to achieve by producing Sai Satcharitra, Sri Narasimhaswamiji has accomplished in compiling Sai Sahasranama Stotra. The Stotra starts with the nama 'akhanda satchidananda' - the true nature of Sri Sai Baba; it concludes with the nama 'kshetrikrutashirdikah' – one who made Shirdi his abode and thus converted it into a kshetra or pilgrimage centre. In between, as in Sai Satcharitra, the remaining 998 namas alternately reveal the real nature of Sri Sai Baba, the remarkable incidents in his life showing what all he did to offer protection to his devotees and his teachings.

SAI, SAHASRANAMA VISWASAH

(Sai Sudha – January 2005)

When one goes through the life and teachings of Sri Sai, it will be very clear that the path followed by him and preached by him was essentially Bhakti Marga – Guru bhakti. This is substantiated by the following:

Shri Sai Satcharitra is mainly the manifestation of the total devotion to and staunch faith the author Dabholkar had for the Great Master. In each and every chapter before and after narrating a particular lila of Baba the author has eulogized expansively the divine attributes and remarkable characteristics of Sri Sai Baba. In between he has given in great detail the Master's teachings in general and specific hints on spiritual Sadhana given to a few deserving devotees. Thus a reading of this wonderful book gives the benefit of knowing Baba's unique acts of protection to his devotees, an understanding of his mission and teachings and an insight into his real nature. Baba had revealed on more than one occasion that he should not be identified with the body they see as Baba and that he is the Parabrahman

transcending the phenomenal world and to get an accurate glimpse of his real nature one should go beyond the mind and intellect. For the vast majority of ordinary mortals he has however advocated meditation on his current physical form before their eyes to start with, which should eventually lead to meditation on his formless nature.

What one hopes to achieve by the parayana of Sai Satcharitra in a week (saptaha) can be certainly achieved by reciting with devotion the Sri Sai Sahasranama Stotra, which can be done in about 30 to 40 minutes.

GRADUATE RELIGION INTO A SPIRITUAL FORCE

(Sai Sudha – March 2003)

The President Mr. A. P. J. Abdul Kalam told a gathering of school students at a function "Rashtrapathi Ke Sath" organized in February 2003 by the South Indian Education Society in Central Mumbai that "religion has to graduate into a spiritual force and the disparities in development should be removed". He said that after discussion with Jain Sage Acharya Mahapragya he was convinced that religious forces can be transformed into spiritual forces. He also very rightly asserted that for communal riots to be brought under control 'the way is to create enlightened citizens'. It is remarkable and praiseworthy that the head of the largest democracy should take it upon him to interact with the young students and make them repeat with him "Intensive learning leads to knowledge and knowledge makes me a great human being'.

What a wonderful message from one of the greatest scientists of the day! Can there be a better forum than the one chosen by him to share his thoughts with? Definitely the message when repeated by the young children with uncorrupted minds will enable almost everyone of them to emerge as glorious citizens of the future. It is for the schools and colleges, those who are entrusted with the noble task of teaching and moulding the children to spread the message effectively and create 'enlightened citizens' at least for the future to usher in a harmonious society.

The President said that 'religion has to graduate into a spiritual force'. Religion as is seen todayappears to be only a commercial activity. Religion is understood and recognized mainly by the externals;the names, forms, rituals, marks you wear and do not wear. The soul of every great religion, i.e. 'Love', islost. Followers of these religions sans spirituality, sans the soul, seem to have formed different groupsvying with each other to increase their numerical strength. Means do not matter for them as long as theend is achieved. This frenzy brings in its trail intolerance and hatred leading to conflics among groups. Terming them as communal riots, setting one against the other, politicians thrive. Accusations arelevelled, but solutions are not sought for. Political parties sitting in opposition are happy in blaming theruling party for the situation.

In reality, but for the din and noise raised by the politicians, pseudo-secularists and a section ofthe Press, by and large the masses in our country continue to live with total amity, with good relationshipwith their neighbours regardless of caste, creed, etc. with a spirit of 'live and let live'. There is one family,the head is a staunch Vaishnavite to whom Sriman Narayana is the only God; the wife worships the Mother of Pondicherry, the son Sri Sai Baba of Shirdi, the daughter adores Sage Ramana's teachings, the daughterin-law Sri Ramakrishna. Yet all of them live happily, one not interfering with the other's faith, with a total spirit of tolerance, inherited by us from the hoary past. If what is seen in a family circle is extended to a village, town, city and to the state, ultimately to human race as a whole, there can be no cause for a communal riot.

One who is born a Hindu can follow the teachings of Buddha or Jesus Christ without his having to convert into a Buddhist or Christian. Mahatma Gandhi was hailed as a 'Christ-like' Christian. Similarly, a Christian or Moslem can benefit by studying the Upanishads or Bhagavad Gita without becoming a Hindu. The lable does not matter. If this is realized, conflicts over conversions from one religion to another can be put an end to. Conversions are nothing but a trade and have nothing to do with religion.

Until the first two decades of the twentieth century a Wondrous Saint, a Messiah of Universal Religion, lived in our country. He is Sri Sai Baba of Shirdi, a rare Mahapurusha, whose parentage was not known, whose caste was not known, whose creed or community was not known, who professed no faith, whose religion was 'Love' and only 'Love'. He chose for his stay a remote hamlet in Maharashtra, Shirdi, inhabited by both Hindus and Muslims, surrounded by similar villages. His abode was a dilapidated mosque, he dressed like a Muslim, but received worship from a large section of the Hindus, totally the Hindu ceremonial form of worship. In his presence all differences were totally forgotten. On one and the same day, Sri Ram Navami day, Hindus and Muslims go on with their celebrations side by side happily. The procession of 'Flags' by the Hindus and that of 'Sandal' by Muslims are taken out simultaneously without any hitch, converging in the Temple of Love. The Hindus hailed Baba as a 'chalthe bolthe dev', Walking, Talking God and the Muslims as an Avalia. In effect Baba's mission was to see that religion graduated into a spiritual force, a force of Life and Love, with no cause for any conflict. In summing up the life and teachings of Sri Sai Baba, Sri Narasimhaswamiji, his foremost apostle, writes: "Differences between religion and religion are found to be matters of doctrine and dogma. All religions must unite in adoration of one common God whose nature is Love, and who with his limitless power creates all and loves all he created equally. Baba made no distinction between Hindu, Muslim and Christian, and treated them all as his children. All religions were united before Baba. Love is a principle on which all religions must unite. That love gets identified with God and perfection in man".

Sri Swamiji further writes: "Baba took great care to see that there should be no such bitterness as would be caused by conversions or intolerance. He put down intolerance and conversions. On one occasion when Bade Baba (Malegaon Fakir) introduced to him one Ibrahim as a recent convert to Islam, Baba slapped him (Ibrahim) on the cheek and asked him 'have you changed your father'."

By reading and hearing the message of Sri Sai Baba of Shirdi and other great saints who traversed this earth and by instilling its essence in the minds of children, the students, our nation can boast of 'enlightened citizens' in the not too far away future.

CONVERSIONS

(Sai Sudha – May 2003)

Recently when an anti – conversion Law was enacted by the Tamil Nadu Government, there was vehement and vociferous opposition not only from the Christian religious heads but also from the parties in the opposition. There was ciriticism in a section of the media too.

This is not a new problem that has arisen. This has been there for the last five centuries. Let us see what The Hindu had reported on April 22, 1953 (fifty years back), republished on April 22, 2003 under the caption 'This Day That Age':

"Missionaries Welcome, But …..

Dr. Kailas Nath Katju, Home Minister, said in the House of the People in New Delhi on the 21st, it had been made clear to all foreign missionaries working in the country that if they engaged in social welfare work, medical and educational, they were welcome, but if they indulged in proselytization that would be undesirable. That was the basic Government's attitude. The Minister was replying to a question by Mr. Judge whether Government had received any complaints from the Madhya Pradesh Government, or the local population, that in many places in the Sarguja and Bilaspur districts of Chattisgarh, Adibasis were given monetary temptations, sometimes threatened, and then converted to Christianity."

So, it is clear that even the Congress Government, headed by Jawaharlal Nehru categorically stated that their Government's basic attitude was that indulging in proselytization by foreign missionaries would be undesirable.

Nevertheless, the situation did not change and proselytization was still going on. Under the circumstances, the State Governments, which enacted legislation forbidding proselytization respecting the genuine concern and sentiments of the majority religious community, cannot be found fault with, whichever is the political party that runs the Government.

Whereas religion is actually a quest after Truth, Peace, Tranquility, the ultimate aim being Godrealisation, it is now more a social phenomenon. In India what was being followed was called Sanatana Dharma, the origin of which could not be established, which included a variety of paths to suit the mental attitudes of different people. This has later come to be called Hinduism. Taking advantage of this diversity, missionaries of the later day religions, particularly Christianity, were successful in getting large number of people converted to their religion. The country being under British Rule for over three centuries was also an added advantage to them.

The shabby treatment given by the caste Hindus to people of lower castes, discrimination shown on economic considerations, low level of literacy, oppressive attitude of a few rich people over the poor, were all taken advantage of by the Christian missionaries. They did offer monetary assistance, education, medical facilities, etc. and ultimately a status in society in return for which what people had to do was just to convert to their religion. The change is in the label.

One cannot expect anyone who suffers due to lack of food, clothing, shelter and basic needs, to follow a religious path. That is the reason why almost all the religions lay special emphasis on annadhan, vidyadhan and offering of loving help to people in distress. Once a person is relieved of his misery, he gets ready to talk or hear about God or religion. For a vast majority of religious people, prayer or worship or other religious activity is mainly to get material benefits only. According to Sri Narasimhaswamiji, 'God is that which you appeal to when you are in trouble, and that which helps you when you cannot help yourself and when your friends on whom you depend cannot help you, something superhuman, something kind, something all-powerful which comes to your rescue just at the moment when without it you are totally at a loss'. The All India Sai Samaj, Sai Mission was founded by Sri Narasimhaswamiji, essentially for Sai prachar, i.e. taking Sri Sai Baba and His message of Universal Love to people. Sri Narasimhaswamiji followed the dictum of Swami Vivekananda,

'First food, then religion'. So Swamiji's prachar work included poor feeding, free medical assistance to the poor and needy and vidyadhan. Serving the poor is actually serving Baba. It is, therefore, time that people who have taken up the responsibility of running the All India Sai Samaj, recall the laudable objects of the Founder, Sri Narasimhaswamiji, and utilize the large sums of money being received by the institution in Sai prachar work which included developing the Dispensary into a good hospital, the Sai Vidyalaya as a model educational institution and annadhan. When relieved of miseries, distress, the minds of people will be receptive to the idea of taking to spiritual path. There will be no necessity for 'conversions' and as insisted upon by Sri Sai Baba, each one will follow his own dharma and will realise that his svadharma is as effective as any other dharma.

In Chapter VI, Sai Baba and the Future of Religion, *Part IV of Life of Sai Baba*, Sri Narasimhaswamiji writes:

"Live and let live; freedom to all people as far as possible to adopt their ideas of approach to God" must be the basis on which society must be founded. Any compulsion in religion will destroy religion and society also. This cardinal principle is noted to be one of the main features of Sai Baba's dealings with his multifarious devotees including Hindus, Muslims, Christians, Parsis and others. Anything like compulsion or for that matter any attempt for conversion is absolutely destructive of the work of religion. We can have neither religion nor unity where compulsion is adopted. Conversion is very often the result of either compulsion or low motives, and Baba, who knew this fact very well, on one occasion when a Hindu convert to Islam was brought by Bade Baba to him saying, 'Baba, this man has been converted to Islam', struck him (the convert) on the cheek and asked, 'Have you changed your father?' Changing one's father is absolutely unthinkable, and an absurd idea. Each religion makes God the father of its followers, and when one has got a father according to accredited lines which are useful, it looks absurd to think of changing either the physical father who begot one or the Universal Father that is adored in religion. So, Baba always dissuaded people from changing their religion either from Hinduism to Islam or from Islam to Hinduism or from Christianity to Hinduism vice versa. What is more important is not mere external conversion but conversion of the heart, which makes a man lose his sinful and bestial nature and climb up to Godhood. That real conversion is not called conversion by people because it generally has no external marks to denote it. Baba's object was that all people should be really converted and should have God in their hearts, and get firmly attached to God so that all of them will be soaked through and through with the idea of God, and in consequence there will be no friction between one person soaked in God and another person soaked in God."

The following report has appeared in The Hindu dated May 2, 1953 (53 years back):

FOREIGN MISSIONAIRES AND CONVERSION

H. S. Narasiah, Founder, Gandhian Brotherhood, said in a letter to the Editor, "It will be interesting to recall what Gandhiji said on the subject. Opening a discussion amidst a fellowship of faiths and nationalities assembled on January 19, 1928, Gandhiji said: 'I came to the conclusion long ago, after prayerful research and discussion with as many people as I could meet, that all religions were true, and also that all had some error in them; and that, whilst I hold my own religion, I should, hold others as dear as our nearest kith and kin, and make no distinction between them. So, we can only pray if we are Hindus, not that a Christian should become a Hindu, or if we are Mussalmans not that a Hindu or a Christian should become a Mussalman, nor should we even secretly pray that anyone should be converted; our inmost prayer should be that a Hindu should be a better Hindu, a Muslim a better Muslim and a Christian a better Christian'. When asked to clarify this statement, Gandhiji stated: "I would not only not try to convert but would not even secretly pray that anyone should embrace my faith".

Gandhiji had only reiterated what saints like Sri Sai Baba had said.

SAI SEVA

(Sai Sudha – January 2003)

According to Swami Vivekananda, feeding the poor, annadana, is Narayana Seva. In worldly parlance, the giver of anything is always considered to be on a higher level than the one who receives. The giver's ego is flattered and ultimately no merit accrues. But when one feeds the poor with the thought that he is actually serving Narayana, the Supreme Lord, he becomes in reality the receiver, that is the recipient of the Lord's Grace. Sri Sai Baba who had become one with the Paramatma time and again declared his oneness with all living beings, particularly the poor, lowly and wretched. Once Mrs. Tarkhad gave a piece of bread to a hungry dog that came to her quarters. Later when she went to take darsan of Baba at the mosque, Baba told her, "Mother, you have fed me sumptuously up to my throat, my afflicted pranas (life-forces) have been satisfied. Always act like this and this will stand you in good stead. Sitting in this mosque, I shall never speak untruth. First give bread to the hungry and then eat yourself. Note this well". He further declared, "The dog which you saw before meals and to which you gave the piece of bread is one with me. I am roaming in their forms, He who sees me in all these creatures is my beloved".

According to our scriptures, daana is the effective means for men to get rid of the trait *lobha* (greed), which leads to other evil tendencies. On this subject Sri Narasimhaswamiji writes: "Prajapati was approached by his three sets of children, the Devas, the Naras and the Asuras. Each of them came and said, 'Please give us instruction as to what we should do',

Prajapati answered *'da', 'da', 'da'*, to each of these. In the case of the gods, the *da* required for them was *dama*, that is self-control, moderation. In the case of Asuras, the '*da*' required was *daya*, i.e. mercy. Their excessive cruel nature had to he met by the spirit of compassion, which was antidote for their cruelty. In the case of men, human beings, the '*da*' was *daana*, i.e. charity. Man's natural instinct is to grasp, to be greedy and to get more and more, and the best way of checking this greed is by making man give up all that he has got. *Daana* forces a man to part with his money, etc. and by constant parting, he will get accustomed to feel quite nonchalant, quite unaffected while parting with moneys or when moneys are lost. Thus daana is the recipe given to men as the rule of their life by Prajapati.

daatavyam iti yat daanam diyate anupakarinc
desa kalecha patrecha tad daanam saatvikam smritan

Quoting the above sloka from Srimad Bhagavad Gita (XVII -20), Sri Narasimhaswamiji further writes, "According to Hindu religion, the beggar is God himself. You have to treat him as Narayana, coming to you to give you an opportunity to serve him".

There are number of types of *daana*, each of which has its own intrinsic merit. Of these, two are considered more meritorious than the rest, i.e. *Annadaana* and *vidyadaana*. *Annadaana* is to appease the hunger of the stomach and *vidyadaana* is to satisfy the thirst for spiritual knowledge. Only when the hunger is appeased, one will be ready to accept *vidyadaana*, i.e spiritual knowledge or religious teachings. So Swami Vivekananda once declared, 'First food, then religion'. When we read the Life of Sri Sai Baba, we find that on several occasions when devotees came to Shirdi from outside to have Baba's darsan, Baba invariably asked them to have food first. Once on a Ekadasi day one devotee came just before Noon Arati time; Baba made him have his food immediately and even went to the extent of assuring him that the Arati would wait till he came back after food. Pujyasri Gnananandagiri Swamigal of Tirukoilur, Tapovanam used to ask the devotees who came to have his darsan to have food first. Pujyasri Gopalakrisha Bhagavataswami, who strictly followed the unchavritti dharma gave prominence to feeding the devotees.

Sri Sai Baba who lived on food collected through bhiksha only till the last, in the earlier years of his stay at Shirdi used to throw the food collected to be taken by dogs, cats and crows freely. Every day the woman who swept the floor of the masjid used to take a few pieces of the bread collected by Baba through bhiksha. In the later years, when the number of devotees grew, lot of prasadams were brought as naivedya which was freely distributed. Hundreds of beggars gathered in Shirdi and they were all fed. Baba felt highly pleased with this kind of *annandaana*. Baba is hailed in Sri Sai Sahasranamavali as *annadaana sada nishtah* (one who was determined to feed others) *athithi bhukta sesha bhuk* (one who always ate whatever was left after guests were fed, *daanasoundah* (expert in giving away daanas), *durbhikshebi annadatre* (even in times of scarcity or famine Baba distributed food *nityannandaana dharmishtah* (who stuck to the dharma of giving away food to the needy every day), *bhiksha annadaana sesha bhuk* (ate only what remained after giving annadaana out of food collected by him by way of bhiksha), *bhikshadharma maharajah* (a great king among those (saints) who took bhiksha as dharma), *bhikshvougha datta bhojanah* (who gave food to a large number of beggars daily), *yajna daana taponishtah* (steadfast in following the dharmas of sacrifices almsgiving and austerities). This was done by a Samartha who ate food only to keep body and soul together (ate to live and not lived to eat) – *dehayaatraartam anna bhuk.*

Sri Narasimhaswamiji followed the system of Narayana Seva or Sai Seva on all festivals like Mahasamadhi, Gurupurnima, Sai Jayanthi (Sri Rama Navami) etc. Later on this seva was continued for several years on all Full Noon (Pournima) days and whenever specific requests were made by devotees with contributions. For some years, even before the Government introduced the Mid-day meal scheme, food was given by the Samaj to the poor children studying in the Corporation school adjacent to All India Sai Samaj.

In the past, the Kings of yore made endowment to almost all temples for carrying on annadaana. By passage of time this dharma was totally forgotten and given up. The Tamil Nadu Government, the Hon'ble Chief Minister in particular, should be complimented for reintroducing the institution of annadaana in a large number of temples. This should be considered a step taken in the right direction for establishing dharma.

IMPORTANCE OF ONION

(Sai Sudha – June 1999)

Strange things do happen in this world. Very commonplace things sometimes assume great importance and change the course of events. Onion is one such thing. People in Government dread this product. Scarcity and rise in price of onion saw to the exit of ruling parties in three states where Assembly elections were held in November last. Even charges of corruption and nepotism at high places pale into insignificance compared to scarcity of onion. This shows how important and valuable onion has become to the people of our great Nation!

Orthodox Hindus shun onion as it is considered to be a food of people of rajasic nature. Even people who consume onion avoid them on specific days like Ekadasi and New Moon Day. These people can do without onion and they do not mind if onion becomes scarce or costly. Perhaps the politicians who rule the country thought of only these people and ignored the importance of onion, and onion had the last laugh. Those who rule, and who want to rule, this great country, should have learnt a valuable lesson. They should see, if they want to be in power, that they give onion its due importance. They may even consider making onion the National Food! Truly, onion is the King Maker!

Some devotees of Baba were averse to onion and thought that they are above the others in their religious advancement by not consuming onion. Avoiding onion is to develop satvic nature necessary for spiritual quest. But if people become egoistic and consider themselves superior by not taking onion, the purpose is defeated since their nature still remains rajasic. Baba wanted to correct this in the case of some devotees.

Baba once asked Das Ganu Maharaj who disliked onion to prepare pitla of onion and offer him a part and take the rest. Das Ganu prepared the onion dish, but just pretended to have taken it by touching it with the tip of his finger and drawing it near the nether lip. When he went to Baba, the omniscient Master exposed Das Gupta's pretension to everyone present. He showed what Das Ganu did. He then asked Das Ganu not to pretend but to actually eat the onion dish. From then on Das Ganu was eating onion while at Shirdi except on important days like Ekadasi.

On an Ekadasi day, Kusa Bhav, an orthodox Brahmin, was asked by Baba what he ate that day. When Kusa Bhav told Him that he did not take anything since that day happened to be Ekadesi, a day for upavasa, Baba asked what he meant by upavasa. Kusa Bhav answered that upavasa meant fasting – not eating anything except kanda moola (sweet potatoes, etc.) Baba exclaimed, "Oh! Kaanda (onion)! Here you have, eat it", and produced some onion dish. The embarrassed devotee told Baba that he would eat it if Baba ate first. Baba ate some and Kusa Bhav had to follow suit. When other devotees came, Baba wanted to have some fun and told them, "Look at this bamniya (corrupt and contemptuous equivalent to brahmin)! He ate onion on Ekadesi!" Kusa Bhav said that he ate it because Baba ate. Baba protested and said that he ate only kanda (sweet potato) and vomited out sweet potato. Seeing this chamatkars of Baba, Kusa Bhav swallowed the vomited potato as Prasad. Baba first admonished him for doing this, but His heart melted later and He blessed Kusa Bhav with a rare boon. Whenever Kusa Bhav thought of Baba and held him empty palms open, warm udhi from the Dhuni kept by Baba fell in his palms as Prasad. This boon Kusa Bhav enjoyed throughout his life.

Dada Kelkar, an overzealous Brahmin, abhorred onion and even objected to use of onion by visitors to Sathe Wada. Once he was harsh on S.B. Nachne's mother in law for taking onion, Dada Kelkar's grandchild developed sore eyes and he went to Baba and asked him what he should do. Baba advised him to apply onion and foment the eyes. Where would the onion-hater Kelkar go for onion? Baba advised him to take it from Nachne's mother-in-law who was present there. But that lady told Baba that she would not like to give anything to Kelkar who earlier abused her

for taking onion, but would do so if Baba ordered. Baba advised her to give and she gave it. Baba taught a lesson to Dada Kelkar for his intolerant over-asceticism.

Baba's message is clear. Avoid onion if required to help in your religious pursuits; but do not make a show of it and be intolerant towards others who use onion. It should not be construed that Baba did not want His devotees to avoid onion.

FIRST IMPRESSION

(Sai Sudha – August 1998)

"First impression is the best impression", it is generally said. It is absolutely necessary that one acts or behaves in such a manner that the impression he or she creates in the minds of others at first contact is always good. In life we see practically that when one goes to somebody else seeking some help or a job, what matters is the first impression he or she creates in the mind of that person. If the first impression is bad, it is very difficult to change it. It creates a prejudice and prejudices die hard.

An impression about a person is created in the minds of people first by his appearance, then demeanour and finally by what and how he or she speaks.

Impressions are also passed on. When two people talk about a person, if one gives a bad opinion, a bad impression is created. It needs lot of efforts to change that impression.

One has to be very careful in talking. What and how one talks creates an impression in the mind of the listener. Spoken words convey what goes on in the mind; words reflect thoughts and thoughts reflect the personality. Unless a person's thoughts are pure, words coming out of the mouth cannot be pure. A person harbouring harmful thoughts can only utter words which would hurt others. That is why Baba advises His devotees to eschew kama and krodha (desire and anger) which make the mind and thoughts stray from what is right. His prescription to get over this is first satsangh and then nama japa, parayana, which are bound to remove all impurities.

In Ramayana, we can see how Rama got a very good impression about Hanuman at the very first meeting. Rama was immensely impressed by the manner in which Hanuman spoke.

Noonam vyakaranam kritsnam anena bahudha srutam
Bahu vyaharataanena na kinchidapasabditam

Rama's these words earned the accolade '*navavyakarana pandita*' to Hanuman. 'He speaks auspicious words that make the heart dance with joy', says Rama. Further, 'If a king does not have an emissary like him, how can he get his jobs accomplished? He who has such emissaries endowed with innumerable good qualities and talented to get jobs accomplished, prompted by the words of such emissaries, will attain success in all endeavours'.

Yevam gunaganaryukta yasya syah karyasadhakah
Tasya siddhyanti sarve artha dootavakyaprachoditah

Again we see Mother Sita, after hearing the wonderful words of Hanuman exclaims, 'Oh, the Great Vanara! You deserve to be engaged in conversation by me' and 'I do not consider you, who has no fear even about Ravana, an ordinary Vanara'. This is how Hanuman impressed the Mother at his very first contact.

Now let us see how a person gets impressed by words of others. Drawn by Rama's wonderful form, Sroopanakha introduces herself to him. She says, 'I am Rakshasee Soorpanakha. My brother is Ravana about whom you should have heard. He has two brothers, one the mighty Kumbakarna always immersed in sleep and the other one Vibhishana who is righteous and does not possess the qualities of Rakshasas'. *Vibhishanstu dharmatma na tu rakshasacheshtitah*. These words which came out of the mouth of even a wicked Rakshasi like Soorpanakha gave Rama the first impression about the great bhakta, Vibhishana.

Hanuman was impressed by the words of wisdom emanated from Vibhishana in the court of Ravana who ordered that Hanuman be killed. Hanuman recognized a great bhakta in Vibhishana. When Vibhishana sought refuge at Sri Rama's feet, Rama first sought the counsel of Sugriva and other Vanara leaders. Sugriva stoutly opposed giving refuge to Vibhishana and gave several reasons for that. The sycophancy or herd mentality which is now seen in today's political culture was there even in the days of Ramayana. All leaders, with the exception of Hanuman, just echoed what Sugriva, their king, said. Most of them had heard about Vibhishana from Hanuman immediately on his return from Lanka after seeing Sita. Hanuman referred to Vibhishana as *Vibhishano nama tasya bhraata mahamatih*. Still once the king gave an opinion, all of them fell in line. Their sycophancy or herd mentality prevented them from thinking on their own and giving a considered opinion. Only Hanuman who spoke in the end set a different trend and argued why Vibhishana was right in seeking refuge in Rama. The first impression Rama got about Vibhishana from the words of Soorpanakha must have got reinforced by the sane counsel of Hanuman. Brushing aside all arguments against accepting Vibhishana, Rama gave refuge to him spontaneously and even crowned him, as the future king of Lanka. Not only that, Rama promised refuge to anyone who seeks refuge in Him and asserted that it would be his vrata (resolve) to protect him always. Rama got the encomium '*saranagatavatsala*'.

WEST TO EAST

(Sai Sudha – March 2005)

In narrating his impressions about Sri Sai Baba, Professor G.G. Narke says, "As even in this flesh – in this earthly life – he was not confined to his physical body, it may be truly said of him, 'Sai Baba is alive, He is where he was then. Even then he was where he is now". He also made occasional reference to what his function is and was in the terrestrial sphere and other worlds". (Devotees' Experiences of Sri Sai Baba)

Rao Bahadur S.B. Dhumal says, "The best way of understanding Baba is to experience him oneself. Where is Baba gone? He is still alive and active – more active, if that were possible, than he was before his Mahasamadhi. Anyone in downright earnest can get into touch with him today and at once".

Similar are the conclusions of several other devotees who had the privilege of sitting at the feet of Sri Sai Baba at Shirdi before his Mahasamadhi. The ever-increasing number of devotees resorting to Baba and temples being erected for Sai in several villages and towns in every nook and corner of this country, nay, even abroad, clearly substantiate the fact that Sri Sai Baba is more active today even after his Mahasamadhi. In fact, as years roll by his powerful presence is more and more manifest.

It is inappropriate to refer to Baba as 'Sai Baba of Shirdi' or 'Shirdi Sai Baba'. As there cannot be several Gods – God is One – there cannot be several Sai Babas. It is said that Sai Baba first came to Shirdi and then went away for some years to return later. “The date of Baba’s first arrival at Shirdi cannot be fixed. A very old lady, the mother of Nana Chopdar, said in 1900 that when she was young she saw Sai Baba first at Shirdi, and then he was a prepossessing and attractive lad” writes Sri Narasimhaswamiji. Das Ganu Maharaj writes that he was told by an old lady Salubai Shelke of Shirdi around 1895, then aged 65 or 70, that when she was about eight or ten years old she saw Sai Baba first coming to Shirdi. There are several stories about Sai Baba’s earliest periods, i.e. the periods before he made Shirdi his abode, but none of them can be said to be authentic. Since none of the people who were living at the time Baba was young could be contacted nor did Baba himself reveal much, it is difficult to arrive at definite theories.

One fact, however, is clear. There was a gap of a few years between Sai Baba’s first visit to Shirdi and his second or final visit. Even after coming to Shirdi, Baba often went into the nearby woods seeking solitude. According to Sri Ganeshnathji Maharaj, a siddhapurusha of Sri Gorakhnath cult having his ashram at Bhimashankar (one of the Jyotirlinga Kshetras, situated in Maharashtra, off Pune), Sri Sai Baba after his first visit to Shirdi was wandering throughout the country for seven years. Finally, he came to Shirdi and by making it his place of stay transformed the unknown hamlet into a venerable place of pilgrimage. It is learnt from Sri Ganeshnathji Maharaj that during his wanderings Sri Sai Baba also traversed the Eastern Region through dense forest areas. Baba spent some time in contemplation underneath a panchavati, cluster of trees, in a place about 20 Kms. from Dhenkanal, en route to the famous tourist spot Kapilaas. Kapilas, situated atop a hill surrounded by flora and fauna, is said to be the abode of Sage Kapila, an incarnation of Lord Vishnu and here is housed the shrine of Lord Chandrasekhara with a number of other temples around it. Shri Ganeshnathji Maharaj visited Kapilas in 1997 and on his way back to Bhubaneswar, about 5 kms. from Kapilas, he stopped the vehicle abruptly and entered into the adjacent woods and later was found to be seated under the Pancha-vriksha, on a stone. Sri Swamiji by his power of *dooradhrushti* or wonderful divine knowledge, revealed that was the identical place where Sri Sai Baba halted during his wanderings before settling down at Shirdi. Coming from the mouth of a siddha-purusha like Sri Ganeshnathji, one cannot entertain any doubt about its veracity. A staunch Sai devotee of Bhubaneswar who had the privilege of taking the Swamiji to Kapilas was given the mandate to construct a temple for Sri Sai Baba at this sanctified location. Since Sai and Dattatreya are believed to be identical, the mandir was to be dedicated to Dattatreya and Sai. It is said that this chosen devotee was also sternly advised by the Swamiji that this project should be completed without getting assistance from the government and going in for public contributions.

Then it is history. In 1997 vast area of several acres surrounding the sacred panchavriksha was acquired. Situated nearly 15 Kms. away from the nearest town Dhenkanal, no water, electricity or any other basic facility was available. Materials, even water, had to be brought from remote places. The road is only about 10 feet wide with no habitation. By the tireless and sincere efforts of the chosen devotee Sri Dwarika Mohan Mishra and his gurubandhus and friends, a huge complex has come up. It will not be an exaggeration to say that it is the greatest of Baba's chamatkars. Like the palace in Indraprastha for the Pandavas, this complex appears to be a creation by gods. Besides the main mandir for Sai and Dattatreya, the complex includes Dwarakamayee with dhuni, Gurusthan with Padukas, a Dhyana Mantap, Library, a mantap around the holy Panchavruksha (referred to as Kalpavruksha), kitchen, dining hall, guest rooms, etc. Bhaktanivas is a massive structure with rooms and other facilities for visiting pilgrims. Several cows are well taken care of in a separate Go-shala. The buildings are surrounded by rich vegetable and flower gardens meticulously tended and a number of bilva and other trees, tulsi groves, herbal plants etc. According to Sri Mishra this accomplishment has been possible only by the inspiration and grace of Sri Ganeshnathji Maharaj.

In Sai Sahasranamavali, Baba is invoked as *Kshetrikrutashirdikah*, i.e. One who has made Shirdi a Kshetra. The number of pilgrims visiting Shirdi, a remote place in the West, has crossed all bounds. The Master, in His mercy, should have decided on a balancing act and has by his gracious sankalpa brought into existence a Kshetra of equal potency in the East. He is now also *Kapila kshetra-nivasah*. The place is ideally christened as Tarana Kshetra – a pilgrim centre that helps the devotees to cross the samsararnava, bhavasagara, the sea of samsara.

That Sri Sai Baba is pervading every inch of this sacred place can be felt by the aura of love enveloping the whole area. One can feel the bliss of love issuing forth from every Sai sevak, every volunteer, every devotee, nay, even the plants and trees. This is a place ideally suited for carrying on spiritual Sadhana – meditation, dhyana or contemplation. Baba had chosen earlier one place of abode near Dwaraka in the West; now he has chosen another in the East, near Puri, the abode of Lord Jagannath.

When we go through the experiences of various devotees of Sri Sai Baba, meticulously collected and published by his great apostle Sri Narasimhaswamiji and also Baba's periodical utterances, what comes to the fore is his ubiquity. In 1968 seeing the grand celebration of Sri Sai Baba's 50th Mahasamadhi Day (Golden Jubilee) at Chennai, Sri Rege with tears flowing down exclaimed, 'See the Glory of the Master! Who says He is at Shirdi alone?" The Glory of the Master is manifest in no small measure at the Dattatreya Sai Ashram.

IN THE COMPANY OF A SAINT

(Sai Sudha – October 1967)

"You have a vast ocean to give you abundantly whatever you need. What need is there for you to come to a river?" Thus spoke Sri Gnananandagiri Swamigal of Tapovanam when the writer went to the Swami with a few others on September 24th. "When Baba is there, what need have we to go after Sadhus after Sadhus?" was the idea of the writer. It looked as though the Swami read the writer's mind when he spoke as above.

Our stay with the Swami was only for a few minutes, but it was very valuable and educative. In fact, one can consider only such moments in life as 'life lived'. After asking the writer about the All India Sai Samaj, the Swami narrated to the small gathering of about 50 devotees there how our Founder- President Sri Narasimhaswamiji left his home, went to Ramanashram, why he had to leave that place and finally how he got the Grace of Sri Sai Baba and started distributing same to the whole of humanity.

We have read in the biography of Sri Sai Baba that the Master identified himself with many saints and sages of the past and present, such as Sri Akkhalkote Maharaj, Sri Tajuddin Baba, etc. Sri M.B. Rege once told how Sri Madhavanath Maharaj identified himself with Sri Sai. While in the presence of Sri Gnananandagiri Swamiji, I was wondering whether the Master's Spirit was manifesting in the Swami also. 'Yes. The same Spirit, Power, manifests itself in different forms at different places' said the Swami.

"The mother bird keeps its little ones in a nest, feeds them, brings them up and bestows its attention till they grow. Once they grow the little ones fly away, leaving the nest. They think of their mother no more nor does the mother-bird think of the little ones any longer. Similarly, the jiva (bird) does not need the body (nest) once it grows spiritually with the aid of the Guru", said the Swami.

As the majority of the devotees of Sri Sai, the devotees of Sri Gnananandagiri Swami mostly approach him for getting relief from their worldly problems and difficulties. With a beaming countenance, the Swami talks individually to each one of the devotees who approach him and gives them solace. It is a feast to the ear to hear the Swami talking in and it is a feast to the eye to see the Swami walking hither and thither swiftly, carrying his bulky body.

The devotees of the Swami say that he is over 100 years old. I am only amused at their claim. Where does the question of age come for such great ones who are ageless? Were they ever born and will they ever die? Can we say that our Master Sai is now dead and gone?

SRI GNANANANDA SWAMIGAL OF TAPOVANAM : A CONTEMPORARY SAINT OF SRI SAI BABA

(Sai Sudha – July 2012)

We have read that Sri Sai Baba identified himself with many saints who appeared in our country during his time, like Sri Akkalkot Maharaj, Sri Tajuddin Baba of Nagpur, Sri Madhavanath Maharaj and a few others. There was one saint who lived in Tapovanam near Tirukoilur in Tamil Nadu whose ways of dealing with devotees were almost similar to the ways of Sri Sai Baba. By about 1965, when the writer was privileged to serve as the Honorary Secretary of All India Sai Samaj, he came to know about him. By the grace of Sri Sai he got an opportunity to go to Tapovanam and have darshan of the saint living there – Sadguru Gnanananda Swamigal, who it was reported was more than hundred years old. No one could say definitely how old he was. In September 1967, this writer went to Tapovanam. When he reached there we were told to have our food first and then come for darshan. Sri Sai also never wanted his devotees to come for darshan with empty stomach. In the ashram under the pleasing shade of huge tree, in an open meadow devotees were asked to assemble. Sri Swamigal who had a bulky physique, majestically came and sat on a stone with his left leg touching the earth and the right leg folded on the left, exactly as we see Baba's posture in pictures. Fruits, Sweets, etc., which were brought by devotees as offering were placed before Sri Swamigal. His attendants collected them and then distributed to all present then and there. Sri Swamigal, with a smiling countenance, talked to each one of the devotees assembled and enquired about their welfare. When the writer's turn came and he told him that he was coming from Sai Samaj, Mylapore, he was very pleased. The writer wrote about this valuable meeting with a Sai-like saint in flesh and blood, as editorial in October 1967 issue of Sai Sudha.

The writer went to Tapovanam again in 1968 to meet Sri Swamigal and to invite him to participate in the celebration of Golden Jubilee of Mahasamadhi planned to be conducted in an exemplary manner. When the writer invited him, his first question was 'who else are coming?' The writer started replying, "Sri Gopalakrishna Bhagavataswami of Pudukkottai", Sri Swamigal stopped the writer and said, "That should be more than enough". He, however, assured that he would be present with us, throughout the celebrations. We were told that Sri Swamigal would be present in Sukshma Sarira (invisible form). Sri Sai, though he physically never left Shirdi, appeared in various places and he once said that he needed no train or bus to travel. It was only by the grace of Sri Sai, darshan of a saint of almost identical stature, was possible to the writer.

BABA AND BHAGAVATASWAMI

(Sai Sudha – October 2000)

In this age of Kali, namasankirtana is considered to be the easiest and most suited sadhana for one and all to attain God-realisation. *Kalau sankirtya Kesavam* – In Kali sing the glories of Kesava. The Lord Himself has made it very clear that He does not dwell in Vaikunta, nor in the hearts of Yogis, but He stands where His bhaktas sing His glory. *Naham vasami vaikunte na yogihrudayeshu, madbhaktah yatra gayanti tatra tishtami Narada*. It was Sri Chaitanya Mahaprabhu who gave a tremendous momentum to namasankirtana or Bhakti movement. This bhakti movement was well nourished by saints like Mira, Kabir, Tulsidas, Tukharam, Namdev, Saint Tyagaraja, Purandaradasa, Bhadrachala Ramadas and several other great ones.

It is well known that in the early years of last century large number of devotees were attracted to Sri Sai Baba by hearing the wonderful Harikathas of Das Ganu Maharaj. Das Ganu, while expounding the lives of great bhagavata-saints like Tukharam, Namdev, Gnaneshwar and others, used to carry with him a picture of Sri Sai Baba and in concluding his Harikatha tell the audience, "If today you want to have darshan of a great saint like the ones I talked about, go to Shirdi".

Though Baba was a great Siddha, Gnani, Karma Yogi and all in one, he essentially preached Bhakti Marga or Prema Marga. That is why the great Bhakta Sri Narasimhaswamiji was drawn from the South in stages to the Great Master and chosen as the Apostle to flood the world with Sai Bhakti. Sri Narasimhaswamiji spread the name of the Master by taking Baba (in the form of pictures) to several households, conducting Nama Sankeertan and giving lectures on Baba. "Nama Sankeertan is the life of Sai Movement", he declared. Bhajan was an important item in all celebrations introduced by Swamiji in All India Sai Samaj and other Upasamajas founded by him.

Swamiji writes: "In his earliest days (even upto 1890) Baba had a youthful love of art and music, and at night he went often to the Takia, the resting place for visiting Muslims. There he would, with his very sweet and appealing voice, sing songs mostly of Kabir or songs in Persian or Arabic, which the local people could not understand. He tied tinklets (gunguru or salangai) to his ankles and danced about in joy while he was singing his songs with rapt devotion".

According to Sri Narasimhaswamiji the essence of Sai Baba's Marga is Bhakti or Prema. "God is pleased by bhakti alone and bhakti can capture Him. This contains the essence of the doctrine of bhakti or devotion".

"Baba must have enjoyed what Tyagaraja says is enjoyed by the devout bhakta in moments of musical laya, *Gitarthamu, mokshamu galada*, asks Tyagaraja, i.e. "Is it possible for a man whose mind does not melt with music, into laya, to obtain laya in any other way into God". Baba told Rangari that on the night previous to his coming, there was bhajan and music, and all night he was in rapture".

In 1958 two years after Sri Swamiji attained Nirvana, dhanurmasa bhajan was introduced in All India Sai Samaj. Some local bhagavatas who volunteered to participate in the bhajans told the Sai Sevaks that they could consider themselves extremely fortunate if they could get Pudukottai Sri Gopalakrishna Bhagavataswami in the presence of Sri Sainath. Sri Bhagavataswami being a very orthodox person, a gentleman who was closely associated with him, told the Sai Sevaks that the Swami would not accept our invitation. But when the Sai Sevaks made their pranams to Sri Bhagavataswami and invited him to do bhajan in Sai Samaj, to their pleasant surprise Sri Bhagavataswami spontaneously agreed to conduct Radha Kalyanam in Sai Samaj and said: "During the course of his prachar Sri Narasimhaswamiji very kindly visited our residence in Pudukottai and asked me to conduct bhajan in Sai Samaj. But I have got the opportunity to do so only now!"

Today after reading Sri Sai Baba's life, as written by Sri Narasimhaswamiji, it transpired that there was nothing strange in Sri Bhagavataswami's spontaneous pleasure in agreeing to do bhajan in Sai Samaj. Sri Bhagavataswami enjoyed what Baba enjoyed in moments of musical laya. Sri Bhagavataswami was a preeminent saint among musicians and a preeminent musician among saints according to one leading professor. "He is a Tower of Bhakti" according to Sri Rege. Sri Basheer Baba used to say that Saint Tyagaraja, Bhadrachala Ramadas and Purandaradasa were all rolled into one in the form of Sri Bhagavataswami.

FORERUNNER OF MAHATMA GANDHI

(Sai Sudha – November 1967)

Mahatma Gandhiji's 98th birthday was celebrated in a grand manner all over the country. But how many people have really understood Gandhiji the Mahatma? People call him the Father of the Nation and the liberator of the country from foreign yoke. In that case he would get a place only in the history of India. But he was something greater. By constant Sadhana in Satya and Ahimsa, which are synonyms to him, he transcended the human level and from there he chose to serve humanity as a whole. He taught by practice, more than precept, what wonders can be wrought by sacrifice, self-control and prayer, based on unshakeable faith in the Lord. His name is thus carved in letters of gold in the history of humanity.

We see many, particularly those in Politics quote Gandhi for anything and everything. But, nay, how many of them try to follow the Gandhian ideals? One friend frankly expressed that it would be very difficult to follow Gandhian ideals. Of what use is it to celebrate Gandhi Jayanthi with all pomp and show after burying deep his ideals? The ideals set by Gandhi are not exclusive for one nation and for one time. When practised, they are bound to benefit the whole humanity for all ties. But they will be too bitter to be swallowed by those who have plunged headlong to attain the peak of material prosperity. If only at least a few earnest men and women join together in each village, town and city, study intently Gandhiji's works, first try to follow his ideals in their lives and then patiently educate other people and draw them into their fold, the country is sure to emerge out of the present economic crisis and life of uncertainty into a nation of peace and plenty.

Everyone knows how much Gandhiji strove to bring about complete unity between Hindus and Moslems. Sri Sai Baba's advent in Maharashtra was in a period in which hostility between Hindus and Moslems was raging in those parts. Sri Sai, living in a mosque was claimed and attracted by both Hindus and Moslems and eventually they learnt to treat each other as brothers serving the same Master. Thus Baba had created an atmosphere favourable to Mahatmaji's work later.

Sri Sai Baba laid great emphasis on Truth and Non-violence, the two great weapons of Mahatmaji. Being divine in nature Baba could know what was in the minds of various people coming to Him and with such knowledge He could make people not to swerve from Truth. Time and again Baba identified himself with all living beings and He taught various devotees to see Him (God) as the *antaryami* of all living beings like ants, flies, dogs, cats, etc., and to treat them with kindness. One Hansraj who was suffering from asthma was advised by Baba not to take curds. Being very fond of curds, he did not heed to Baba's advice and he was stealthily taking too much of same. But to his dismay, every day a cat was drinking away the cuds kept by him. He got angry and one day he beat the cat mercilessly. That noon when he went to see Baba in the mosque, Baba exclaimed to those present, "I wanted to help this chap by preventing him from taking curds which is harmful to his health; but this fellow beat me mercilessly and drove me away. See here." So saying, Baba showed His back where red stripes were seen as marks of the beating given to the cat by Hansraj. Sai devotees would have read from the Life of Baba how Baba saved a buffalo from being butchered. Sri Sai was the very embodiment of Ahimsa. Can we not say that Ahimsa was the legacy left to Gandhiji by Baba? It may be noted that Gandhiji approached Sri Upasani Baba, disciple of Sri Sai Baba in the twenties seeking his advice.

Sri Sai Baba essentially preached Prema Marga and he laid great stress on the efficacy of chanting "Rama" nama. How many thousands were made to chant Rama Nama ecstatically in the Prayer Meetings held by Mahtmaji?

Those who read the life of Mahatmaji will find it to be a commentary on the life and teachings of our Master Sri Sai Baba.

HOMAGE TO SAINT TYAGARAJA

(Sai Sudha – March 1968)

Devotees may remember that Saint Tyagaraja's Birthday Bi-Centenary was celebrated in a grand manner last year for three days by the All India Sai Samaj under the guidance of Sri Gopalakrishna Bhagvataswami. Many eminent musicians rendered the nectarine kirtans of Sri Tyagaraja. When Sri Bhagavataswami conducted the Divyanama sankitan followed by Dolotsavam the whole of the night, when he went on *unchavritti* and performed the *aradhana* ceremony the next day, one could visualize a Tyagaraja and a Purandaradas. No doubt one hears the kirtans of Sri Tyagaraja throughout the year. But in a special function arranged in honour of this great saint, when the whole atmosphere is electrified with the presence of an eminent personality like Sri Bhagavataswami, the very same kirtans inspire the hearers in a greater measure and reveal the intense *bhakti* and *bhava* of the saint who rendered them.

In response to the desire of many devotees, it was decided to celebrate the Aradhana Utsavam in honour of Saint Tyagaraja for a week this year also. Actually the aradhana of Saint Tyagaraja falls on the Bahula Panchami Day (Panchami following the Full Moon) in the Tamil month of Thai (January-February), when it is observed in all solemnity at Tiruvaiyaru on the banks of Cauvery in Tanjore District where exists the Samadhi Mandir of the Saint. Sri Tyagaraja's Day is however observed subsequently at different places by his devotees to suit their convenience.

According to Sri Narasimhaswamiji, "Tyagaraja, who like most Hindus reveled in meditating on the details of form of God, attained laya, or mystic absorption, especially with the aid of music." Swamiji writes in the *Life of Sai Baba* (Vol. I), "Baba similarly expressed his approval of the use of music also for purposes of enabling the Jiva to get laya in bliss. Baba himself in his early days used to dance with tinklets tied to his feet singing rapturously songs of Kabir, some of which undoubtedly referred to the beauty and blissfulness of infinite Godhead. Baba must have enjoyed what Tyagaraja says is enjoyed by the devout bhakta in moments of musical laya. Tyagaraja asks, 'Is it possible for a man whose mind does not melt with music into laya, to obtain laya in any other way into God?' (*Mokshamugalada*). Baba told Rangari that on the night previous to his coming there was bhajan and music and all night he was in rapture".

In a previous article we observed that in Baba's school one should develop *nishta* and *saburi* with love and humility. If one follows the life of Saint Tyagaraja, he can easily find that Tyagaraja got Rama sakshatkara with the aid of these qualities only. His love to Sri Ramachandra, his chosen deity, was so intense and unassailable that he was not moved a bit by the inconveniences caused to him by his brother; his faith (*nishta*) in the Lord was so firm that he remained undaunted by the difficulties he had to encounter. Patiently and courageously bearing all the difficulties and inconveniences (*saburi*), Tyagaraja got laya in his Lord by the nectarine music that flowed out from his heart, a fountain of Love. One need not elaborate on the humility he showed to one and all. This is perhaps the reason why of all the musician-saints who appeared in our land Sri Tyagaraja appealed most to Sri Narasimhaswamiji and appeals to many Sai devotees.

Further, Sri Tyagaraja is an ardent devotee of Rama and when one thinks of Tyagaraja he cannot but think of Sri Rama also. Likewise, devotees of Sri Sai also cannot think of Sai without Rama. Nay, to them Sai is Rama and Rama is Sai – Sairama. How fitting it is to celebrate the day of Sri Tyagaraja just one month before the birthday of Sri Sai Rama, - Sri Ramanavami! Sri Sai never mentioned to anyone anything about his birth, parentage, etc. In fact nobody knew for certain when exactly he was born. But when some devotees repeatedly requested him to tell them when he was born so that they could celebrate his birthday every year, Sri Sai without directly giving them the information advised them to observe

Rama Navami as his birthday. That is how the famous Sri Rama Navami Urs at Shirdi started and Sai Jayanthi is being celebrated everywhere.

Let us pay our homage to Saint Tyagaraja and pray to him to bless us with a fraction of his devotion to the Lord so that we may, at least in a small measure, try to taste the Bliss of Love.

MOTHERS AMONG SAI DEVOTEES - I

(Sai Sudha – February 2002)

Baba wanted his devotees to develop nishta and saburi – unswerving faith and perseverance for spiritual advancement. Even for achieving success in the mundane plane, these two qualities are absolutely essential. While generally it requires sustained efforts to develop these qualities, they are to some extent naturally ingrained in women. Women, as a rule, are seen to show lot of resilience in adverse situations and have proven to be a source of solace and inspiration to men in day-to day life. It is said that there is a woman behind every man's success.

It is known that today after eight decades of Baba's attaining Mahasamadhi, devotion to and faith in Sri Sai has attained monumental heights. Many ascribe this to the tremendous prachar work done by Sri Narasimhaswamiji and the propagation in their own way by his forerunners like Nana Chandorkar, Das Ganu Maharaj, Rasane, Sathe, Dixit, Khaparde and others. But the world of Sai devotees should remember with a sense of deep gratitude the remarkable service and devotion of some women devotees to Baba right from the day he set foot in Shirdi soil first.

No authentic information is as yet available about the parentage of Baba nor as to when he was actually born. From the hints given by Baba later from time to time, inference was drawn that he was born of Brahmin parents in Patri Village in the erstwhile Nizam State adjoining

Maharashtra. It is also said that as an infant he was handed over by his parents to pious Muslim (Sufi) couple. When he was about five, the fakir who initiated him in the path of Love died and as per his direction, his wife took the child and left him to the care of Sri Gopalrao Deshmukh of Selu (known as Venkusa because of his staunch devotion to Lord Venkatesa). First and foremost, the Muslim Mother who brought up child Baba and led him to his Spiritual Guru, Venksua, is to be remembered with reverence.

Obeisance of Sai devotees is next due to Mother Baijabai. When Baba first came to Shirdi as a lad of about sixteen, donned as a moslem fakir, it was this lady who spontaneously recognised the divinity concealed in him. In the early days, this lad was staying under the tree-shades and mostly wandering in the neighbouring woods totally oblivious of food and other comforts. Bayajabai used to go to the woods every noon with a basket on her head containing bread and vegetables, roam miles after miles in search of the fakir and after tracing him fall at his feet. "The fakir sat calm and motionless in meditation, while she placed a leaf before Him, spread the eatables, bread, vegetables, etc. thereon and fed Him forcibly. Wonderful was her faith and service. Every day she roamed at noon in the jungles and forced Baba to partake of lunch. Her service, upasana or penance, by whatever name we call it, was never forgotten by Baba till His Mahasamadhi. Remembering fully what service she rendered, Baba benefitted her son magnificently. Both the son and the mother had great faith in the Fakir who was their God". (Shri Sai Satcharita).

"Baba recognised that sisters of his former janmas gave him support, and took birth in this janma again to continue the support. Tatya Patil's mother, Baija Bai was a sister of his previous birth and by that strong tie she took immense pains to see him fed, especially in his young nomadic days at Shirdi, when he used to wander into the jungles not caring for food", Writes Sri Narasimhaswamiji. Baba would be the last person to forget a life-long support for food, etc, such as Bayaja Bai gave him. Her son Tatya enjoyed Baba's special affection. Tatya would call Baba "Mama" that is maternal uncle and Baba would refer to Tayta as 'Puthna' or nephew. Even on occasions when Tatya went on doing things without heeding to Baba's warnings, Baba went out of the way to save him from coming to harm. Baba's love to his Sister Baija Bai was so great that it is said that in 1918 Baba gave up his own life to save that of Tatya, son of his sister.

In writing about Baba's Lovers, Sri Swamiji observes, "Of the orders possible among Sai's lovers (order of chronology, order of merit, etc.) luckily all the orders coincide in the case of Baija Bai, the first and greatest lover of Baba".

Bayaja Bai was a very simple unlettered village woman living far from the so-called civilised world. This provided her with a totally pure, uncorrupted, untainted heart which enabled her to spontaneously recognise the saintliness in the rustic lad, a new-comer to the village, who was taken to be a nomadic pagal fakir by the villagers. This recognition, the inherent maternal instinct and ties of earlier births prompted her to render service to the saintly lad with Love and affection, a bargainless and unalloyed love. Baba reciprocated this with his love and affection not only for her but also for her son and heirs. What better reward one can get than a permanent place in the heart of Samartha Sadguru Sainath? Pranams at the Feet of this Wonderful Mother!

MOTHERS AMONG SAI DEVOTEES - II

(Sai Sudha – March 2002)

Radhakrishnabai or Radhakrishna Ayi or Ramakrishni, as she was known, was one of the rare gems among Baba's intimate devotees. It was a thrilling experience to hear a first-hand account from no less a person than Sri Rege himself about the remarkable selfless service she offered to Sri Sai Baba. Sri Rege used to speak very highly about her devotion and spiritual advancement. Baba's daily morning routine included a walk to the Lendi. The route was through the village and Radhakrishna Aye would sweep the road backward so as not to step on the swept portion. Her reverence to the Master was such that she could not bear to see that he set his feet on the road which was trodden by her or any other person! Let us see what Sri Rege says:

"In my first visit, the Master asked me to go to Mother Radhakrishna whom He described as His mother and mine. My association with her – and I owe my spiritual life to her – left no doubt in my mind that she was the Yoga Maya like the Yogini who gave Sri Ramakrishna Paramahamsa his training in 'Tantra'. Mother Radhakrishna, whom the Master always referred to as Ramakrishni, was to me an ideal of the Madhura Bhakti of the Gopis. All her belongings in the world were a durrie (Cotton mat), a blanket, a pair of dhotis, Eknath Maharaj's Bhagawat, abhangas of Sri Tukaram and a lota. She had an idol of Lord Sri Krishna – she called it 'chhabi' and engaged herself in occasional singing of bhajans in which she would soon get unconscious in a deep trance."

"Sri Das Ganu was a great devotee; and we find in his kirtanas references to the love of Gopis; but he probably thought that what was proper for Lord Sri Krishna was not so for a fakir. Being confined to the residence and company of the mother, I was a persona non-grata and was far from Das Ganu Maharaj until after the Master's Mahasamadhi. He then came to Indore and stayed with me. Then with tears in his eyes, he said, "Bala Saheb, you were very fortunate in living with a devotee of the highest order I Madhura Bhakti. I do Kirtans of Mirabai, Janabai, Kanhopatra, and Gopis, and tears flow from my eyes but I could not appreciate the Madhura Bhakti of Radhakrishna Ayee 'in real life'."

"Mother Radhakrishna was of ordinary build, about 5 feet high, but had an iron will and the strength of a giant. She used to fetch water from a well about a furlong away in large pots, which she picked alone with her hands, when a strong man would need the help of another for the purpose. She once gave me a blow on my chest and said, "You are a samsari. This is hollow". She then asserted that she was much stronger than me. I replied that I was only a child. She then suggested a trial of strength, and insisted on it in spite of me. The road leading to Rahata used to be deserted in the afternoon and she said that each one of us should run with the other on the back. I told her to get on my back and I would run first. I ran about two furlongs and the mother said she was satisfied and I may stop. She then made me get on her back, and ran much more than two furlongs, and asked whether she was not stronger, and when I said it was doubtlessly so, she asked me to get off her back; I said I was happy on the back of my mother and would not leave it. She threatened to throw me off and I replied that the world would stare if a fond mother did so. Eventually I got a promise from her that she would carry me on her back on the spiritual path. It appears to me that this was pre-ordained by the Master, as, when we returned to Mother's residence, I was called by Baba and asked what we were doing. When I told him about our race and mother's promise, the Master said, 'She will take you on her back and so will I'. But then he directed me to give up the practice of yoga. 'Do bhakti', He said, 'nothing more is necessary. Only let your heart, head and hand be in tune'."

"Mother Radhakrishna hated publicity. A gentleman from Bombay took some snapshots of her without her knowledge; but someone spoke of it as the gentleman was leaving Shirdi in a tonga. She ran after the tonga for about a mile, wrested the camera and smashed it. Tatya Koti Patel, an intimate devotee of Baba, told me of this in her presence."

Baba fully recognized the Madhurya bhakti and the spiritual advancement of Radhakrishna Mayee. Select intimate bhaktas like Rege, Avasthe and others were sent by him to stay with this Mother. She lived only on the roti sent by Baba to her every day as Prasad. On days when Rege or other devotees joined her, Baba used to send extra rotis. It was she who prescribed the name of Sai – Sainama – to Rege for japa, which was later approved by Baba Himself.

Purushotham Avasthi, another intimate devotee of Baba, who introduced Sri Narasimhaswamiji to Rege later, narrated his reminiscences about Mother Radhakrishna as follows: "We went to the residence of Mother Radhakrishna Ayi. She appeared to me like the proto-type of my Guru Shanthi Devi. On seeing me Mother Radhakrishna Ayi narrated a few earlier incidents of my life. I was stunned but still did not accept her as a substitute for my Guru Shantha Devi but as her sister. Even as I was thinking on these lines, Mother Radhakrishna Ayi cried aloud, 'I am dying' and fell flat on the ground. I ran up to her and putting her head on my lap loudly chanted one after the other five mantras based on the five letters of 'Shiv Panchakshari' which represented the five elements. I implored the deities to revive her in exchange for all the virtues I had acquired in 16 years of my spiritual sadhana. Mother Radhakrishna Ayi opened her eyes and I felt exceedingly grateful to God for this recovery." In May 1918, after the Mother's passing away, Sri Avasthi went to Shirdi with his sister and niece and they occupied the room that used to be formerly occupied by Mother Radhakrishna Ayi. The fuel was wet and smoke covered the entire room. "Unable to bear the smoke, my sister thought of Mother Radhakrishna Ayi to come and help in kindling the fuel. At once they fancied that Mother had come downstairs and helped them in enkindling the wet fuel and then disappeared. While they felt the ethereal presence of the Mother amidst them, reality dawned that Mother had cast off her mortal coil in November 1917 itself", narrates Sri Avasthi.

Another devotee of Baba, Mrs. Tara Bai of Poona, once came to Shirdi with her husband Sadasiva Tarkhad, "Baba told her to go and put up with Ramakrishni for accommodation. That lady gave it on the strict condition that Mrs. Tarkhad should carry out all the menial labour that might be ordered by Ramakrishni (who was a Brahmin Widow) and the latter had a very sharp tongue and would rebuke her (Mrs. Tarkhad) for shortcomings. So, Mrs. Tarkhad found that Baba had imposed a very painful position on them, but what was their recompense? She found that Ayi (Ramakrishni) possessed powers of clairvoyance and thought reading. Some messages would come for Mrs. Tarkhad. At once Ramakrishni, or Ayi as she was called, would read off the reply from her (Tara Bai's) mind and send a reply. In other matters also, when Baba sent unusual orders, Ayi would have the things ready. Then Ayi related the history of Mrs. Tarkhad's past life. Above all, Ayi lived only for Baba's service. She was very deeply devoted to Baba and rendered very great service to the Sansthan. It was therefore an education in service that she got by staying with her." (*Life of Sai Baba, Volume III, by Sri Narasimhaswamiji*).

Another very intimate devotee of Baba, Purandhare, when he was suffering from unbearable headache, requested Mother Ramakrishni to intercede on his behalf and persuade Baba to give him relief. This devotee also was being asked by Baba to stay with Ayi during his visits to Shirdi.

One Bhikubai of Ahmednagar, a childhood friend of Radhakrishnabai (Ayi) got married to a person in Sangamner but unfortunately she became a widow at the age of 14. As she knew Ayi was staying in Shirdi serving Sai Baba, she came to Shirdi and was asked by Baba to stay with Radhakrishna Ayi and be busy serving.

Sri Rege recollects that once when Baba was coming from Lendi, after washing the floor of the Masjid, the mother was in a trance, and Baba stroked her on her back and asked her not to worry. The Mother passed away in 1916 and Rege got intimation from a friend. Two months after her death, he went to Shirdi and not knowing where to stay went straight to Masjid. Baba asked him to go to Dixit Wada where Shama and some others came and offered him a sort of condolence. At that time, a message came from the Masjid that Rege and all others sitting with him in the wada should come to the Masjid. When Baba heard about what Shama and others were talking about Mother Radhakrishna Ayi, He told Rege, "What do these fools know? She was your Mother and mine. She wanted to be freed from her Karma and you know I gave her my assurance. One night she came saying she would not wait and lifting up my kupni got in here (pointing to His heart). You will see her here when you desire". Rege concludes, “My Divine Mother is now merged in the Master. Let people in their own way imagine what they will. I cannot forget what I owe to her. Of the devotees, Sri Mahlsapathi, Sri H. S. Dixit, had great reverence for her, and I feel I am in good company”.

In his foreword to Sri Sai Satcharitra, Sri H. S. Dixit pays glowing tributes to Ayi. “When Maharaj went to Chavadi, musical instruments, horse, palki, chopdar, singers of bhajans, flags and banners and all such paraphernalia accompanied him. All the credit for this goe to Sundarabhai Kshirasagar alias Radhakrishna Ayi. It would not be out of place to say that she was the Guru of loving bhakti. She did not have wealth but surrendering her body and mind to Maharaj, she had obtained from different devotees of Maharaj different items and well established the Shirdi Sansthan. By ill luck her life ended early, that is when she was only thirty five. She was here only for eight or nine years, but in that short time she achieved what perhaps might have taken another twenty five years or more. It was due to this lady, Maharaj's night aratis and Kakad aratis in the early morning hours started in the Chavadi.

“Radhakrishna Ayi served in all possible ways. Twice in the day, she swept and cleared the path on which Maharaj walked. Consequently, she herself removed all the dirt there.

“Not only did Radhakrishna Ayi rendered all kinds of services to Maharaj, but got several devotees to do all kinds of services. She did various kinds of chores and got involved in them, and the devotees did the work with love and eagerness. Men of all status, and also women were included in them. To carry away earthen stones, sweeping roads, making mud and carrying it, digging trenches and filling them, splitting wood, dusting lands and chandeliers, washing and painting the Masjid, making flowers from paper, holding whisks, peacock feather fans, ornamental umbrellas, flags, stitching flags – all these were done by people of higher status and even ladies coming from noble families were pleased to have got the opportunity to render service”.

Salutations to this great Mother Devotee of Baba!

MOTHERS AMONG SAI DEVOTEES - III

(Sai Sudha – April 2002)

Mrs. Tara Bai Sadasiva Tarkhad of Poona was also one of the Mother devotees of Baba who derived very peculiar and very great advantages, mostly in temporal matters, but partly in spiritual matters also. Pujyasri Narasimhaswamiji has devoted a separate chapter for her (Chapter IV) in *Life of Sai Baba*, Volume III. Chapter IX of Shri Sai Satcharitra deals with Mrs. Tarkhad. This lady had already a fairly good grounding of religious experiences by contact with other saints, and her first impressions of Baba are the most valuable on that account, writes Sri Swamiji. She found the most prominent feature about Baba was his eyes. She says:

"There was such power and penetration in the glance that none could continue to look at his eyes. One felt that Sai Baba was reading him or her through and through. Soon one lowered one's eyes and bowed down. One felt that he was not only in one's heart but in every atom of one's body. A few words, a gesture would reveal to one that Sai Baba knew all about the past and present and even the future, and about everything else. There was nothing else to do for one, except to submit trustfully and to surrender oneself to him. And there He was to look after every minute detail and guide one safe through every turn, and every vicissitude of life. He was the antaryami, call Him God or Satpurusha in Sahajasthithi or what you like. But the overpowering personality was there, and in His presence no doubts, no fears, no questionings had any place, and one resigned oneself and found that was the only course, the safest and best course".

Here is one lady devotee who had submitted to Baba two pice of dakshina which Baba wanted, that is nishta and saburi. The conviction with which she had issued the above statement reveals clearly the depth of her total surrender and devotion to Baba. Tara Bai had become Baba's Ankita, by complete surrender, with full faith, to him. She had given, when contacted by Sri Narasimhaswamiji later, a number of instances to show Baba's antaryamitva and the manner in which He looked after His devotees wherever they were and saved them from all troubles and calamities.

Once when Tara Bai was sitting in the Masjid with Baba, a leper devotee, whose disease was very far advanced, who was stinking all over, with great difficulty got up the three steps of the masjid, took udhi from the Dhuni and placed his head on Baba's feet. Tara Bai was seized with revulsion on him and heaved a sigh of relief when at last the leper devotee left the place. Baba who could fathom what was going on in her mind shot a piercing glance at her and then sent for the leper devotee. When he came back, Baba took from him a dirty parcel which he had in his possession which contained some pedas. Baba picked up one piece, put in his mouth and gave another piece to Tara Bai asking her to eat. She had no option but to obey. Baba used the occasion to teach her valuable lessons in humility, fraternity, sympathy, endurance and trust in Baba's supreme wisdom.

There have been numerous instances where Baba helped this ankita devotee in the temporal plane. Once she was sick, her eyes were paining her and water was freely flowing from them. "Baba looked at her. Then the eyes ceased to pain and water ceased to flow. But tears were tickling down from Baba's own eyes. The accurate diagnosis of disease takes doctors much time and effort, and to discover the appropriate remedy takes more time and more effort. In the case of Baba the diagnosis, the remedy and everything were instantaneous. A deep-seated organic disease abruptly and suddenly got cured, and the power of drawing disease from her to himself, by pure will power, was something marvellous and something uncommon". (*Life of Sai Baba, Volume III*)

"One important difference between Sai Baba and several other saints she had seen is mentioned by Tara Bai. Some other saints used to get into Samadhi or trance conditions, and then they would forget their body. They

would utter things in the trance state revealing supranormal knowledge or power. But in the case of Sai Baba, he never had to go into trance to achieve anything or reach any higher position. Every moment he was exercising a double consciousness, namely, (1) the Ego called Sai Baba and (2) the Antaryamitva of all, superseding all egos and resting in the Paramatma. He was at the same time exercising and manifesting the powers and features of both states of consciousness. Some other saints with much trouble would read other men's minds for a time, and then lapse into their original condition. But with Sai Baba, his knowledge of other people's minds was not a matter of effort. He was in the allknowing state always."

Let us read a portion from Shri Sai Satcharitra which narrates an incident concerning Mrs. Savitri Bai Tarkhad, sister in law of Tara Bai, to her conviction about Baba's *antaryamitva* and All-pervasiveness:

"Once Mrs. Tarkhad was staying in a certain house in Shirdi. At noon, meals were ready and dishes were being served, when a hungry dog turned up there and began to cry. Mrs. Tarkhad got up at once and threw a piece of bread, which the dog gulped with great relish. In the afternoon when she went to the Masjid and sat at some distance, Sai Baba said to her, 'Mother, you have fed me sumptuously up to my throat, my afflicted pranas (life forces) have been satisfied. Always act like this, and this will stand you in good stead. Sitting in this masjid I shall never, never speak untruth. Take pity on Me like this. First give bread to the hungry and then eat yourself. Note this well: She could not first understand the meaning of what Baba said. So she replied, 'Baba, how could I feed you? I am myself dependent on others and take my food from them on payment'. Then Baba replied, 'Eating that lovely bread I am heartily contented and I am still belching. The dog which you saw before meals and to which you gave the piece of bread is one with me, so also other creatures (cats, pigs, flies, cows, etc.) are one with me. I am roaming in their forms. He who sees Me in all these creatures is my beloved. So abandon the sense of duality and distinction and serve Me as you did today'. Drinking these nectar-like words, she was moved, her eyes were filled with tears, her throat was choked and her joy knew no bounds".

In the narrative about Mother Radhakrishna Ayi, a detailed account has been given as to how Tara Bai was afforded by Baba an education in service by sending her to stay with Mother Radhakrishna Ayi.

Volumes and volumes can be written about the help given and being given by Him to His devotees, but let us conclude with what Tara Bai says as to why she regarded Shirdi as a veritable paradise, a real Bhuloka Vaikunta.

"Directly we went there, we felt safe that nothing could harm us. When I went and sat in his presence, I always forgot my pain – nay the body itself with all mundane concerns and anxieties. Hours would pass, and I would be in blissful unconsciousness of their passing. That was a unique experience shared, I believe, by all His real devotees. He was all-in-all and the All for us. We never could think of his having limitations……".

"Baba has not altogether vanished. He is still living now, and gives ample proof of His powers and protecting care in many matters off and on, though the impressions about these, because of His body being invisible, are not so great as those that the devotees enjoyed when they sat in His presence at Shirdi".

Tarabaiya surakshakaya Namah – Salutations to One who offered protection to Tara Bai. This namavali is seen in Sri Sai Sahasranamavali.

Reading or learning about ardent devotees like Mother Tara Bai would do a lot of good, especially in strengthening our faith in and devotion to Baba.

MOTHERS AMONG SAI DEVOTEES - IV

(Sai Sudha – May 2002)

Let us now read about another Mother devotee through whom Annasaheb Dabolkar or Hemadpant who was the author of Shri Sai Satcharitra got his doubt clarified by Baba. When Baba blessed Sathe who read Guru Charitra for a week only, why he, Dabholkar, who was reading it for forty years was not rewarded? When this thought arose in his mind, he was directed by the Master to go to Shama and chit-chat with him. When the two devotees met they were talking about the wonderful leelas of Baba. Shama then narrated to Dabholkar the incident about how a lady devotee by name Radhabai Deshmukh got Baba's grace.

Radhabai Deshmukh, an old woman, hearing Baba's fame as a Samartha Sadguru, came to Shirdi with some people from Sangamner. At her first darshan she was drawn to Baba and started loving him intimately. She resolved in her mind that she should make Baba her Guru and take some upadesh from Him for her spiritual advancement. Baba never accepted anyone as a disciple and gave upadesh. This lady was adamant. She decided to fast unto death if Baba did not condescend to give her upadesh. She went without food or water for three days. Shama took pity on her and interceded with Baba on her behalf and told Him, "Deva, what is this you have started? You drag people here. This lady who depends on you solely has resolved to fast unto death if you do not give her upadesh. If she meets with death, people will blame you. So take mercy on her, bless her and instruct her".

Baba sent for that lady and in His own unique way addressed her as follows (Shri Sai Satcharitra): "Oh Mother! Why are you subjecting yourself to unnecessary tortures and hastening your death? You are really my mother and I am your child. Take pity on me and hear me through. I tell you my own story, which if you listen carefully, will do you good. I had a Guru who was a great saint and most merciful. I served him very long; still he would not blow any mantra into my ears. I had a keen desire, never to leave him, but to stay with and serve him, and at all costs receive some instructions from him. But he had his own way. He first got my head shaved and asked me to give two pice as dakshina. I had no money and asked him what he, a perfect desireless man, would do with two coins. His two pice were (1) *Nisha* - Firm faith and (2) *Saburi* - patience or perseverance. I offered these two at his feet and he was pleased.

"I resorted to my Guru for 12 years. He brought me up. There was no dearth of food and clothing. He was full of love, nay, he was love incarnate. He loved me the most. When I looked at him, he seemed as if he was in deep meditation and then we both were filled with bliss. Night and day I gazed at him with no thought of hunger and thirst. Without him, I felt restless. I had no other object to meditate nor any other thing than my Guru to attend. He was my sole refuge. My mind was always fixed on him. This is one pice dakshina. Saburi (patience or perseverance) is the other pice. I waited patiently and very long on my Guru and served him. This saburi will ferry you across the sea of this mundane existence. Saburi is manliness; it removes all sins and afflictions, gets rid of calamities in various ways and casts aside all fear, and ultimately gives you success. Saburi is the mine of virtues, consort of good thought. Nishta (Faith) and Saburi (Patience) are like twin sisters loving each other very intimately."

"My Guru never expected any other thing from me. He never neglected me but protected me at all times. I lived with him and was sometimes away from him; still I never felt the want or absence of his love. He always protected me by his glance, just as the tortoise feeds her young ones whether they are near her or away from her on the other side of the river bank by her loving looks. Oh mother, my Guru never taught me any mantra, then how shall I blow any mantra in your ears? Just remember that Guru's tortoise-like loving glance gives us happiness. Do not try to get mantra or upadesh from anybody. Make me the sole object of your thoughts and actions and you will, no doubt, attain Paramartha (the spiritual goal of life). Look at me whole-heartedly and I in turn look at you similarly. Sitting in the Masjid, I speak the truth, nothing but the truth. No sadhanas, nor proficiency in the six Shastras, are necessary. Have faith and confidence in your Guru. Believe fully that Guru is the sole Actor or Doer. Blessed is he who knows the greatness of his Guru and thinks him to be Hari, Hara and Brahma (Trimurti) incarnate".

This is the essence of Baba's teachings. This is the path shown by Baba – Prema Marga, Guru Marga, i.e. loving service to Guru, surrender – total and absolute surrender – to Guru. Baba has only reiterated and reinforced what Sri Ramanuja, the great Vaishnavite Acharya, taught centuries ago.

Instructed as above, the old lady Radhabai was convinced. She bowed to Baba and gave up her fast.

Baba's above advice to Radhabai Deshmukh is the most valuable of all of Baba's teachings and applies to humanity as a whole irrespective of whatever religion or sect or school one may belong to. For imparting this most valuable advice if Radhabaï Deshmukh is chosen by the Master, she must be a special devotee far ahead of many others in spiritual attainments deserving Baba's love and concern. Hemadpant felt that he was blessed by Baba in having been made to hear this narrative from Shama.

Baba thrust into the hands of Hemadpant a handful of sugar candy and gave him (and through him to all Sai devotees of all times) the categorical assurance. "If you take this story to heart and remember it well, your state will be sweet as the sugar candy, all your desires will be fulfilled and you will be happy".

Salutations to this Mother Devotee who was the receptacle of Baba's Grace as above!

Laxmibai Shinde was another intimate devotee of Baba. Laxmibai, a good and well-to-do woman, was working in the Masjid day and night. Bhagat Mahlsapathi, Tatya Patil and Laxmibai were the only devotees who were allowed to enter the Masjid at night.

"Once while Baba was sitting in the Masjid with Tatya in the evening, Laxmibai came and saluted Baba. The latter said to her, 'O Laxmi, I am very hungry'. Off she went saying, 'Baba, wait a bit, I will return immediately with bread'. She did return with bread and vegetables and placed the same before Baba. He took it up and gave it to a dog. Laxmibai then asked, 'What is this, Baba, I ran in haste, prepared bread with my own hands for you and you threw it to a dog without eating even a morsel of it? You gave me trouble unnecessarily'. Baba replied, 'Why do you grieve for nothing? The appeasement of the dog's hunger is the same as Mine. The dog has got a soul; the creatures may be different, but the hunger of all is the same, though some speak and others are dumb; know for certain that he who feeds the hungry, really serves Me with food. Regard this as an axiomatic Truth'. From that time onward Laxmibai began to offer Him daily bread and milk with love and devotion. Baba accepted and ate it appreciatingly. He took a part of this and sent the remainder with Laxmibai to Radhakrishna Mai, who always relished and ate Baba's remnant Prasad."

"Baba remembered Laxmibai's service. How could He forget her? Just before leaving the body, He put His hand in His pocket and gave her once Rs.5/- and again Rs. 4/- , in all Rs.9/-. The figue (9) is indicative of the nine types of devotion (*sravanam kirtanam vishnoh smaranam padasevanam, archanam vandanam dasyam sakhyam atmanivedanam*). Or it may be the dakshina offered at the time of seemollanghan. Laxmibai was a well-to-do woman and so she was not in want of any money. So Baba might have suggested to her and brought prominently to her notice the nine characteristics of a good disciple mentioned in the 6th verse of Chapter Ten, Skanda XI, of the Bhagawat, wherein first five and then four characteristics are mentioned in the first and second couplets. *amanya matsaro daksho nirmamo dhrudasouhrudhah, asatvaro arththajijnasuh anasooyah amoghavak* – My devotee should be free from pride, jealousy, sloth and attachment, should be firmly devoted to his preceptor and cool, a seeker after knowledge, should not be fault-finding and one indulging in useless talk. Baba followed the order, first paid Rs. 5/- and then Rs. 4/-, in all Rs. 9/-. Not only nine, but many times nine rupees passed through Laxmibai's hand, but Baba's this gift of Nine she will remember" – (Shri Sai Satcharitra).

Oh, Mother Laxmibai, Salutations to you, the privileged devotee of the Master!

MOTHERS AMONG SAI DEVOTEES - V

(Sai Sudha – June 2002)

It is a well-known and established fact that generally it is the wife who helps the husband to tread the path of dharma. In giving Sita in marriage to Rama, King Janaka says, *iyam Sita mama Suta sahadharmachari tava*, according to Sage Valmiki. Especially in religious pursuits, even today we can see many women striding along with their husbands. Faith and perseverance being the natural traits of women, they at times are able to move ahead of their husbands and lead them from the front. We shall, therefore, take up for our study some such Mother devotees who came to Shirdi with their husbands and earned the love and affection of Baba.

Hon'ble Dewan Bahadur G.S. Khaparde, Advocate of Amraoti, was a trusted lieutenant of Bal Gangadhar Tilak, in the freedom struggle. Being considered to be an extremist, he was being watched by the then British Government and he faced the prospect of being arrested for trial and conviction. Having heard about Baba's powers, he moved to Shirdi with his family and sought asylum with Baba. He got total protection from Baba. During their long stay, Khaparde's wife served Baba with love and affection and enjoyed His grace.

From December 1911 for three months plague raged at Shirdi. Balwant, son of Khaparde, got an attack and developed bubo and fever. Mrs. Khaparde went to Baba and with tears asked Him whether it was to sacrifice her child that she had come to Shirdi. Baba spoke in parables assuring her that all would be well. She could not understand Him, and later Baba showed on His own person bubos and told her that He had to bear all these to save her son. He also said that He had saved Balwant and that His orders were supreme – *ajna aprati hata*.

One day when a number of naivedyas were placed one after another before Baba, He did not touch any one of them. When Mrs. Khaparde's naivedya was brought, He at once put it into His mouth.Then Shama, who occasionally took liberties with Baba, asked why He was so partial to Mrs. Khaparde's naivedya. In giving an account of Mrs. Khaparde's love and service to Him birth after birth, Baba said, "She was formerly a cow of a bunya and gave (Me) plenty of milk, Then she was born of a mali (gardener) and later went to Kshatriya. Then she married the bunya. Then she was born a Brahmin. After a long spell of time, I am seeing her again, and the food she gives Me is sweet (with her love)". Sri Swamiji writes: "Mrs. Khaparde's prema more than Mrs. Khaparde's self -interested visit to Shirdi, was that which operated powerfully on Baba and made him take so much trouble of each member of that family". Baba did not give mantra upadesa except in exceptional cases. Baba gave it to Mrs. Khaparde, thus; Go on saying "Raja Ram Raja Ram", Baba's help to Khaparde's family was partly temporal, but the most notable part of it was the development of Mrs. Khaparde's soul stage after stage in furtherance of which He gave her Rama mantropadesa. Baba used to call Mrs. Khaparde 'ajibai' which means grandmother or old lady. Baba's use of that term conveyed to her husband that he should no longer regard his wife as one for purposes of sex gratification or reproduction but he must treat her as a soul companion for spiritual purpose mainly.

Mrs. Khaparde when presenting naivedya at the Mosque was daily inviting Baba to go to her lodgings for a meal. Baba promised, but did not come. One day when she was preparing dishes, a dog came near her and as she viewed it as an unclear and polluting animal, flung burning fuel at the dog and it ran away. That day at naivedya time at the Mosque, when Mrs. Khaparde again invited Baba to come to her lodgings for a meal, Baba told her, "Yes, When I came, you threw burning fuel at Me!"

** ** ** ** ** ** ** ** ** ** ** **

Rao Bahadur Moreswar Pradhan, Mumbai was listening to an enthralling Kirtan by Das Ganu Maharaj along with his family when Mr. Chandorkar and a few other friends were also present. The Kirtan went on for the whole night. Mrs. Pradhan was very much moved and she got a burning desire to visit Shirdi at the earliest. She told her husband that Baba came to her in a dream and this she considered as a sufficient indication that she should be taken to Shirdi, but what would they do with her sister-in-law who was in advanced stage of pregnancy? After due consideration, the couple decided to take her also to Shirdi, When they reached the mosque at Shirdi, Baba told Madhava Rao Deshpande, pointing to Mrs. Pradhan, "This is the mother of my Babu", Mr. Chandorkar thought it must refer obviously to her sisterin- law who was believed to be pregnant and asked Baba, pointing to that lady. "This is the lady, is it not. Baba replied "No, it is this" and He again pointed to Mrs. Pradhan. Exactly twelve months from that date Mrs. Pradhan delivered a male child and was named 'Babu' (the name mentioned by Baba). Babu was the nephew of Dada Kelkar and was treated by Baba as a pet. This boy was serving Baba devoutly even neglecting his official duties and died at an early age.

Once when Mrs. Pradhan was doing her puja of Baba at Dwaraka Mai, Baba suddenly stopped her and asked her to go to the wada [their lodging]. When she went there, she found her baby crying, she then comforted put the child to sleep and came back to Baba to continue her puja. Baba had heard the lady's cries by his antarjnana.

Mrs. Pradhan depended on Baba for all her wants, Baba helped her in many ways. Once Baba appeared in her dream and told her to place turmeric and saffron on His feet. She worshipped them in the dream. She mentioned about this to Nana Chandorkar and as advised by him, she took silver padukas to Shirdi and placed them before Baba. Baba asked her to place the Padukas on each of His stretched feet and worship, she did so. Then Baba handed them over to her. What a unique privilege!

On the day of Baba's Mahasamadhi, Mrs. Pradhan who was at Mumbai dreamt that Baba's body was in a dying condition and cried 'Baba is dying', Baba told her 'people do not talk of saints as dying, but as attaining Samadhi'. Mrs. Pradhan writes in her experiences "On the 16th night (day next to Mahasamadhi day) I dreamt that Baba came and gave me three rupees and that I felt distressed as receipts of money in dreams are not auspicious. Baba said, 'Receive this and give Me all the money you have stored up in your box', I woke up and sent all the money for the ceremonies".

** ** ** ** ** ** ** ** ** ** ** **

Once when Chandrabai R. Borkar, a lady devotee of the Master, was at Kopergaon during Sravan or Chaturmasya of 1908, an unknown fakir appeared before her and wanted garlic chatni and bread. She said that she would not take garlic during Chaturmasya and the fakir disappeared. Having heard of Sri Sai Baba and his taking onion every day, she thought that the fakir might be Sai Baba. So she went to Shirdi for the first time and bowed before Baba. Baba told her, "You have not given garlic chatni and bread! And why have you come here?" This confirmed her idea that the fakir who came to her was Baba and she answered, "Yes, I have come to give garlic chatni and bread." Baba said that Mrs. Borkar was his sister for seven generations and had always sought him out.

While at Shirdi, once Baba asked Chandrabai Borkar to go to Pandharpur where her husband had his official work. She went to Pandharpur and found that he had gone away on transfer, and sat dejected at a dharmasala. A fakir appeared, told her of the transfer of Mrs. Borkar to Dhond, gave her tickets to Dhond and a male escort to take her there.

Baba once advised Chandrabai Borkar, "We should not harbour hatred, envy, rivalry or combative disposition towards others. If others hate us, let us simply take to Nama Japa and avoid them." Chandrabai Borkar was the devotee specially deputed by Baba to do worship to Upasani Baba also on Guru Poornima day.

The wife of one Vinayak S. Giridhar of Malad was a great devotee of Baba. Once when Giridhar was proceeding to Shirdi, she took special pains to prepare a nice flower garland and sent it to Baba through her husband. Baba received it and in recognition of the love with which it was prepared and offered, he kept it on his neck for a long time, and said, "This is prepared with great devotion. Let her thus garland my picture every week in her house".

A woman of Bassein (name not known) was very much devoted to Baba. She was blind. She made a visit to Shirdi and while entering the mosque, prayed, "Baba, my wish is to see you with these eyes". She at once got sight and was able to see Baba. She then went out and blindness returned.

There were a few other women devotees in Shirdi who were used as instruments by Baba to carry on his mission.

Baba once wanted to give Sadgati to a buffalo. He called Mrs. Jog and told her to give plenty of pooran poli with lot of ghee to a buffalo that would come and knock at her door. Baba said that when she finished making the required number of polis, the buffalo would come to the southern door of her residence. Exactly when she finished making the polis, as informed by Baba, the buffalo came and Mrs. Jog placed all the pooran polis before it. The animal ate the whole lot with gusto and fell down dead. Mrs. Jog was scared. She rushed to Baba and informed him of what happened. Baba allayed her fears saying, "That she-buffalo has exhausted all her vasanas except the desire to eat plenty of pooran polis with ghee and when that desire was satisfied, her vasanas were exhausted and she passed away, getting released from the buffalo body".

Dada Kelkar, an over-zealous Brahmin, abhorred onion and he was very critical of people using onion. Once he was very harsh to Nachne's mother-in-law as the conduit. Once Kelkar's grandchild got sore eyes and Baba advised him to use onion for fomenting the eyes. Where would Kelkar, an onionhater, get onions? Baba suggested that he could get it from Nachne's mother-in-law who was present there. But she was not willing to oblige Kelkar. However, she told Baba, "Dada Kelkar abused me for using onion. So I do not like to give him onion. But if you so order, I shall give". Baba told her to give, the lady gave onion to Kelkar and through her Baba made him feel humiliated for his over-zealous asceticism and intolerant behaviour.

MOTHERS AMONG SAI DEVOTEES - VI

(Sai Sudha – July 2002)

In Sri Sai Baba's Charters and Sayings, Sri Swamiji has mentioned about a few other ladies. One is Mrs. T (Tendulkar) from Bandra, Mumbai. Let us go through them.

Bandra lady came and sat before Baba with chronic (seven years) headache. Touching and gently stroking her head, Baba enquired whether her head was aching. The lady replied that it was aching and it had stopped then. Baba told her that she had been feeding Him well for many years and the surprised lady replied that she was seeing Him only then. Baba said, "I have been seeing you ever since your infancy". The puzzled lady, to a query from Baba, told Him that in her house as well as in her mother's house they had been worshipping Ganapathy, offering flowers, fruits and eatables. Baba told her that all that had come to Him and that He had been seeing her from her girlhood.

In May 1914 addressing Mrs. T., a Bandra lady, Baba said that He had to go thrice a day to her house. A lady of Shirdi who was present was surprised as she had been seeing Baba at Shirdi daily. Baba said, "I do not speak falsehood. I am Mahalaxmi. Mother! I came to your house. You gave me things to eat, is this not true?" That lady and her son replied in the affirmative. Baba then said, "Yes, mother, I go easily to Bhav's house (i.e. that lady's house at Bandra). In the middle, there is a wall. Jumping over it, next comes the Railway line, and then Bhav's house. I have to fly across walls and excavations". (Here Baba described the crow's fight from Shirdi to the lady's house at Bandra).

Mrs. Tendulkar of Bandra daily heaped up garlands of bakul over Baba's picture in her house at Bandra for two months and then went to Shirdi. Baba told Dixit, "These two or three months I have not been at Shirdi at all. This mother has smothered me with bakul flower and I was quite dizzy, and unconscious of myself. Now I am slowly coming round".

Baba once asked Mrs. T. to give Rs. 6/- as dakshina. She told her husband that it was painful to be asked for money when they had nothing. Her husband told her that what Baba wanted was the surrender of six internal enemies (*kamadhishadripu*) – Kama, Krodha, Lobha, Moha, Mada, Matsarya. When Baba asked her whether she would pay the dakshina of Rs. 6/-, she told Him that she had given them. Baba cautioned her to ensure that she does not wander off.

Once when Mrs. T went to Baba with her son, Baba told her that He had to take the entire responsibility for her son. The lady submitted that He had to take care of all of them. Baba said, "I have to take thought for my devotees. And if a devotee is about to fall, I stretch out my hands, and by four hands lift him and support him thus, I will not let him fall". Once Baba told this lady and her son, "How often, in the past janmas, have I been with you! And how many more shall I remain with you! We shall meet again and again. I have to give an account of every pie (i.e. every soul committed to My care) by God".

Baba gives instructions to each one of His special devotees to suit his or her nature, bent of mind and receptivity. When in October 1917, a lady from Mumbai came to Shirdi, Baba asked her to tell Him what she wants. The lady replied that she should be saved from the whirl of births and deaths and Baba, laughing, asked her, "Is this all you want? What! Have you come here to die?" The shocked lady confessed to Baba that she did not at all understand Him. Baba advised her, "Think who you are". When the lady did not grasp, she was advised by Baba that her husband would tell her what Baba meant. Once the couple reached their lodgings, following conversation took place between them.

Husband: Baba's words are mysterious. I cannot be sure I have made out his meaning. Probably he means something like this. The Jiva goes on reincarnating any number of times till it gets sakshatkar, i.e. sees or realizes God. Baba is God but people seeing him do not get full faith and do not see him, i.e. feel him to be God; and hence they do not get Mukti.

One must learn from the sastras, that essentially Jiva and Siva are one. You think yourself to be a Jiva, is it not?

Lady: Yes.

Husband: Baba and the Sastras want you to regard yourself as Siva or God.

Lady: No, No, I am a pretty sinner – a Jiva and not the great God Siva.

Husband: No doubt that is your feeling. But Baba means that by constantly regarding yourself as God, your deeply ingrained belief that you are only a finite Jiva will be removed. This process continued, may be through numerous births and strengthened and helped by contact with saints, will give you the firm belief that you are Brahman. That must be Baba's meaning.

When the couple late returned to Dwarakamayi, Baba told the lady, "Mother, I have listened (from here) to all that your husband told you. Keep that in mind.

One lady in Burhanpore saw in her dream Sai Baba coming to her door and begging for Khichadi (rice cooked with dhal and salt) for his meals. On awakening she saw nobody at her door. However, she was pleased with the vision and told it to all, including her husband. He was employed in the Postal Department and when he was transferred to Akola, both husband and wife, who were devout, decided to go to Shirdi. Then on a suitable day they left for Shirdi and after visiting Gomati Tirth on the way reached Shirdi and stayed there for two months. Every day they went to the Masjid, performed Baba's worship and passed their time happily. The couple came to Shirdi to offer Khichadi as naivedaya but for the first fourteen days, somehow or other, it could not be offered. The lady did not like this delay. Then on the 15th day she came at noon to the Masjid with her Khichadi. There she found that Baba and others were already sitting for meals, and that the curtain was down. Nobody dared enter in when the curtain was let down, but the lady could not wait. She threw up

the curtain with her hand and entered. Strange to say that Baba seemed that day hungry for Khichadi and wanted that thing first, and when the lady came in with the dish, Baba was delighted and began to eat morsel after morsel of Khichadi. Seeing the earnestness of Baba in this respect, everybody was wonderstruck and those, who heard the story of Khichadi, were convinced about His extraordinary love for His devotees. (Shri Sai Satcharithra).

In 1914 one poor old woman (like Sabari in Ramayana) undertook a journey to Shirdi to have Baba's darshan. She took with her one loaf of bread and an onion to be offered to Baba. On the way, she felt tired; she was feeling hungry and on the banks of a rivulet she ate half the loaf of bread and half the onion, leaving the remaining halves, and drank some water. At last when she reached Shirdi, it was Ramanavami season and the crowd was so huge that she could not go anywhere near the Masjid to have Baba's darshan. She was shouting out "O Baba! Take pity on me, an old woman. Give me your darshan!" The old lady's fervent prayer reached Baba the sarvantaryami and He bade Shama to go out, search for the old woman and bring her to His presence. Shama went out and elbowed his way back with the old woman to Sai's presence. She melted into tears and held Baba with both her arms round His waist. Baba, the Embodiment of Love, exclaimed, "Mother! How long have I waited for you! Have you brought anything for me to eat?" The old woman gave Him the remnants of the loaf of bread and onion. Munching the stale bread and eating it with gusto, Baba said, "How sweet, O Mother, is your bread!"

Sincere devotees, especially lady-devotees, by nature are very unassuming and they shun publicity. Steeped in bargainless devotion engaged in service with Love, they spontaneously surrender their *tan, man, dhan* to the Master. Baba, as promised, undertakes their welfare here and hereafter. While we have made a study of only a handful of such privileged Mothers among Sai devotees, in the millions that sought refuge at Baba's Feet there should have been many more exalted Mother devotees, details about whom are not available. Salutations to all of them!

GURU PUJA

(Sai Sudha – June 1998)

In the month of Ashada falls Guru Poornima which is also known as Vyasa Poornima. On this day Vyasa puja is done since Vyasa is considered to be the foremost among Gurus. Lord Vishnu Himself has taken the form of Vyasa. Vishnu Sahasranama parayana commences with invocation to Vyasa –

Vyasaya Vishnuroopaya Vyasaroopaya Vishnave
Namo vai brahmanidhaye vaasishtaya namo namah

Guru Poornima has added significance to Sai devotees since Baba Himself asked His devotees to offer puja to Him on this day. According to Baba, worship of Guru is the highest of all spiritual sadhanas. The essence of Baba's teachings is that nothing is more efficacious than pouring out one's love wholeheartedly on the Guru, serving the Guru steadfastly and surrendering oneself completely at the Feet of the Guru. Baba's marga is known as Bhakti Marga, Bhakti to Guru, i.e. Guru Marga.

Baba says "For 12 years I waited on my Guru….. I meditated upon nothing but the Guru and had no goal or object other than the Guru. Unceasingly fixed upon him was my mind. That Guru blew no mantra into my ear". In this process, without getting any upadesa, any teaching in the common sense, simply by total surrender to His Guru, Baba gained the knowledge of all scriptures, all sastras, essence of all religions and everything to be known.

Having attained divine state through His Guru's Grace, Baba categorically assures His devotees: "If you make me the sole object of your thoughts and aims, you will attain Paramartha, the supreme goal. Look at me with undivided attention; so will I look at you. This is the only truth my Guru taught me. The four sadhanas and the six sastras are not necessary. With entire confidence, trust your Guru. That is enough".

In the First volume of "Life of Sai Baba", Sri Narasimha Swamiji has devoted a full chapter (Chapter IX) to Guru Worship. He says that Guru Worship must form an important feature of Sai movement. "Many asked and ask whether Baba was a Yogi or a Jnani or a Bhakta or followed any marga peculiarly His own. Several thought and think that Baba cannot be classed under any of the divisions applying to saints and sadhus. As a result of study, aided by His own Grace, one sees at last that He was an adept of all the margas though His chief marga was Bhakti Marga, that special form of it that is described as Guru Marga in the Guru Gita and that Jnana and Siddhis including yoga siddhis come in the wake of His Guru bhakti".

Sri Swamiji explains how Guru Gita classifies Gurus under seven heads, the greatest being Parama Guru. Parama Guru is one "who enables the sishya to thoroughly absorb the truth of the Mahavakyas to realize for himself the Mahavakyas and thus escape samsara or rebirth. He is also called the Moksha Guru".

There are Gurus "who give definite undertakings and carry out the same at all costs and if necessary life after life, proceeding to seek the sishya in subsequent lives for the purpose. The best instance of such a Guru is Sai Baba".

"The Guru who teaches something secular or religious is merely called Guru. He who teaches about God or Sat is called Sadguru. He who uses all his siddhis and superior powers to carry the sishya right up to the goal is called Samartha Sadguru. Ramdas, Guru of Shivaji, and Sai Baba belong to the class of Samartha Sadgurus. Parama Guru is a Samartha Sadguru who looks after the entire welfare (Secular and spiritual) of his disciple".

"Sai Baba, a Samartha, has proved in a good number of cases (several of which are recorded) that he could provide everything and that he undertook to provide everything", asserts Sri Swamiji.

By dedicating his life to the mission of propagating the greatness of Samartha Sadguru Sai Baba, projecting Him as such to the entire world and thus enabling thousands of people to approach Sri Sai Baba successfully for their material and spiritual benefits, Sri Narasimha Swamiji has become a Sadguru and is so hailed by his followers.

Let us, therefore pay our obeisance at the Holy Feet of Samartha Sadguru Sri Sainath Maharaj and His chosen apostle Sadguru Sri Narasimhaswamiji on the occasion of Guru Poornima and pray to them to endow us with the much needed Guru bhakti.

GURU WORSHIP

(Sai Sudha – July 1999)

We are entering the Dakshinayana with the advent of the month Ashada. It is in dakshinayana we have all important religious festivals one behind the other. With a view to give due importance to the observance of religious functions in dakshinayana, social functions like marriages are generally planned in Uttarayana commencing from the month of Thai or Paush.

It is very significant that the religious functions start with Guru Puja on the Guru Poornima or Vyasa Poornima day. Krishna Jayanthi, Vinayaka Chathurthi and other festivals follow Guru Puja.

Sanyasins observe Chaturmasya vrata from Guru Poornima Day. During Chaturmasya, they generally stay in one place although they are parivrajakas, wandering monks. In this period many sadhus, eminent scholars and devotees gather around them creating a very valuable atmosphere of satsang. This satsang affords an opportunity for all to gain knowledge about our religious scriptures and truths and advance spiritually.

We all know that Sri Sai Baba attached great importance to Guru Vandana. He told some devotees that by simply worshipping His Guru He attained all the siddhis and powers without having to engage in studies or spiritual pursuits or taking any formal upadesa or initiation. Baba's dictum is that there is nothing which one cannot achieve through single-pointed devotion and love to one's Guru. He also said that without the guidance of Guru, it is very difficult to achieve one's goal, here and hereafter.

Baba preached only what He Himself practised. That is why He is hailed in Sahasranamavali as "*sarvadharman parithyajya gurvisam saranam gatah*", i.e. one who cast aside all observances according to Sastras and only sought refuge at the feet of His Guru.

Therefore, Baba advised his devotees to do special puja to the Guru on Guru Purnima Day. "Baba's (group) arati and puja on ordinary days was started in 1909, but for some time, there was no celebration of Guru Purnima by special worship of Baba on that day. Baba himself sent for Dada Kelkar one Guru Purnima day and said, "Do you not know that this Guru Purnima! Bring your worship materials and do your Guru Puja!" Then Guru Puja was done on that day and this practice of celebrating Guru Purnima by all the devotees worshipping Baba, then begun, has continued up-to-date. (*Charters & Sayings, 552*)

Guru Purnima is thus observed as a very important celebration by all Sai devotees over the last nine decades. Pujyasri Narasimhaswamiji introduced Vyasa Puja strictly conforming to scriptural injunctions at the Sai Mandir in All India Sai Samaj on Guru Purnima day and this is being followed every year. Worship of and prayers to our Master Sri Sai on this day will definitely confer greater benefits to devotees.

Sri Sai Sahasranamavali hails Baba as:-

Guruvangritheevrabhaktischeththa devalamitheerayathah – One who declared that it is sufficient for one's welfare and advance if he has intense faith in the Guru.

Gurupremasamalabdha paripoornaswarupavat – One who attained perfection by loving his Guru.

Guruvathmadevathabudhdhya brahmanandamayah – One who attained the bliss of becoming one with Brahman by perpetual concentration on the identity of Guru with Self and God.

Guruparamparapraptha satchidanandamurthih – One who became the embodiment of Divinity – Sat Chit Ananda – by the Grace of successive Gurus.

Gurumarga pravarthakah – One who followed the path of placing entire faith in and dependence on the Guru.

Theevraprema viragaptha venkatesa krupanidhih – One who received abundant kindness and mercy from his Guru Venkusa through his intense love for that Guru and detachment from everything else.

VYASA PUJA

(Sai Sudha – July 2000)

The month of July marks the beginning of series of festivals. The six-month period of dakshinayana commences in July. The festival season begins rightly with puja to Guru – Vyasa Puja on – Guru Purnima Day, i.e. The Full Moon Day in the month of Ashada or Adi.

This year Guru Purnima and Dakshinayana Punyakala, the beginning of the Tamil month Adi, fall on the same day. On this day, in the evening, there will be a lunar eclipse.

Since Baba Himself directed Dada Kelkar and Sathe to do puja to Him on one Guru Purnima day, Sai devotees celebrate this day in a grand manner.

In Sai Mandir at All India Sai Samaj, Chennai, on Guru Purnima Day – Vyasa Puja is done as specified in Sastras, as established by the Founder – President Pujyasri Narasimhaswamiji. This is followed by Abhisheka, Archana and Puja to Samarth Sadguru Sainath. Every year large number of devotees participate in the function.

Baba attached great importance to Guru worship. According to him everything can be achieved by the grace of Guru alone. He advocated absolute surrender to Guru with implicit faith. He is hailed as Gurumarga pravarthakah. Therefore, for all devotees of Sai, - Guru Puja on Vyasa Purnima day is very important.

It is Sri Krishna who is hailed as Jagadguru, Master of the whole

Universe. Sage Vyasa is considered to be one of the avatars of Sri Vishnu according to Srimad Bhagavata.

Thathah saptadase jathah satyavatyam Parasarath
Chakre vedataroh Sakha drushtva punso alpamedhasah

The seventeenth avatara of the Lord is as Veda Vyasa born to Satyavati from Sage Parasara; he divided the Vedas into several branches seeing people ignorant.

Vyasaya Vishnurupaya Vyasarupaya Vishnave
Namo Vai Brahmanidhaye Vaashishtaya Nama Namah

Veda Vyasa is the author of eighteen great Puranas. These puranas are mainly the cause for upholding the greatness of our ancient religion, the Sanatana Dharma. Mahabharata contains Gitopadesa by Lord Krishna and Vishnu Sahasranama. Gita is considered to be the essence of all religions and Vishnu Sahasranama the most potent sthuthi for parayana.

The most valuable among Vyasa's creation is Srimad Bhagavata. This is the basis for the Bhakti Movement. It is said that Sri Krishna Himself has taken the form of Bhagavata Purana. According to Bhagavata Mahatmya, the six-month period dakshinayana is best suited for the parayana or hearing of Srimad Bhagavata.

Nabhasya aswinorjou cha margaseershah suchirnabhah
Ethe masah katharambhe srothrunam mokshasuchakah

Baba advised many devotees to do Bhagavata Saptah. After doing Puja to Vyasa and to Samartha Sadguru Sri Sainath, parayana or hearing of Srimad Bhagavata will be very valuable and fruitful. Doing Puja to Vyasa or participating in Vyasa Puja which is essentially puja to Jagadguru Sri Krishna Himself is bound to shower immense benefits on one and all.

GURUMARGA PRAVARTAKAH

(Sai Sudha – July 2010)

Sri Sai followed and preached Gurumarga; his Sadhana was absolute surrender to Guru, dedicating himself totally to loving service of the Guru. He preached this path to his followers. Sai was one who never preached anything that he himself did not practise. His precept did not vary from his practice.

Before Sri Narasimhaswamiji started Sai prachar, there were some eminent Sai Bhaktas whose influence, talks and writings were cause for Sai Baba being known to more and more people. While most of them highlighted the divine powers that Sai possessed and used in alleviating the hardships of devotees who approached him, it was Swamiji who collected details from several contemporary devotees of Baba, screened them, made a thorough research and came to the conclusion that Baba preached *Gurumarga – Guru-bhaktimarga*. Therefore, in compiling Sri Sai Sahasranama, Swamiji, besides hailing Sai as *Gurumarga Pravartakah*, also invokes him as *Gurvangri teevra bhaktih chet tadevaalam iteerayatah*, Sri Sai categorically declared that for one's welfare and spiritual progress, intense devotion and faith at the feet the Guru alone is sufficient. Because he himself attained that divine stature, the stature of a Samartha Sadguru, endowed with all siddhis by being *Gurupada-parayanah*, always contemplating on the feet of the Guru, *Gurvisangri sada dhyayan*, ever meditating on Guru's feet, *Gurusantoshavardhanah*, by his loving dedicated service his Guru was highly pleased.

By single-pointed love to his Guru, Sai attained perfection – *guruprema-samalabdha paripoorna swarupa*; he achieved success in his spiritual Sadhana by dedicating himself to his Guru heart and soul, *Guroopasana-samsiddhah*. He became a *Brahmanishtha*, attained self-realisation or God-realisation, ever remained in a blissful state of Brahman by perpetual concentration on the identity of Guru, God and Self – *Guruvaatmadevata buddhya brahmanandamayah*. His heart was ever merged in the feet of the Guru who was delighted at the undiverted love of the disciple – *Ananya Prema-samhrushta Gurupada Vileenahruddah*.

To the lady devotee Radhabai Deshmukhin who was determined to get upadesa from Baba and undertook a fast, Baba expounds the greatness of Guru. When the Guru's grace is there, no upadesa is required; the loving glance of the Guru is enough. Baba tells Dabholkar: "The mother tortoise is on one bank of river. Her young ones are on the other bank. They get neither milk nor warmth – only her glances give nourishment to them. The young ones always think only of their mother. They don't need milk nor do they need food. The mother beholding them attentively is their only nourishment. This caring through just looking by the mother tortoise is actually like the showering of nectar. The young ones get happiness and they flourish. Similar is the case of the Guru and the disciple.

On another occasion Baba narrates how he found his Guru or rather how his Guru sought him and how he got transformed into the likeness of his Guru. Baba and three others were wandering on their spiritual quest. They were met by the Guru (Vanajari) on the way who offered them help. While the companions persistently declined to accept the offer, Baba readily accepted. Baba describes how the Guru tested his sincerity. "He took me to a well, tied up my legs with a rope, and suspended me, head downwards, from a tree by a side of the well. My head was about three feet off the water, which I could not reach. And my Guru left me there and went away, God knows where. He returned after four or five hours and asked me how I fared. 'In great bliss was my time passed' I answered. This was the 'entrance' test and Baba passed it remarkably well. Arthur Osborne explains this thus: "Tying him head downwards over a well is overturning the ego, binding it and holding it within sight of the cool water of Peace. It is because of this that the ordeal is blissful; it is suffering beatified by the end for which it is endured. This absorption in the Guru is the Sadhana or path followed and the final 'in silence I bowed down' is the extinction of the ego in Realization."

Having come out in flying colours in the 'entrance' test, Baba's development under the Guru followed. Baba says: "For 12 years I waited on my Guru who is peerless and loving. How can I describe his love to me? When he was Dyanastha (in love-trance) I sat and gazed at him. We were both filled with Bliss. I cared not to turn my eye upon anything else. Night and day I pored upon his face with an ardour of love that banished hunger and thirst. The Guru's absence even for a second made me restless. I meditated on nothing but the Guru, and had no goal or object other than the Guru. Unceasingly fixed upon him was my mind. Wonderful indeed, the art of my Guru! I wanted nothing but this intense love from me." Baba concludes. "Making the Guru the sole object of one's thoughts and aims one attains Paramartha, the Supreme Goal. This is the only truth the Guru taught me. The four sadhanas and six sastras are not necessary. Trusting in the Guru fully is enough".

Later, when Baba was taken from Shirdi to Rahata by Moulana Jawar Ali for being initiated into Islamic religious Sadhana, Baba showed how a disciple should conduct himself in serving a Guru. No type of service rendered to the Guru was mean. In explaining the meaning of Gita verse (Chapter IV, Verse 34), Baba told Nana what 'Seva' actually meant. "As for 'seva', mere service, e.g. massage etc., is not enough. To be effective, there must be no lingering idea that one is free to yield the service or refuse it. One must feel that one is not the master of the body, which has become the Guru's and exists merely to render him service."

Service to the Guru with love and devotion is the spiritual Sadhana prescribed by Sri Sai. That was why he exhorted his devotees to do Guru Puja or Vyasa Puja on Guru Poornima Day.

GURU POORNIMA: VYASA PUJA

(Sai Sudha – June 2012)

Vedaat sastram param naasti, na daivam kesavat param. There is no scripture greater than Vedas nor is there any God superior to Kesava (Lord Vishnu). The Vedas originated from Lord Vishnu. As a part manifestation of the Lord Himself, Sage Vyasa appeared in Dwapara Yuga and classified the vedas in four sections, under the titles, Rig, Yajur, Sama and Atharvana. Besides this, Vyasa Bhagavan also authored the eighteen puranas and the *ithihasa*, the great Mahabharata. Out of compassion to men of poor wits, Sage Vyasa did all these so that even the dull-witted might be able to retain the vedas. Therefore, Sage Vyasa is looked upon as the Guru of all the Gurus, the primary Guru, and he is first worshipped on the Guru Poornima day, which is also called Vyasa Poornima, the poornima in the month of Ashada.

By worshipping one's Guru as the embodiment of Sage Vyasa, the Guru of Gurus, on the Guru Poornima Day, one is sure to derive immense benefits, both temporal and spiritual. Baba himself called one of the devotees, Dada Kelkar, father-in-law of H.V. Sathe, on a Guru Poornima day, sometime around 1908, and told him, "Do you not know that this is Guru Poornima? Bring your worship material and do your Guru Puja". Guru Puja commenced on that day at Shirdi and is continued in all Sai Mandirs.

In the Age of Kali (Kaliyuga), bhakti is said to be the easiest to be taken as a spiritual sadhana. To exemplify and make even common people understand the glory and efficacy of bhakti, Sage Vyasa, inspired by Sage

Narada, created the ambrosial bhakti sastra, Srimad Bhagavatam. If we witness today the ever-growing Hari Bhakti – Krishna bhakti – in this world, the sole source of inspiration is Srimad Bhagavata; and for this, Sage Vyasa will always be remembered.

If there are millions of Sai devotees in the world and thousands of places of worship for Sai in India and abroad, it is preeminently because of the voluminous literature on Sri Sai Baba like Charters and Sayings of Sri Sai Baba, left as inexhaustible legacy by Pujyasri Narasimhaswamiji. No wonder that Sri Rege Maharaj called Swamiji the "Vyasa" of Sai. Sri Rege also said that as long as the name of Sai there, the name of Swamiji will also remain linked to the same. Therefore, all Sai devotees have to offer worship to Samartha Sadguru Sainath and Sri Swamiji when Vyasa Puja is done on the Guru Poornima day.

How can we celebrate Guru Poornima? Let us read and try to assimilate what Sri Swamiji had written in his Guru Poornima message in the year 1955:

"The importance of a particular day for Guru worship is not enough to note. One must carry out everything, necessary for the success of the celebration. The purpose of Guru Puja on that day being special illumination, the earnest bhakta must observe all rules, forms and procedure that are best fitted for development of spirituality – early bath, purity, reduction of attention to worldly concerns, abstemious diet, or a careful fast (or phalahara), devotion of every available minute to contemplation on and immersion in the Guru Deva. Every reading, parayana, manana, stotra, keertana, bhajana, katha, etc., that tends to develop and deepen one's bhakti should be strenuously and scrupulously adopted. Frivolity, idle gossip, indulgence in every form of loose and low mentality should all be shunned. Above all, meditation, preferably in solitude or at least in holy company under auspicious and favourable circumstances such as proximity of the Guru Deva, should be developed. If on the Guru Poornima Day, for instance, 30 minutes of intense unbroken concentration on Guru Deva is achieved, that ought to be maintained or increased during subsequent periods. The end of concentration is tanmayatva (becoming That). Thinking of Brahman, the soul becomes Brahman. In fact, we are nothing but our thoughts. The more we avoid loose and worthless thoughts and confine ourselves to noble thoughts, preferably to the noblest thought of Guru Deva, the more assuredly we shall achieve the goal of life, namely, our transformation into the likeness of the Guru Deva. This is the basis of Tukaram's famous saying that saints turn their ardent bhaktas into their own likeness. Apna sarika karitat tatkal, i.e. immediately they (saints) make them (the adorers) like unto themselves. This is the grandest achievement possible for us, and the Guru Poornima day is the day when we should not only recall that fact but make every possible effort to help on that consummation."

"Sri Sai Baba is ever present and near us and will assuredly respond to our call."

SATSANG

(Sai Sudha – July 1998)

Sri Sai Baba led most of his devotees on the path of devotion, bhakti marga. First, devotion should be to one's own Guru, which will lead to devotion to God. But how is one to get this devotion?

It is known that Sai Baba laid stress on the nine modes of devotion, nava vidha bhakti as propounded by Prahlada. The first two are sravanam and kirtanam, that is, hearing the Lord's leelas and attributes and singing His Glory. These two can be had only in satsang, that is in the company of the devotees, the learned, the virtuous. Devotion is built on faith. Faith develops when one is in good company, satsang. Sai Baba, therefore, directed people who came to him to places where scriptures and puranas were being read, where namasankirtan was going on and also to great devotees like Kaka Dixit. In satsang the seeds of faith are sown leading to the sprout of saplings of bhakti. Atmanivedanam, the last of the nine modes of devotion, is possible only when faith and bhakti grip the heart.

In Bhajagovindam Sri Sankara says that it is satsang which ultimately leads one, in stages, to the state of Jeevanmukti. *Satsangatve nissangatvam, nissangatve nirmohatvam, nirmohatve nischalatatvam, nischalatatve jeevanmukthi*. He prescribed recital of Gita and Vishnu Sahasranama, *geyam gitanamasahasram*. This is also possible only in satsang. When people come to a place where Gita or Sahasranama Parayana goes on, they first hear (sravanam) and gradually they switch over to parayana (Kirtanam). Congregational prayers develop bhakti fast. This is being seen in many places like Sri Sai Spiritual Centre at Bangalore where late

Sri Saipadananda Radhakrishnaswamiji had introduced Sahasranama and Gita parayana as a daily routine in the evenings. In such congregational prayers, worldly thoughts are taken away from the mind and one could feel a sense of peace – shanti. That is the effect of satsang.

"Both good and evil are infectious. Persons who lead highly moral lives naturally affect their neighbourhood and all persons that come in contact with them rise in their grade of morality and spirituality. Some of them may get the position of Gurus for others", writes H.H. Narasimhaswamiji. Regular prayer meetings conducted by Mahatma Gandhi afforded an opportunity to millions of people to taste the effect of satsang, LOVE, which is essential to tread the path of Ahimsa.

In writing about the need for Guru Worship, H.H. Narasimhaswamiji says: "The need (for Guru Worship) is questioned as a rule by persons not yet fit to be sishyas, i.e. those without humility, reverence, patience, receptivity and other virtues or the proper attitude towards the great saints. They must be advised to have satsang. That is, they must move with bhaktas and fit themselves for further progress. When they are fairly fit, they will get their Gurus. It is not the truth that sishyas always go out to find the Guru. The reverse is often true. There are many noble souls waiting to be approached by persons who want to become sishyas and have the proper attitude and training".

Many people are found to lead a mechanical way of life, a life without a purpose, a life without a goal, a life without any aim. It is the duty of everyone who has become fortunate to come under the influence of a Great Master or Samartha Sadguru like Sri Sai Baba to help such people and direct them towards satsang. This is what H. H. Narasimhaswamiji means when he says, "they must be advised to have satsang".

MARGAZHI – SACRED MONTH

(Sai Sudha – December 1997)

The month of December has become very important to one and all ever since the British started ruling India. It is the last month in English calender year. For Christians all over the world, the celebration starts with Christmas Eve on the 24th and lasts upto 1st January, the New Year. This sentiment has caught up with Indians also irrespective of what religion they belong to. The New Year Eve is celebrated merrily with gay abandon on the 31st December by all fun loving folk. The religious also celebrate the day by offering prayers at midnight at temples of their choice, welcoming a prosperous and Happy New Year. Hill temples attract devotees participating in Padi vizhas chanting the Names of the Lord.

The month of December has been very important and significant to Hindus also from ancient times. In December, the month of "Margazhi" or "Marghasirsha" is born. "Marghasirsha" is the last month of Dakshinayana. The pre-eminence of this month over all the other eleven months is emphazised by Lord Krishna's proclamation in the Bhagavad Gita that "Masanam Marghasirshosmi" (I am Marghasirsha among the months.)

Dakshinayana starts with the month Ashada (Adi) and concludes with "Marghasirsha" (Margazhi). The entire six month period of Dakshinayana is devoted to worship and religious pursuits. All major festivals take place during this period, commencing with Ashada Poornima – Guru Poornima or Vyasa Poornima. Ascetics start their Chaturmasya Vrata on this day. Sri Sai Baba exhorted His devotees to offer Puja to their Guru (Sri Sai Himself) on Guru Poornima day since it is only with the Guru's grace the devotees can reap the fruit of their religious pursuits. This is followed by Sri Krishna Jayanthi, Sri Ganesh Chathurthi, Varalakshmi Puja, Upakarmas for the twice-born or dwijas, Dusserah or Navaratri (Devi Worship), Durga Pooja, Narakachaturdasi or (Deepavali) Skandhasashti, Karthigai Deepam, Vaikunta Ekadasi, Arudra Darsanam, etc. concluding with "Bhogi".

It is in Dakshinayana that Lord Krishna assuming the role of Jagadguru, handed over to humanity as a whole the quintessence of Vedas and Upanishads, the Bhagavad Gita through His chosen instrument, His Sakhya-bhakta (friend-devotee) Arjuna.

Sri Sai Baba attained Mahasamadhi – in His own words "crossed the border" – in Dakshinayana on Vijayadasami Day (Ekadasi thithi). The Mahasamadhi celebrations are very important to Sai devotees, like Brahmotsava in all Hindu temples.

There are festivals in almost every month of Dakshinayana. But all the 29 days in the last month Marghasirsha, are spent in devotion. In all temples "Dhanurmasa Puja" is done in the pre-dawn hours. Devotees engage themselves in bhajans circumambulating various temples in the early hours when the weather is very chill and the mind is very fresh and receptive. This is the month which Mother Andal chose to sing the glorious Tiruppavai and observe the "Paavai Nonbu" or Karthyayni Vrata to propitiate Mother Durga for fulfilment of her desire to get Lord Krishna Himself as her spouse.

It is during this month that the wounded Bhishma spent his life on a bed of arrows thinking about the lilas of the Lord. From this bed of arrows, Bhishma endowed to the world the most sacred "Vishnu Sahasranama". Sri Sai prescribed Vishnu Sahasranama chanting as the panacea for all our worries.

Sri Sai Baba attached great significance to 'namasankirtan". Let us, therefore, engage ourselves in namasankirtan during the month and attain the Grace of our Master Sri Sai. Those devotees who are not in a position to participate in bhajans can chant the Lord's Name, the mahamantra "Sairam", even while engaged in their mundane activities. No ritualistic discipline is required; only attunement of the mind to the Divine Name is needed.

Welcome to New Year – Uttarayan – Sankranti – Pongal. May Sri Sai Baba – the Master – Sadguru Narasimhaswamiji – bless us all with peace, happiness and prosperity. Let us follow the guidelines of Sri Sainath and Swamiji.

THE IMPORTANCE OF MARGAZHI MONTH AND ENTERING THE NEW YEAR 2001

(Sai Sudha – December 2000)

We will shortly be entering the New Year 2001, the first year of the twenty first century. The New Year will dawn in the middle of the month Margazhi (Margasirsha).

This month, the last one in Dakshinayana, will be full of religious fervour. For the Hindus this is the most sacred month as Sri Krishna Himself proclaimed in Gita that He is Margasirsha among months. It is during this month the Lord expounded the Gita to humanity as a whole through His devotee friend Arjuna. It is during this month Sri Bhishma Pitamah bequeathed Sri Vishnu Sahasranama to mankind lying on a bed of arrows. That is why Samartha Sadguru Sainath Maharaj attached great significance to Vishnu Sahasranama parayana by all and the study of Srimad Bhagavad Gita by his chosen devotees.

Margazhi is the first month in Hemantha Rithu, after the conclusion of Sarat Rithu (rainy season). In this month the Vanara King sent his emissaries in various directions in search of Mother Sita. Sri Hanuman who was part of the mission sent in the Southern direction headed by Prince Angada crossed the ocean and met Mother Sita in Lanka.

The Jayanthi of Sri Hanuman is also celebrated during this month. Hanuman is both a Bhakta and Dasa of Sri Rama. His service with devotion to the Lord has no parallel. That is why Vaishnavas worship him as "Siria Thiruvadi", younger Sevak of the Lord's Feet while the elder one is Garuda. His great devotion to the Lord earned him a place in the heart of Mother Sita who always dwells in the heart of Sri Rama; Sri Rama dwells in the heart of his dear bhakta Anjaneya. That is why he is the only bhakta for whom separate temples have come up throughout the country. Let us chant Rama Nama and invoke the blessings of Sri Hanuman since he is present wherever Rama Nama is sung.

During this month the devotees of Sri Ayyappa observe vrata and proceed on pilgrimage to Sabarimala. In the mornings and evenings devotees carry on puja and bhajans. Shedding their ego, high or low, these devotees address each other with love as "Swami".

It is in Margazhi the Gopis observed Katyayini Vrata and worshipped Mother Durga to get Sri Krishna as their spouse. Sri Andal who vowed that she would marry only the Lord also followed the Gopis and observed Katyayini Vrąta. The immortal Tiruppavai of Goda Devi forms part of the daily Bhagavad Aradhana by Sri Vaishnavas and is sung every day during Margazhi by all devotees of the Lord with devotion.

This period also witnesses the celebration of Christmas by Christians and Ramzan by Muslims.

It is said that during this month, in 1886, our Master Sri Sai Baba went into Samadhi leaving his lifeless body in the care of his devotee Mahlsapathi and returned to life after three days for upholding dharma through his life and teachings.

Let us worship the Lord and carry on Nama Japa and Namasankirtan during this month for entering a very happy and prosperous New Year.

MARGAZHI AND NAMASANKIRTAN

(Sai Sudha – December 2001)

Hemanthe' prathame' mase' Nandavrajakumarikah I
Cherur havishyam bhunjanah katyayanyarchana vratam II

Katyayani Mahamaye' Mahayoginyadheeswari I
Nandagopasutam Devi patim me' kuru te' namah II

[Srimad Bhagavatam, Canto X, Ch. 22]

"Goddess Katyayani! The Great Maya (deluding potency of the Lord) possessed of infinite yogic powers! Oh Supreme Ruler! Pray, make the Son of Nandagopa (Krishna) my husband (Lord)! I bow to you!"

With this prayer, in the first month of Hemantha season (Margasirsha or Margazhi), the maidens of Nanda's Vraja observed Katyayani Vrata and worshiped Devi.

Mother Andal, Sri Goda Devi, donning the role of a Gopi also observed the Pavai Nonbu or Katyayani Vrata in the month of Margasirsha, her aim being the same as that of the Gopis, that is praying to Devi Katyayini to make Sri Krishna as her husband. Her thirty songs starting with Margazhi Thingal, known as Thiruppavai, are most sacred to all Srivaishnavites. Thiruppavai is recited every day by ardent Vaishnavas and millions of devotees in the month of Margazhi. It is said in Vaishnavite circles that it is a burden for the Earth to carry a person who does not know Thiruppavai. Recital of Thiruppavai will remove all sins and lead to the Holy Feet of the Lord; it is the source for all Vedas.

Thus the ananya bhakti, bhakti with nayaka-nayaki bhava, moved from the Gopis of Brindavan to Mother Andal in Srivilliputhur in the southern part of Tamilnadu. Bhakti movement flourished in Tamil Nadu with the advent of Vaishnavite Alwars and Saivite Nayanmars.

At the time Kali Yuga commenced, according to Srimad Bhagavata-Mahatmya, Sage Narada wandered throughout the country, observed the evils of Kali Age and came to Brindavan, on the banks of River Yamuna. There he met Bhakti who had taken the form of a young maiden. She told Sage Narada that she was born in the Dravida country, attained maturity in Karnataka, was respected here and there in Maharashtra and became very old in Gujarat; finally when she reached Brindavan, she regained her earlier youthful form.

"In the age of Kali, righteous conduct, the path of yoga and austerities have vanished under its influence. Engaged in rowdyism and evil deeds, people are turning out to be like Aghasura (the Asura who took the form of a boa constrictor); righteous men get dejected and the unrighteous feel elated", says Narada. "How is this adharma tolerated by the Lord Sri Hari?" Thus questioned by the Damsel Bhakti, Narada answers: "In the age of Kali simply by chanting the name of Kesava, Harinamasankirtan, one attains the fruit which cannot be attained by askesis, meditation, yoga, etc. Perceiving Kali to be very valuable for this one reason, considering the ultimate happiness of people born in Kali Yuga, the Lord allowed the spirit of Kali to stay".

If one has to live in peace in the midst of all sorts of evils being perpetrated by persons of Asuric nature under the influence of Kali Age, the only course open is namasankirtan.

The month of Margazhi is the most suited for one to engage in namasankirtan. That is the reason why devotees get up in the early hours and engage themselves in bhajans, circumambulating the temples in the area. Participating in the namasankirtan, listening to the bhajans, is itself soul elevating. During this month Radha Kalyanam is celebrated everywhere with devotion. Radha Kalyanam symbolises the union of Radha Mata, representing the Gopis (jivatmas) with Sri Krishna, the Supreme Lord (Paramatma).

Sri Sai Baba himself was engaging himself in namasankirtan, singing and dancing throughout the night, in the early years of his stay in Shirdi. He exhorted his devotees to do namasankirtan.

Following the traditions, early morning Dhanurmasa bhajan was introduced at the Sai Mandir (All India Sai Samaj), Mylpaore, Chennai on December 16, 1958. For the first time of Pongal Day, January 14, 1959, Radha Kalyanam was celebrated in Baba's sannadhi by the great Bhagavatottama Sri Gopalakrishna Bhagavataswami. It is gratifying to note that this is being continued so as to give an opportunity in all devotees to taste the nectarine sweetness of Hari Namasankirtan.

NAMAMRITA

(Sai Sudha – December 2002)

In the month of December, the month of Margazhi according to Tamil Calendar or Margasirsha begins. The whole of this month is devoted specially to namasmaran, namasankirtan, bhajans and the whole atmosphere is charged with devotion. To most of his devotees Sri Sai Baba prescribed namasankirtan. Bhajan was the primary means through which Sri Narasimhaswamiji carried on the Sai Mission. 'Bhajan is the life of Sai Movement' he declared once. No wonder, one of the greatest Bhagavatas, Maha bhagavata, Sri Gopalakrishna Bhagavataswami, who lived amongst us during the last century, was inseparably attracted to Sri Sai Baba. In the last twelve years of his life, Sri Bhagavataswami did namasankirtan in Sri Sai Mandir at Mylapore very frequently enthralling thousands of bhaktas.

In 'Life of Sai Baba' Swamiji writes that Baba was not merely a teacher or trainee, but a school or a college in himself, nay, a University in himself, with postgraduate courses leading ad infinitum to unknown horizons. When one reads the 'Life of Sai Baba', he is sure to realise that Sri Swamiji was also transformed by the Great Master completely unto his own likeness. What a wide range of religious, philosophical and spiritual subjects has been handled in this work with total felicity by Sri Swamiji! Let us now endeavor to benefit to the extent possible by reading what Swamiji has written on the subject of namasmaran or namasankirtan:

"Etavata alam agha nirharanaya pumsam
Sankirtanam bhagavate gunakarma namnam
Vikrusya putram aghavan yat Ajamilo api
Naarayana iti mriyamanaiyaya muktim"

This Bhagavata verse means: "To wipe off sins of men, it is enough if they go on with sankirtanam, that is good singing or recital of God's gunas (qualities), karma (deeds) and nama (names). (For Example) Ajamila, though a great sinner, by barely calling out the name of his child Narayana at the moment of death attained mukti. This seems a basis for saying that the bare utterance of God's Name, even though the utterance was only of the name of the child bearing God's name, at the moment of death, would have the effect of saving a man. The proposition thus stated seems too wide and too wild. In the case of Ajamila however, the man had been formerly a great bhakta leading a very pure life and would have constantly used the term Narayana with very holy associations. Some of those associations might have dawned upon his mind when he uttered the name with reference to his child Narayana and therefore made Lord Narayana send his angels to save Ajamila who was just about to be dragged away by the myrmidons of Yama to hell for punishment for his numerous sins."

Here what Sri Narasimhaswamiji observes should be noted with special attention and be guided thereby. It is not just chance that Ajamila called out 'Narayana', though the name of his child, at the time of death, Ajamila had been in Satsang, holy associations in the early years of his life. This association only should have made him name his child as 'Narayana', the holy name of the Supreme Lord. And it is the vasana, the effect of his having spent his early years in satsang or holy association that surfaced and made Ajamila to call out the name of that particular child Narayana. It is, therefore, absolutely essential that we keep good company, satsang, engage ourselves in namasankirtan or namasmaran now itself, and thus make the repetition of the Lord's Name a habit. Again Swamiji says:

"Coming back to the question of the use of God's Name for eradicating sins from one's nature, we find that Valmiki and other authors of great works on ethics, ancient and modern, stress the importance of the constant recall to the mind of God and His qualities, especially through japa, japa being so holy as to make the mind get drowned in God so as to justify the remark of Lord Krishna – *yajnaanaam japa yajno asmi*, that is, "Of all yajnas, I am the yajna consisting of japa". Japa is the sankirtanam above referred to. When the name is uttered, the guna and karma above referred to follow immediately into the mind of the japa karta by the law of association of ideas. That is why people are content to begin with a repetition of the holy names even when not attended with perfect realization of the holiness of the name as in the case of the hunter who repeated '*mara, mara*' and became the Rishi Valmiki. Many a man goes on repeating like a parrot the names he finds either in a book or uttered by some other persons. But gradually, as the repetition goes on, the sacred influence pours in especially if he has the good fortune of having the company of the other person or persons who are inspired by that holy influence and if the surroundings as in a temple or bhajan hall are specially favourable".

Baba loved bhajan. Swamiji writes: "Baba in the earlier years used to visit the Takia which was a place for travelling Muslims arriving at Shirdi to rest. At nights he would tie 'salangai' or tinklets to his feet and sing rapturous songs with kanjira in hand. He would sing songs of Kabir, Arabic and other songs, giving him full scope for expressing his overflow of love. This trait was in him many decades after he stopped his nightly dance at the Takia, for in 1910 when Rangari of Thana visited him, he mentioned that the singing by the devotees the previous night of holy songs drowned him".

No other period of the year affords so much opportunity of being in satsang as the month of margazhi or margasirsha. Let us avail the opportunity as much as possible and invoke the blessings of Sri Sai, Sri Krishna.

MARGAZHI – NEW YEAR
Baba, An avatar of Datta

(Sai Sudha – December 2004)

In the last few years editorials in Sai Sudha were highlighting the extraordinary importance the month Margazhi assumes, starting from the declaration of the Lord in Gita that he is among months the month of Margasirsha.

A vast majority of the human race celebrate a very happy New Year, following the Merry Christmas of the Christians, during this month.

While we see a festive fervour for ten days in the month of Poorvabhadra (Purattasi), i.e. Dusserah or Navaratri, the whole of the month Margazhi the atmosphere is charged with devotional fervour. The Vaikunta Ekadasi of Vaishnavites, Arudra Darshan of Saivites, Hanumad-Jayanthi of Anjaneya Bhaktas, bhajans and Radha Kalyanams of Bhagavatas, rendering of Tiruppavai and Tiruvempavai, Swami Saranam of Ayyappa bhaktas, etal. No other month offers such a unique opportunity for a large number of people, to lose themselves either in spiritual ecstasy or in entertainment galore.

For devotees of Sri Sai Baba, this month is significant because during this month only in 1886, the Master went into Samadhi leaving his body in the care of his loving devote Mahlsapathy for three days and returned with a resolve to uplift mankind.

Another event of great significance to Sai devotees is that this month is privileged to be chosen by the Trimurthis – Brahma, Vishnu and Siva

– to take birth as Lord Dattatreya, the son of Maharshi Atri and Anusuya Devi. The Lord appeared on the Full Moon Day, Poornima, in the month of Margasirsha. The Lord offered Himself (Datta) to the Holy couple Atri Maharshi and Anusuya, revered by all for her remarkable chastity, a Pativrata par excellence.

Lord Datta became the son of Atri (Atreya) and thus Lord Dattatreya. He appeared with three heads and six hands. The four Vedas are said to follow the Lord in the form of dogs of different hues. Just as Lord Dakshinamurthy and Lord Krishna (Jagadguru), Dattatreya is considered to be universal Guru. According to tradition, He assumed several forms, Avadhuta and Digambara among them, to dispel darkness and bring light to discerning devotees. Datta Guru worship is widely prevalent in the North, particularly in Maharashtra and neighbouring States. The Guru Charitra which extols the greatness of Datta Avadhuta is one of the prominent granthas (holy books) being taken for parayana with utmost Shraddha. Samartha Sadguru Sainath had prescribed the parayana of Guru Charitra to many devotees for their spiritual advancement.

By a vast section of devotees who were privileged to have direct contact with Sri Sai, Baba is firmly believed to be Datta Incarnate, Datta Avatar. If we go through the Arati songs, Sri Sadguru Sainatha Sagunopasana, one can see that the composers had addressed Sai Baba as Datta.

In the song '*Gheuniya pancharati*', the author Sri Bhishma invokes the Master in the last stanza as '*Krishnanatha Datta Sai*'. In the next song, '*Kakada Arati Karito*' the Master is told '*tochi Datta Deva tu Shirdi rahuni pavasi*' i.e. 'You are also the Datta deity, who lives in Shirdi and blesses us'. In the bhajana, the prayer runs as '*Dattaraja Guru maje ayi, majala tava dhyana patee*', i.e. 'Guru Dattaraja, my Mother, grant me a place at your feet'. In the famous Arati song of Madhav Adkar, in stanza 4, '*Kaliyuga Avatara*', Sri Sai is praised as *Swami Datta Digambara*. And also we see '*Jaya Deva Jaya Deva Datta Avadhuta, Sri Sai Avadhuta*'.

"Devotees' Experiences of Sri Sai Baba" presented by Pujyasri Narasimhaswamiji reveal how many of the devotees associate Sri Sai Baba with Datta Guru.

Santaram Balwant Nachne says "my father attended Das Ganu's Kirtan, wherein Sri Sai Baba was described as a veritable Avatar of Datta with wonderful powers and wonderful kindness". Then he visited Shirdi to take Sri Sai Baba's darshan.

M.W. Pradhan's narrative contains an interesting incident. Once his child Babu was seriously ill. His family priest Madhava Bhat carried on mantra japa and puja in Mr. Pradhan's house to get relief for the sick child. "Bhat fancied that Babu's illness was due to our worshipping a Moslem saint, viz. Sai Baba, but he dared not give utterance to his thought. One night he had a dream. He saw a figure (which from the photo we had, he recognized to be Sai Baba) sitting on the top of the staircase, holding a baton (sota) in our hand. That figure (Baba) told him, 'What do you mean? I am the Lord of this house'. The priest kept this dream to himself for a time. (He had asked us to go and make a vow to Datta for the child's cure but he had been told that Baba was Datta himself). Later, Babu's condition was much worse than before, he priest noted with concern. He ran up at once to Baba's photo and loudly prayed thus: 'If the child should improve sufficiently by 4 p.m. so as to be brought downstairs, then I will agree that you are Datta'. Within a short time of this prayer, the child's temperature was getting lower and by 4 p.m. he wanted to be carried down for amusement and his mother took him downstairs. Madhav Bhat was convinced and felt that Sai Baba was really Datta".

Rao Bahadur H.V. Sathe says: "Once about 1916 or so, in pitching a tent for me at Kothrud (a suburb of Poona) certain Mangs (untouchables) went and put it up under a sacred Audumbur tree, touching it and tying ropes to it. I did not know it then. Finding that I was having mishaps thereafter, I enquired into the cause and learnt of that regrettable incident. I prayed to Sai Baba to help me and he advised me in a dream to get a Brahmin first to perform the purification ceremony of that tree and next to install Datta Paduka there. I have done both".

Police Sub-Inspector Nagesh Atmaram Sawant: "I dreamt one night that a big strong man with a black dress on his body and a black cloth on his head caught hold of me and was dragging me. I shouted 'Baba, Baba'. Immediately a white individual in white dress appeared and struggled with the black man and I escaped from the clutches of the black man. I shouted 'Baba and Datta Maharaj'. Suddenly Baba appeared before me out of the frame of the picture that I worship and disappeared".

Vinayak Daji Dhave: "I was a clerk in 1932 in the B.B.C.I. Rly.

Co. on Rs.90 p.m. I was anxious to find a Guru and read Guru Gita from 13.04.1932 for one month. I had not found any guru or obtained a vision of Datta in that period – as I had hoped to find. Then one Thursday, sacred to the Guru, I went to a Datta temple. When I went there in the place of Datta's image a Samadhi, neatly sculptured, was what I saw. Next morning, I went to a friend's house and opened Anna Saheb Dabolkar's book on Sai Baba and my eye lighted on the picture of Sai Samadhi found in that book – a picture I had not seen before. That was an exact picture of the tomb I saw at the Datta temple. So, I inferred that Sai Baba was to be my guru".

Kusha Bhav: "During that period of nine years (stay at Shirdi), he (Baba) told me to see a person with three heads. That, of course, I took as a direction to go and see Datta at Gangapur. Every year I visited Gangapur twice, once in Guru Poornima and next in Magha Poornima. Then, once he told me to do 108 parayanas of Guru Charitra taking three days to finish each parayana. I did this at Gangapur and stayed there 10 or 11 months for this purpose".

Sankar Balwant Kohojkar: "My father went to Shirdi only once. During his stay at Shirdi in 1911, Datta Jayanthi occurred. About 5 p.m. or so, Baba was seated at the mosque with devotees around him. At once, he said, 'I am having the pangs of labour. I cannot bear it. I am about to be delivered'. Evidently, he was identifying himself with Anasuya, mother of Datta, who at that time had her pains of labour and was undergoing sympathetic pain. At twilight time (i.e.) shortly after the above incident, he drove out all people from the mosque and again after a little while he called all people to come unto him. Then he was in glee. This is according to Purana the time of Datta's birth. People all went in and among them my father directly entered the mosque. What he saw on Baba's seat and in place of Baba's figure was a small child, charming three-faced figure of Datta, i.e. Datta as an infant. That vision he had just for a moment. Then, instead of Datta figure, he saw at the identical spot Baba in his usual dress and form. Just imagine what his feelings must have been at that time. He vividly realized that Baba was Datta".

Ramachandra Vasudev Ghaisas: "I was very uneasy in my mind at not getting a decently high position or higher grade (called selection grade) in my department. At that time I got a dream. In the dream, I was talking with someone else on financial matters. Suddenly someone appeared and told my companion, 'Why do you not grant him what he (i.e. myself) wants? Let him prepare Vanki (i.e.) upper armlets of ladies'. He disappeared after my companion said to the third person 'yes, that will be done'. That was my dream. This like other dreams and experiences of mine, I communicated to Kaka Saheb. The third person was obviously Baba. The reason why three armlets were to be prepared, while only pairs are worn, I did not first understand. But, Kaka Saheb explained, saying that the third person was Baba – a Datta Avatara having three bodies in one. So three vankies were wanted. I accordingly got three silver vankies prepared and I placed them in my box of Pooja, after making Prana pratishta. The fourth day thereafter, I was given the selection grade!'.

In some cases, when devotees, who vowed to offer some money to Lord Datta and failed to do so, come to Sri Sai Baba, Baba had collected the vowed amounts from them as Dakshina.

Let us all pray to Datta Digambara Sri Sainath for overall peace and prosperity for the entire universe.

AN IDEAL MONTH FOR SADHANA

(Sai Sudha – December 2007)

We have entered the Hemanta Ritu (season). The two months of this season Margasirsha (Margazhi) and Paush (Thai) are very significant. Dakshinayana ends in the first month and Uttharayana begins in the second month.

While the entire six-month period of Dakshinayana starting with the month of Aashada (July-August or *Aadi*) is devoted to spiritual saadhana and is full of religious festivals, one following the other in quick succession, the last month Margazhi (December-January) is unique – the entire month being devoted to the worship of the Lord with nama-sankirtan, nama-japa.

In Srimad Ramayana, Sage Valmiki has devoted a full sarga (Chapter) of 43 slokas (verses) to describe the Hemanta Season, which follows the Sarat or rainy season. Lakshmana tells Sri Rama, 'The season which is liked by you very much has come'. Thus, this season is very dear to the Lord. Therefore, the Gopis, the guileless maids of Vraja, chose the first month of this season to observe a vow of worshipping Goddess Katyayani, with the prayer, "Pray make Sri Krishna, the Darling of Nanda my husband (Lord)" (*Nandagopasutam Devi patim me' kuru te' namah*). This prayer fructified. The following autumn (sarat season), on a full-moon day, Sri Krishna, the Lord, enacted the Rasa Leela with the Gopis.

Sage Vyasa has devoted five chapters to describe the Rasa-Leela of Bhagavan Sri Krishna – the inexplicable soul-elevating sport of the

Paramatman with the Jeevatmas. This happened in the last age – Dwapara Yuga.

In this age, the Kali Yuga, Sri Goda Devi or Sri Andal of Srivilliputtur re-enacted the episode of Katyayani Vrata in the month of Margazhi one year. The girls who were born in Srivilliputtur and were the friends of Sri Andal were very fortunate. Sri Andal endowed them also with Gopi Bhava. Srivilliputtur was transformed into Vraja or Brindavan; the maids of Srivilliputtur were transformed into Gopis. Sri Andal left to the succeeding generations the immortal 'Garland of Songs' – Paamaalai – Thiruppavai. Andal became one with Lord Ranganatha – jivatma merged with Paramatma.

This is the month in which Bakri-Id of Muslims, The Christmas and New Year of Christians fall.

During this month all the Hindu temples in the South are opened very early in the mornings and special pujas are offered. In the early hours one can witness scintillating bhajans by many bhagavatas along the four streets surrounding the temples. Radha Kalyanam – the marriage of Sri Radha Rani with Bhagavan Krishna - the unification of Jivatma with Paramatma – is being celebrated everywhere with surcharged emotion in many places.

The season Hemanta, particularly the month of Margasirsha, converts the earth into a perfect stage with needed acoustics and when namasankirtan is conducted with devotional fervour on this stage, the whole atmosphere seems to glow with vibrations of Bhakti. Those who sing and those who hear -why those disinterested passers-by in the vicinity also – get the benefits of the bhakti vibrations consciously or unconsciously. An ideal month to take onward steps in one's spiritual Sadhana.

PRAY FOR PEACE AND PROSPERITY

(Sai Sudha – January 1968)

We have entered the New Year 1968 but not very enthusiastically. We see trouble everywhere and consternation writ large on almost every face. The common man is struggling for the very existence due to an inflated economy. The Government does not seem to be in a position to do much to arrest the steep rise in the prices of essential commodities.

In a thickly populated country like India, unemployment has always been an incurable malady. Introduction of machines has worsened the situation and the future looks very gloomy. Gandhiji, whose name is always spoken but whose ideas are seldom thought of foresaw the havoc that mechanization would play. Let me quote a few excerpts from his writings:

"Today machinery merely helps a few to ride on the backs of millions. The impetus behind it all is not the philanthropy to save labour, but greed".

"I can have no consideration for machinery which is meant either to enrich the few at the expense of the many, or *without cause to displace the useful labour of many*"

"Mechanisation is good when the hands are too few for the work intended to be accomplished.

It is an evil when there are more hands than required for the work, as is the case in India".

"Whatever the machine age may do, it will never give employment to the millions whom the wholesale introduction of power machinery must displace".

As in so many other matters, if serious thought is given by those in the power to Gandhiji's ideas, it will go a long way in bettering the lives of millions and thus bringing about lasting peace.

The other phantom that threatens the unity and solidarity of the nation is the question of language. Only when the people of the country emerge out of the present economic crisis, time will be congenial to think of issues like common language. The policy of the Government should be not to give any consideration to any proposition at any time if it should disrupt the harmony of the country and endanger the unity of the nation. Everything should be done individually and collectively to maintain the harmony prevailing in this Bharatavarsha of ours from time immemorial amidst people speaking different language. We in India have all along been proud of one excellent quality 'tolerance', even to alien religions, which should not be sacrificed at the altar of the 'language phantom'. History has proved that nothing can be achieved by force. Only that which is got by love lasts forever. What is first needed is a language of Love. Attracted by Great Masters like Sai Baba, when people come together and mingle with each other, all differences vanish and there remains only one language and that is the 'language of Love'. Sri M B Rege a direct and intimate devotee of the Master and Sri Gopalakrishna Bhagavataswami met. The former did not know Tamil or Telugu which were the only two languages the latter was conversant with. But how well they understood each other through the unspoken language of Love!

Let us, therefore, pray with all our hearts to Lord Sai, the Embodiment of Love, for the Peace and Prosperity of the nation as a whole!

TOWARDS HARMONY

(Sai Sudha – January 1998)

In his inaugural address at the recent three-day seminar on 'Religion, Politics and Society in South and Southwest Asia' at Delhi, Dr. Karan Singh, eminent scholar and former Indian Ambassador to the U.S., said, "Religion and culture are profound impulses that affect and transform a society at all levels. Religion should at no cost be equated with bigotry and fanaticism. On the contrary, it could be a powerful force for social and spiritual revival".

All religions are based on Love and only Love. To see unity in diversity is our religious heritage. There is no place for bigotry and fanaticism in any religious faith. As all rivers enter into the ocean, all religions take us to the same goal albeit through different paths, according to our Sanatana Dharma. Harmony is the undercurrent of all great religious faiths.

There can be no other unifying force as Love. Love presupposes tolerance and sacrifice. This is the essence of life and mission of our Great Master Sri Sai Baba. Attired like a Moslem fakir and making a mosque as His abode, He brought under His benevolent grace millions of people from various faiths cutting across all barriers of religion, caste, creed, sect and strata of society. Over hundred years back, He made both Hindus and Muslims celebrate a festival in His honour on Sri Rama Navami Day which is continued even today happily.

Every Sai devotee should take a vow to emulate this Message of Love and Harmony and infuse the same in all those with whom she or he comes into contact; to talk to them about the wonderful life and message of Sri Sai. It is also the duty of every Sai institution to take the Message of Sri Sai to every nook and corner of the country through regular congregations, bhajans, etc. A Sai empire has to be created not with brick and mortar but with selfless love and dedicated service. It is to be understood that service to Sai is service to humanity and vice versa. Parents and teachers should take a leading role in impressing upon the children the necessity to speak Truth and follow Dharma (Satyam vada, dharmam chara). The media has to take the responsibility to avoid giving undue publicity to provocative acts of violence and take a positive lead in promoting harmony.

MESSAGE OF LOVE

(Sai Sudha – January 2000)

"We have to break down barriers of caste, language and religion. We have to erase artificial boundaries that separate Indian and Indian. We have to remove all forms of discrimination, especially discriminations against women". Thus spoke Sri. A. B. Vajpayee, our Hon'ble Prime Minister in his message to the nation on the eve of the advent of new millennium 2000.

Hundred years back our Master Sri Sai Baba said: "This is the Teli's wall that parts you from me; pull down this wall, and then we see each other clearly face to face". "Saints do not recognize this differentiation. To serve me, remove this differentiation. Continue to think in this way and then you will realise it".

Two thousand years after the supreme sacrifice of Jesus Christ, His message of Love is still as potent as ever. What Jesus taught was only an extension of what the Buddha taught six centuries earlier. The same message is again being repeated by saints of all religions in later years.

First and foremost, the determination to erase the artificial boundaries, to pull down the Teli's wall of differentiation, must come from people, particularly, people involved in politics. Today, sadly, we see that the politicians want these artificial boundaries. To keep their vote bank intact, they encourage the differences among people, setting one community against the other, one caste against the other. Harmony among people is sacrificed by their thirst for power. Unless there is a change in their hearts, this trend will always continue.

It should be the earnest endeavour of all religious minded people, peace-loving people to bring about a change in the hearts of those who create dissensions. Artificial boundaries can be erased only with the solution of love; the wall of differentiation can be pulled down only with the axe of Love.

"Love is itself a training, in fact, the highest training, and is at the same time the end and goal of all training. Baba taught (without oral instructions generally) this Love and trained his devotees to develop this Love to the fullest extent of their capacity", wrote Sri Narasimhaswamiji.

Let us therefore start the new millennium 2000 with the firm resolve to undergo this training in Love and thus erase the artificial boundaries that separate people from people, pull down the Teli's wall of differentiation, leading to peace and harmony.

MALADY AND REMEDY

(Sai Sudha – January 2002)

In the middle of the month Margasirsha or Margazhi, which brims with divine fervor, the New Year according to the English Calender is born. This day, the First of January, is being celebrated throughout our country with great joy. The whole of the night of December 31st is devoted to fun and frivolity. The religiously minded people visit various temples for offering prayers and puja at the dawn of the New Year. In recent years the presiding deities in many Hindu temples are forced to keep awake till midnight! Even the New Year Days of the Hindu Calendars, be it Tamil, Telugu or Kannada, is not given so much importance.

In the last two or three decades we have been witnessing a gradual moral degradation, growing lawlessness and increasing threat to peace, not only at the national level but also at the universal level. Every New Year dawns with a hope that the situation will change for the better. Year by year the situation becomes worse. The root cause is the ever-increasing thirst for self-aggrandisement among people at the helm, people in public life, nay, even among some people preaching religion. The main cause for the recent attack on the World Trade Centre in New York, the parliament building in India and ruthless massacre of innocent people at various places is sheer craziness born out of greed, hatred, intolerance and fanaticism.

The cure for this malady lies within. It will not come from somewhere. It needs a thorough metamorphosis in the hearts of individuals as they are the vital components of society. This change can be brought about only through sincere prayer. Sri Narasimhaswamiji writes: “Sincere prayer draws the Grace of the Lord. Prayer sharpens the brain and the intellect. Prayer elevates the mind. It can reach a realm where reason dares not enter, the Kingdom of God. Prayer is a mighty spiritual force. Prayer generates good spiritual currents and produces tranquility of the mind. If you pray regularly, your life will be gradually changed and moulded. Prayer purifies the mind and the intellect of man and fills them with sattwa."

In the last century the efficacy of prayer was unambiguously demonstrated to the world by Mahatma Gandhi. For freeing the nation from the yoke of foreign domination, the weapon exclusively used by Gandhiji was ahimsa; satya or truth was his shield, but prayer was his most effective means. Gandhiji's prayer meetings were memorable and millions of people were attracted and they felt a change in their hearts. It was mainly the power of this prayer that worked in the minds of the British and induced them to transfer the governance of the country to us. It was while proceeding to participate in a prayer meeting that Gandhiji sacrificed his life.

When adharma is at its peak, generally the meek are the casualty. In response to the earnest prayers of the afflicted, the Lord, as promised in Gita, appears on the earth from time to time for the protection of the good and the annihilation of the wicked. In this age of Kali, He appears in the form of saints, messiahs, sages, like The Buddha, The Christ, The Prophet, Sri Chaitanya Mahaprabhu, the three great Acharyas – Sankara, Ramanuja and Madhwa. In the last two centuries India has seen the advent of the Great Masters like Sri Ramakrishna Paramahamsa and Samartha Sadguru Sai Baba. Both by precept and practice, they were able to pull human race out of chaos, remove the wickedness from the hearts of the wicked by the process of Love and restore peace. The Missions started in the names of such Great Ones are engaged in spreading their teachings among people. The mission started by Sri Narasimhaswamiji in the name of his Master Sri Sai Baba in the Thirties of the last century with All India Sai Samaj as the nucleus has a role to play in the present situation.

Sri Sai Baba's advent was essentially for bringing together people belonging to various faiths, religions, cults and communities and leading them in the path of Love to lasting peace. Nearly two decades after Baba's Mahasamadhi, Sri Narasimhaswamiji was drawn to Shirdi and chosen as the principal apostle by the Master Himself. Sri Swamiji has left us a legacy – volumes of literature on the wonderful life and teachings of Sri Sai Baba. Sri Swamiji conducted bhajans at various places, houses of devotees, where he presented his Master to the gathering. The gathering of devotees sing the glory of the Lord, participate in namasankirtan and hear the teachings of Saints and Sages; that is real satsang. Being present in a satsang removes the dross in the mind of the participant and leads him or her in the Right Path. Baba exhorted his devotees to take part in satsang. Satsang provides an opportunity for exchange of thoughts and experiences for mutual benefit. Therefore, besides the periodical gatherings, Sri Swamiji introduced the system of holding All India Sai Devotees' Conventions at various places in the country where devotees from all parts of the country gather, learn more about Sri Sai Baba and His Message and make spiritual advancement.

NEW YEAR THOUGHTS

(Sai Sudha – December 2005)

The year 2004 ended with a colossal calamity like Tsunami devouring the lives of millions of human beings and animals and causing huge material losses. All over the world violence and terrorist activities were seen to be growing every day. The year 2005 began with expectation and hope in the minds of people that the havoc being wrought by nature and human species would abate and the world would march towards peace. Events that followed belied all expectations.

Man survives by the bounty of Nature. But man does not remain content with the resources afforded by Nature. Greed prompts man to act against the laws of Nature. Gandhiji said, "Nature is relentless, it will take its revenge". We see Nature's fury not only in India but in other parts of the Globe also. Man should learn to respect Nature. He is most welcome to enjoy its resources but without infringing on its form and course. If this is done, damages caused by storms, floods and the like will be far minimal.

In the last one year terrorist acts have multiplied; everyday massacre by bomb blasts, lethal weapons and mass destruction is reported. To serve their own ends people in politics organize bandhs and agitations; even students are incited into violent acts. Talking about secularism seems to be a myth when one notices the violent clashes between communities, religious groups and castes. Law is helpless because the makers and upholders of the law are also caught in this web.

A change for better in the coming year 2006, the New Year, is what each one of us should hope for and aim at, but this is possible only by a change in the heart, in the heart of every individual. Harmony, ahimsa, tolerance, altruism and LOVE ae the solid stones on which can be erected a glorious edifice of Peace. With this as his mission a saint appeared in Maharashtra in the Nineteenth Century. He was neither a Hindu nor a Moslem; but he was both Hindu and Moslem. In his own way, by infusing the potion of Love silently into the veins of his followers, he brought under one common fold people professing different faiths. He is revered as Sai Baba by millions of people today, but the core of his teaching is not given the thought that is due to it. 'Shun hatred' was his principal message; when hatred is removed, the fountain of Love wells up and peaceful existence results.

In a lecture delivered in All India Radio, Hyderabad, as far back as 1944, as a glorious introduction of his Master Sri Sai Baba, Sri Narasimhaswamiji said:

"Human progress in societies till now has been largely based on the principles of egotism as expressed in individualism and nationalism. Self-assertion in the individual and the nation is undoubtedly essential for progress. But, we have learned to restrict individual freedom by the enforcement of the principle of altruism to the extent necessary for the proper working of a group or society known as a nation. Nationalism, however, is, at present, practically the last word in our political civilization. This has been leading us to terrible errors involving loss of life and property. It is obvious that the principle of Altruism, or, in other words, love must be introduced or developed so as to check and counteract nationalism to the extent necessary to secure the welfare of mankind. Is there any person or means by which this principle of Altruism or love can be enforced on national units today? Most will immediately reply that there is none and that the prospect for humanity is consequently very dark. But some of the more hopeful members of society are able to see through this darkness of the present hour, a glimmer of hope. There appear to be some persons and some forces which will emphasise the principle of love and make it the leaven to leaven all society.

"These men are the great supermen, the Godmen, the modern Rishis. The age of Rishis, some say, is gone, as also the age of miracles. But, believe me when I tell you, the age of miracles is coming and the stream of Rishis is not over, but swelling. These appear bold assertions. But I will mention one clear and startling instance of a modern Rishi as powerful and deep in his love for mankind as Jesus. I am referring to Sai Baba of Shirdi of whom I shall immediately proceed to give a short account."

Swamiji has made a mention about Jesus because no other godman proclaimed Love as the sole principle of any religion as Jesus did. Baba's mandate was identical to his: "Love ye one another even as I love ye all".

In the short pamphlet 'Who is Sri Sai Baba of Shirdi' written nearly seven decades back, Swamiji described in golden letters the pathetic situation prevailing in the world and prescribed the effective remedy also. What Swamiji had written then seems to be more valid today.

"Baba declared that if people hated one another, his heart was smarting with pain and sorrow and if persons forgave enemies and endured the ill-treatment, he was highly pleased. This is the most valuable lesson for this day and for all time. A story is told in Bhagavata of the world going as a cow to Brahma, groaning under the weight of the cruel Asuras harassing innocent people. That is just the spectacle all over the world today. Hatred, destruction, plunder, and absolute disregard for truth and virtue, are the predominant features in the daily history of the world today. Man's claws and teeth are red with the gore of brother man; and the criminal is not apologetic but is blatant. Civilization is in imminent danger of being submerged in pools of human blood and devastating fire leaving the human form a fossil to be discovered within some rocks by some later race. The only thing that can avert this doom is love, a revival of the very ancient message to Asuras from God, 'Dayadwan', i.e. 'Be merciful."

How to start loving? "You must start by beginning with 'Ahimsa'. If you are cruel to creatures, you cannot possibly love them. Himsa and Love are the opposite poles. So to start universal love, avoid hatred of any one. 'Nirvairah sarva bhuteshu' . That is, a man who hates no creature at all is said to be the best devotee of Sri Krishna in Chapter XII of the Gita. Starting therefore by avoiding hatred, proceed next to see in what possible cases sympathy can take more positive and concrete forms than avoidance of injury. Whatever is possible for you to do to other creatures, try and do that. That will be a positive act which engenders a feeling of love and enables you to achieve love to all beings that is Sarvabhuta Hite Ratah."

Let us seriously ponder over the words of Sri Narasimhaswamiji. Let us not stop with just worshipping Baba with fruits and flowers. Let us deeply contemplate more on his teachings. If everyone of us, individually, and collectively, do this, we can definitely make this earth a paradise. In conclusion, let us take to heart these words of Swamiji.

"Love is the one force which upholds the Universe, and Love is that force which can overcome the innumerable obstructions to the manifestation of love which arise in our imperfect civilization between individual and individual, group and group, and nation and nation. All bitterness, hatred, rivalries, and antagonism will melt into thin air at the contact of powerful love, and such love has to be directed to the world in existing conditions in increasing measure to enable it to cast aside the darkening clouds that cover it and restore to it the blissful light of love. The ultimate future of humanity cannot be and should not be mere ruin and wreck. It must be an integral whole, integrated by the force of love. For that, the proper dynamo that can work upon the world is the dynamo that we call Sai Baba". (*Life of Sai Baba, Part I, Ch.XV*).

LOVE, LOVE, LOVE

(Sai Sudha – January 2007)

A new year is born. Only time has moved. There seems to be no change in the world environment. Terrorist activities are seen to be on the increase taking a heavy toll on human lives and causing huge damages to public and private properties. The Government is trying out all measures, in co-ordination with other countries, to control this phantom.

Terrorism is an international phenomenon. What is more disturbing are the frequent clashes among communities, people of different castes and religious groups. The law seems to be helpless. Politicians who are at the helm do nothing to control this, not because they are not able to, but because they do not want to. Their minds are always busy calculating as to how to make use of these clashes in garnering votes.

The only solution is 'Love'. The fundamental of all world religions is 'Love" but what is seen among religious followers of various hues, generally, is bigotry, intolerance. It will do a lot of good to recollect the vows taken by all the strict followers of Mahatma Gandhi in 1935.

"Non-violence; Truth; Non-stealing; Celibacy; Non-Possession; Body-Labour; Control of the Palate; fearlessness; Equal Respect for all Religions; *Swadeshi* (use of home manufactures); freedom from untouchability. These eleven should be observed as vows in a spirit of humility."

These are the virtues extolled by the Lord as '*daivisampat*' in Chapter 16 of Bhagavat Gita.

Let us recollect Gandhiji's words: "I have found that life persists in the midst of destruction. Therefore, there must be a higher law than that of destruction. Only under that law would well-ordered society be intelligible and life worth living.

"If that is the law of life we must work it out in daily existence. Wherever there are wars, whenever we are confronted with an opponent, conquer by love. I have found that the certain law of love has answered in my own life as the law of destruction has never done."

It is a time for all Sai devotees to do some introspection. Millions approach and worship Baba to achieve material benefits. Millions get what they prayed for. But their demands never end; they go on praying for more, more, more, never satiated. At some time or other, one has to pause for a moment, find out what is Baba's mission, the purpose of his advent and his message to the world.

Baba's religion is a religion of Love. By practice and precept Baba, in his own unique way, taught people the need for Love, the potency of Love. It goes to his credit to bring together in his mosque – Dwarakamayi as he called – two warring communities, Hindus and Muslims, and trained them to carry on worship and other religious practices each according to their own systems not only without any conflict but also complimenting each other, coordinating with each other. Baba exhorted people to eschew hatred totally; according to him hatred is a poison that slowly but surely kills the hater, not the hated.

Sri Narasimhaswamiji writes: "In reality, the essence of religion, wherever it may be found, is one. It is Divine Power, Knowledge and Love – Love that recognizes no barrier of caste, creed or colour. When people assert that they are following such an amsa of God, be it Christ, Mohamed, Buddha, Sankara or Chaitanya – and in his name slay, burn, torture and 'shut the gates of mercy on mankind', they are really working out not God or the essence of religion but the opposite principle. GOD IS LOVE. HATRED IS ITS OPPOSITE. Where hatred and murder, greed and plunder are the prevailing features, there is no God or real religion. In Baba, hatred and greed had no place at any time. His being, mind, words and conduct were saturated with Love Divine – impartial Love that seeks no reward – Love that sacrifices itself for the benefit of humanity.

"Baba allowed his own worship with the prescience that it would be the means for providing temporal and spiritual benefits to millions of individuals and also the means of solving India's national problems of communal and religious unity, as *sarvaloka malapaha*".

In this New Year, let all Sai devotees take a solemn vow to develop Love, a Love that will drive away the least trace of hatred, a Love that will bring harmony among individuals and groups, a Love that will ensure an absolute existence of Peace. Let us all pray to our Master Sri Sai Baba to see that our vow is fulfilled by His unfailing Grace!

LET US BE WORTHY OF BEING CALLED A SAI DEVOTEE

(Sai Sudha – December 2008)

We are coming to the end of one more year. This year has been more tragic than the previous ones. Terrorism is spreading like a wildfire. Blinded by mad frenzy, a few senseless people resort to barbaric acts resulting in the loss of several innocent lives and properties worth several crores of rupees pushing the country's economy backwards.

While terrorism is a world phenomenon now, in the recent past our nation had to face a series of bomb blasts in various cities. The recent attack by terrorists on prominent hotels in Mumbai killing several people is most gruesome. While the common man is dismayed over the turn of events, politicians seem to seize this opportunity to play blame-game with an eye solely on the vote bank. If a few Muslims are involved in these crimes, one has no justification to blame the community as a whole or find fault with Islam. Similarly, if a Hindu or a Christian is involved, the entire Hindu or Christian Community is not to be blamed.

Terrorist act is a heinous crime and the persons involved are criminals and have to be dealt with severely by the Law. No terrorist can be said to belong to any religion whatsoever. Because no religion preaches hatred and violence; no religion preaches intolerance. A person involved in a terrorist act is not human, is devoid of the faculty of discrimination and hence cannot be a 'religious' person at all. Hence the question of his belonging to Hindu, Islamic, Christian or any other religion whatsoever does not arise.

In India what was being followed in ancient days was not a 'religion' but it was a 'dharma'. It was not founded by any single individual. It preached more of human conduct and ethics; it was all-embracing and extremely accommodative. Tolerance was its main plank; that was why one sees so many later religions could easily enter into and flourish in India. The dharma of our land is totally based on the motto 'Live and let live'.

An article entitled "Making a Mockery of Jihad" written by Sri Asghar Ali Engineer, The Centre for Study of Society and Secularism in Mumbai, that appeared in the *Times of India*, on October 7, 2008, is thought-provoking. He has brought out clearly that terrorist attacks have no sanction in Quran and it is wrong to use the word '*jihad*' in connection with wars and the like. The Quran advises 'And cast not yourselves to destruction with your own hands and do good (to others). Surely Allah loves the doers of good".

There is another revelatory article captioned "Of Dharma Yudh and Jihad" written by Prof. Ishtiyaque Danish (also appeared in *Times of India*, 2-11-2008) has been reproduced. He rightly concludes, "Planting a bomb surreptitiously to kill an innocent is not Jihadi; so, too, burning a handicapped person to death is not Dharma Yudh. There is something seriously wrong with the understanding that terrorism is Jihad or Dharma Yudh".

Till the beginning of the last century a fakir lived in India and remarkably brought together various communities under one fold. He preached love alone. His benevolent influence was so great that today, after ninety years of his Mahasamadhi, several millions of people from all communities, all walks of life, from all countries, worship him, not only in his Samadhi Mandir at Shirdi, but by erecting temples for him at every nook and corner of the country. Lakhs and lakhs of people visit his Samadhi at Shirdi every day. It is most unfortunate that in the State in which he lived, and continues to live in astral form, some people raise a revolt and war cry against people from other States, especially the Northern States. While Sri Sai Baba during his life time at Shirdi in Maharashtra radiated his divine influence to usher love, harmony and peace among human beings as a whole and played a vital role in bringing about national integration, people in that State who engage themselves in acts detrimental

to the goal of integration should pause, ponder and work towards national unity and peace.

The devotees of Sri Sai Baba form a very large fraternity not only in India but in other parts of the world also. Having been fortunate to come under the influence of such a wonderful and great Master, all these devotees should not stop with offering worship to him, but should ponder over his teachings, which are essentially –

"Behave properly"

"Avoid hatred totally"

"Do not talk ill about others".

"All faiths lead to same goal. Stick to your own faith".

We cannot assume a role for reforming society. One should aim at reforming oneself. Bhagavan Sri Ramana says, "Make your outlook right. The Creator knows how to take care of His creation". Sri S.S. Cohen, a very staunch devotee of Bhagavan, in his book "*Reflections on Talks with Sri Ramana Maharshi*", clarifies: "The last sentence makes us think of the politician, social worker, philanthropist, economic philosopher, and even the clergymen who are ever anxious to help the nation and the world, perpetually thinking of how to save humanity from misery and disaster. Bhagavan particularly tells them that there is a power which is making and moving all things. Who are you to imagine that you can make and unmake to your liking? Such worries denote ignorance of Providence, or the arrogation to oneself the duties of Providence….. ."

A new year is approaching. This is the time when each devotee of Sri Sai introspects and makes a resolve to follow his teachings and give thought to altruism, shunning bias and hatred totally, and thus becomes fit to be called a Sai Devotee.

MAHASAMADHI - I

(Sai Sudha – September 1998)

It is now eighty years since Sri Sai Baba attained Mahasamadhi. In these eighty years the spread of Sai Bhakti has been phenomenal. Sai nama is recognized to be as potent as Rama or Krishna or Siva nama. His presence is felt everywhere.

So long as Baba was in his physical frame, he confined his stay to Shirdi and carried on his mission from the remote hamlet. Though large number of devotees flocked to Shirdi to have his darshan and reap benefits from him, temporal and spiritual, his name was known mainly in Maharashtra and border areas. Once Baba cast off his moral sheath, or crossed the border (*seemallanghan*), he became *sarvavyapi*, allpervading.

After Mahasamadhi, "Sai Baba has outgrown Shirdi and his presence is felt in the various temples that have been built for him and in the bhajan halls; and even in the homes. Baba's presence is actually felt and his sakshatkaras also sometimes take place to confirm the feeling of all that He is divine and everywhere", writes Sri Narasimhaswamiji. In 1955 Sri Swamiji prophesied, "Perhaps it is only just now that Baba is getting to be recognized in various parts of India. The more He is known, the more assuredly will He draw groups to His feet. One index of His growing popularity is the large number of children we name after Him in so many families, Hindu and Muhammadan, and the large number of temples and bhajan salas named after Him. So He is sure to equal Tirupati Venkatesa in the matter of attracting people. Incidentally, it may be noted that Tirupati Venkatesa and Sai are not different". He further says, "The followers and worshippers of Baba have derived the same benefits by worshipping Him as the most intense worshippers of Tirupati Venkatesa or Brindavana Krishna or Bhadrachala Rama or Lord Shiva of Kailash have".

Today we see that Shirdi has become next only to Tirupati among the vast number of pilgrim centres in Bharat. Thousands of temples have been built for Baba by ardent devotees in every nook and corner of the country and more temples are coming up every day. On Thursdays and other important festival days we see a large number of devotees patiently waiting in long queue to offer puja to Sai. Baba's pictures adore puja rooms of millions of houses. Millions carry with them Baba's pictures and millions wear lockets bearing the image of Baba. What a grand transformation in the last eight decades! More specifically, in the last six decades after Pujyasri Narasimhaswamiji was chosen to be the Apostle to carry on Sri Sai's Mission!

One of the very intimate, ankita, devotees of Baba, Sri Rege Maharaj (who as a High Court Judge by profession) could categorically say, "I look upon Sri Sai Baba as the Creator, Preserver and Destroyer. I did so before Mahasamadhi in 1918 and I do so now. To me He is not gone. He is even now. To me he had no limitations. Of course, when he was with us, there was the fleshy tabernacle. That was prominently brought to our notice at times. But mostly the infinite aspect of his was what remained before me. I thought of him as a mental or spiritual image in which the finite and infinite blended very perfectly – yet allowing the finite to appear before us at times. Now that the body has been cast off, the infinite alone remains as SAI BABA".

Just as Brahmotsava is celebrated for Lord Venkatesa in Tirupati or festival for Durga in West Bengal during dusserah or Navaratri, Mahasamadhi utsav is being celebrated in a grand manner in Baba's temples all over the country by His devotees. On Mahasamadhi Day, the day on which the finite has integrated into the infinite, when millions of devotees think of Baba, pray to Him, offer worship to Him, engage themselves in namasankirtan and satsang, His presence could be felt more intensely and His response to prayers is bound to be, more spontaneous and positive.

MAHASAMADHI - II

(Sai Sudha – October / November 1999)

Namah Sri Sainathaya mohatantravinascine
Gurave buddhibodhaya bodhamatraswarupine

Pranams to Sri Sainatha who destroys delusion and attachment, the Guru who stimulates the right knowledge, Himself being the Embodiment of knowledge.

Here the most significant attribute of Sri Sai is buddhibodhaya. By stimulating the right knowledge, the right thoughts in the minds of devotees, He destroys delusion and attachment.

Devotees pray to Sri Sai for help in solving various problems and rescuing them from the trials and tribulations they come across. But is there any end to problems and predicaments? If one problem is solved, another one is ready to take its place. If one analyses carefully, these problems or predicaments or miseries do not spring up on us suddenly from somewhere, they are not caused by any external agency, but are the results of one's own actions, the effect of one's own Karma. The actions are controlled by thoughts. If thoughts are good, the actions that follow are bound to be good also. Thus by giving the right knowledge, the knowledge of discrimination, viveka, Baba helps His devotees to think right and act right whereby they are not snared by trials or tribulations.

This prayer to Sri Sai for the right knowledge has to be preceded by total faith. It is only by Baba's grace that one can develop the absolute faith that he will be guided by Baba in all his thoughts and actions. No doubt Baba Himself draws His devotees to Him. But it is for the devotee to make Baba his sole refuge and repose complete faith in Him.

When a rich lady came to Baba with a plate full of money as dakshina and waited for four days with a prayer to be her Guru and give upadesa, Baba told her: "It is not the Guru that makes himself your guru. It is you who must regard him as guru, i.e. place faith in him. Take a potshred and regard it as your guru and see if your goal or aim is reached or not!"

Baba told Radhabai Deshmukhin, "If you make me the sole object of your thoughts and aims, you will attain paramartha, the supreme goal. Look at me with undivided attention: so will I look at you. This is the only truth my guru taught me. The four sadhanas and six sastras are not necessary. With entire confidence trust your guru. That is enough".

Is it easy for all to develop faith? Sri Narasimhaswamiji writes: "Faith seems to be easy to place but when anyone tries to place faith in a particular guru or holy person that he visits or meets, he discovers that there are very sharp limits to the faith that arises. Faith in one sense is voluntary; if one traces the real starting and progress of faith, one sees that it depends upon so many circumstances which are not under one's control. And the growth of faith seems to be peculiar to the constitution of some. The previous mental habits cultivated have a great deal to do with a person's faith. Some people are cussed. They are ever determined to contradict anything and everything and some are skeptic or ever doubting. This habit of doubt or aggressive combativeness is ruinous to the starting or development of faith".

Faith depends on an individual's strength of mind. It is difficult to develop faith in a wavering or oscillating mind. Here satsang, the company of devotees who had already developed faith, will be of help.

When one is in the company of steadfast devotees, his mind gradually absorbs that devotion, when faith becomes easy to develop.

On a day like Mahasamadhi Day, large number of devotees gather at one place and engage themselves in puja, bhajan, dhyana, etc. To be in such a congregation of devotees is itself a blessing and helps in stimulating faith in Baba.

The day of Mahasamadhi is the day on which Baba crossed the border, gave up the finite body to become the apantaratmarupa. When a jivanmukta or satpurusha gives up his body wishing to continue his personality, the soul thereafter surviving in subtle form is called apantaratma. Before giving up his body, Baba categorically declared that he will always be active from his tomb. When in body, he subjected himself to the limitations of the body. By giving up the body, he broke himself away from such limitations to remain as an apantaratmarupa, to confer unlimited benefits to his faithful devotees. As long as Baba had his body, people were talking of Baba, living in Shirdi. After Mahasamadhi, Baba's presence is felt everywhere. Sri Sai Sahasranamavali hails Baba as *apantaratmarupena srashturishtaprovarthakaha* – One who is carrying out the will of the creator as an apantaratma.

Bow to Sri Sai!

MAHASAMADHI - III

(Sai Sudha – September 2000)

Soon we are going to celebrate the Eightysecond Mahasamadhi Day of our Great Master Sri Sai Baba. In all Sai Mandirs, institutions, devotees are planning to make the celebration grander than in the previous years. Efforts are being made to arrange spectacular colourful programmes, cultural events and music performances to turn the celebration into a colourful and attractive show with all pomp and grandeur. There is nothing wrong in doing this since as Sri Narasimhaswamiji says, "In the case of saints, the anniversary of their escape from the flesh is a day of rejoicing. From beyond the veil, they are more clearly discerned as God or fragments of God that will continue to guard, guide and save their loving devotees and answer prayers". It should be our endeavour to look beyond the veil and seek the blessings of the Great One on the Mahasamadhi Day. "It is best to spend this day, the Dasara - Ekadasi day on which Sri Sai Baba attained his Mahasamadhi with thoughts and actions that He would commend".

Baba was an Embodiment of Love. His religion was Love. His message was Love. Perfect and unalloyed Love. Bargainless Love. When one takes his strides in the path of Love towards Baba, he becomes prepared to sacrifice anything, even his ego. The ego merges in the ocean of love and what remains is Bliss. Love and sacrifice are two sides of the same coin. A mother is prepared to sacrifice anything for her child, a husband for the wife he loves, a wife for the husband she loves and close friends for each other. But what is difficult nay, even impossible, is to sacrifice one's ego, one's pet notions, theories, prejudices. It is here a Samartha Sadguru like Sri Sai Baba helps, if only we pray to Him earnestly and abide by His teachings.

Yasmannodvijate Loko Lokannodvijate Cha Yah l
Harshamarshabhayodvega irmukto sa cha me priyah ll

(Bhagavad Gita Chapter XII, 15)

"He who is not a source of annoyance to his fellow-creatures, and who in his turn does not feel vexed with his fellow-creatures, and who is free from delight and envy, perturbation and fear, is dear to Me", says the Lord.

Time and again Baba has reiterated this message. He brought devotees of various faiths under one roof and taught them the importance of loving each other. "Love is itself a training, in fact, the highest training and is at the same time, the end and goal of all training. Baba taught (without oral instruction generally) this love and trained His devotees to develop this love to the fullest extent of their capacity" writes Sri Swamiji.

In the name of castes, creeds, religion, sects and subsects associations are being formed everywhere when politicians continue to speak loudly of a secular state. The politicians cannot bring harmony among people of various religions, various castes, languages, because in their own interest they do not want such harmony. It is only devotees of a Great Master Sri Sai Baba who belonged to no particular religion but at the same time belonged to all religions, that can bring about a harmonious society through love and sacrifice.

"Let us remember on this day of Baba's ascension, this central truth of His life, viz., that a life spent in sacrifice and Loving service is life; and that a life spent in indulgence and other ways is death"

– H. H. Narasimhaswamiji.

MAHASAMADHI - IV

(Sai Sudha – October 2004)

When an ordinary man breathes his last, people say that he is dead, he is no more, his prana had left and so on. But when a saint, a Mahapurusha, dies, we do not say he is dead, we do not say that he is no more. We say that he has attained Samadhi, nirvana that he has given up his body, the mortal sheath. It is because in the case of an ordinary man, he identifies himself with the body or physical frame with which he moves about and he is so identified by others. Naturally, when the body falls, it is said that he is dead, he is gone, he is no more. In the case of a saint he has no body-consciousness, at no time he identifies himself with the body, he is always conscious that he has taken the body for a specific purpose and that he would give it up once the purpose is served.

Let us see what Baba himself has said on different occasions:

"I have no residence. I am the attribute-less Absolute-Nirguna. (Again, in the mood of Duality:) By the action of Karma I got embroiled and came to a body. My name is – 'The embodied-Dehi'. The world is my abode. Brahman is my father and Maya my mother. By their interlocking I got this body. The world is mutable, evanescent".

To Nana: "Does Baba mean to you only this visible body of 3.1/2 cubits height? Is that all? "This body is but my house. My guru Mourshad has long ago taken me away from this".

"What fun will it be (for me) to stand by and see the whole of this (Sai Baba) body burning on a funeral pyre of cowdung cake fuel?"

Mrs. M.W. Pradhan, one of the close devotees of Sri Sai Baba records in her experience: On 16.10.1918, i.e. the night after Baba's departure, I saw his body in a dying condition in my dream and said, 'Baba is dying'. Baba replied, 'People do not talk of saints as dying, but as taking samadhi'.

For saints giving up the body means freedom from shackles. An avatara varishta like Sri Sai Baba showered benefits on his devotees when appearing with the body and continues to do so even after leaving the body. The body was only a symbol; it is the Divinity abiding therein which acted then and which acts now. Sri Rege, ankita devotee of Baba, unambiguously asserts: "To me, he had no limitations. Of course, when he was with us, there was the fleshy tabernacle. That was prominently brought to our notice at times. But mostly the infinite aspect of His was what remained before me. I thought of him as a mental or spiritual image in which the finite blended very perfectly – yet allowing the finite to appear before us at times. *Now that the body has been cast off, the Infinite alone remains as SAI BABA*".

Another intimate devotee, G.G. Narke, states: "Sai Baba occasionally asked (I heard it myself), 'Where are you? Where am I? Where is this world?' Occasionally he declared, pointing to his body or touching it and referring to it as 'this is my house', 'I am not here. My Guru Mourshad has taken me away'. As even in the flesh, in this earthly life, he was not confined to his physical body, it may be truly said of him '*SAI BABA IS ALIVE. He is where he was then. Even then he was where he is now*'.

Rao Bahadur S.B. Dhumal says, "The best way of understanding Baba is to experience him oneself. Where is Baba gone? He is still alive and active – more active, if that were possible, than he was before his Mahasamadhi. *Anyone in downright earnest can get into touch with him, today and at once*".

Mrs. Tarkhad, privileged to enjoy the company of Sri Sai Baba for several days, talks about Baba: "He was all-in-all and the All for us. We never could think of his having limitations. Now that he has passed away, I feel what a terrible loss it is, as I can no longer pass hours together in blissful unconsciousness of time and affairs at his feet. We feel we have lost our soul; our bodies alone are left to us now. Yet it would not be true to say that he has altogether vanished. *He is still living now* and we have

ample proof of his powers and protecting care in many matters off and on ....'.

Both the appearance and disappearance of the 'human form' which was called 'Sai Baba' were part of a divine plan, to achieve a specific purpose – *dharma samsthapana* – upholding righteousness. The one which took this human form existed before appearance and continues to exist after disappearance as is borne out by the various events narrated in the Life of Sri Sai Baba. Sri Anna Saheb Dabholkar (Hemad Pant) has devoted three lengthy chapters, a total of 520 verses, to make the readers understand the significance of Baba's Mahasamadhi – *Leaving of the Body by Sainath – Chapters 42, 43 and 44*.

Baba said on several occasions that he would be active even from the tomb, he would take care of his devotees birth after birth and so on. Yet, when Baba gave up his body, people thought that he was dead and gone, they would no more be able to enjoy the bliss of being in his presence and they felt like destitutes. In the early hours of the night following the Mahasamadhi Day, Lakshman Mama who was in deep sleep at his home had a dream that Baba held his hand and said, "Get up quickly and come. Bapu saheb will not come today. At least you do *Kakad Arati* for me with the *Puja*". The devoted Lakshman Mama did so. Later on, the noon arati of Sai was done by Bapusaheb Jog, as usual, in the Masjid, along with others. Thus, Baba wanted his devotees to get the firm conviction that he is still with them.

Those who worship Sai on this Day of Ascension, who meditate on him on this Holy Day, sing his glories on this Day of His Merger in the Infinite, are sure to derive immense benefits. But it is very important to remember Baba's most valuable teaching on this occasion, which is extracted below from Sri Sai Satcharitra.

"If anyone speaks insultingly to another, then he has hurt me only and pierced my heart. He hurts me immediately who speaks a volley of hard words to another, while I am immensely pleased for a long time if one bears an insult patiently".

Hemant Pant says: Sai is immanent in the whole creation and he likes nothing else than love. This supreme nectar of teaching, which was most auspicious, flowed from Sai's mouth always. This was because of his great love for the devotees.

MAHASAMADHI - V

(Sai Sudha – September 2006)

This year Sri Sai Baba's Mahasamadhi Day falls on 3rd October. Therefore, we have to share our thoughts on Mahasamadhi in this issue itself.

This year's CELEBRATION has a special significance. The "NIRVANA DAY" of Sri Narasimha-swamiji, the foremost Apostle of Sri Sai Baba and the Founder-President of All India Sai Samaj falls on the Full Moon Day, following Baba's Mahasamadhi Day, i.e. 6th October, 2006. This year marks the 50th Nirvana Day of Sri Swamiji. This is a special occasion for all of us to rededicate ourselves to carry on the glorious Mission started by the savant with minds specially focused on the lofty ideals of Swamiji.

In 1956 also, the year in which Swamiji chose to give up his mortal coil, the September issue of Sai Sudha carried the Mahasamadhi message – the last such message – of Swamiji. Swamiji began his message thus, "The Mahasamadhi Day of Sri Sai Baba comes off this year on the 13th October and, as the Sai Sudha of October '06 containing the Mahasamadhi Message would not reach our readers before the 13th October, we have to issue that message in the September issue itself." Perhaps Swamiji was conscious of the fact that he would have attained Nirvana by the time October 1956 issue of Sai Sudha reached the readers!.

In this Message Swamiji wrote, "*So many devotees of Sai are now experiencing His constant and perpetual guardianship, protection and help, in almost every matter, that there is no necessity for pressing this truth further to show that Sai is still there after His Mahasamadhi and is not gone. How can God go and where is He to go? But it is not every one that gets the benefit of His continued existence and protection. The devotee has to attach himself at first with some degree of effort to Sai Baba and then he can get the full benefit.*"

What Swamiji wrote about his Master equally applies to him also. His entire life was wholly dedicated to the service of his Master and like Maruti for Sri Rama he had ananya – single-pointed – bhakti, devotion, to Sri Sai Baba. By constantly meditating on Sai with no other thought for over two decades he became Sai Himself. Sri Krishna said, "Those who attach themselves to Me by their devotion are in Me and I am in them". (*Ye bhajanti mam bhaktya mayi te teshu chaapi aham* – Gita IX – 29). Thus, Sri Swamiji who attached himself to Sai by his devotion is Sai, and Sai is in him. 'As Baba is still active and vigorous as God is in his dealings with bhaktas', Swamiji who has become one with Sai is also very much active and vigorous as far as the faithful devotees are concerned. Twenty days prior to his giving up his body, Swamiji emphatically proclaimed.

"*In the first place the spiritual leadership of Sai movement is of the utmost importance and none but the founder amongst the members could provide it. So the founder still continues to be the spiritual head of the Sai Samaj and of all Sai Devotees. It is to facilitate this work that a cottage has been erected and allotted to the founder to live in and thus become a permanent and always present guide, director and helper of all*".

Swamiji has concluded in his last Mahasamadhi Message thus: "Every one who cares now to think of Baba, to study about him, to contact his bhaktas and to attend proceedings such as puja, bhajan, kathas, etc., impressing people with the nature of Sai gets undoubted benefit and our Mahasamadhi Message this year may close with pointedly drawing the attention of all our readers to this fact that every reader should make his contact with Sai Baba as full and perfect as it can be and then rich will be his reward. As will be seen from the Foreword to Volume II of the Life of Sai Baba, furnished by Sri B.N. Datar, Home Minister with the Government of India, *every portion of his life is covered by Sai Baba and happiness with success is the result*. May similar contact, similar success, and blessings be the lot of every reader!"

B N Datar was Minister for Home in Jawaharlal Nehru's Cabinet. He had intimate contact with Swamiji. Swamiji in his last Mahasamadhi Message made a reference to Datar's total devotion to Sai. It was B.N.Datar who spoke about Swamiji and declared open the *H.H.Narasimhaswamiji Library & Free Reading Room* on the First Aradhana Day/Founder's Day celebrated at All India Sai Samaj in October 1957! In the Foreword to Part II of *Life of Sai Baba*, B.N. Datar has stated: "In a way, Swamiji has been responsible for rousing in me a desire to know Shri Sai Baba and to seek His Grace. It was in or about 1937 while both of us had been at the Ramanashram at Tiruvannamalai that I came to know that Swamiji had visited Shirdi and had been trying hard to collect material for a detailed study of the mysterious of the manifold life of this great saint. It was my conversation with him that enkindled in me a great curiosity to visit Shirdi and to seek His blessings. I did so early in 1938, and have since then been visiting it off and on".

It should be our earnest prayer to Samartha Sadguru Sai Baba and Sadguru Narasimhaswamiji to endow us with devotion and enthusiasm and zeal to carry on the wonderful work carried on by Sri Swamiji.

MAHASAMADHI - VI

(Sai Sudha – October 2007)

It is now eighty-nine years since Baba attained Mahasamadhi, crossed the border, or cast away his mortal sheath, the bondage with which he had to carry on his ministrations thus far. October 1918 marked a new era in the history of Sai movement. The light that was guiding people in the subhra marga – righteous path – encased in a physical frame called Sai Baba and confined to the remote village of Shirdi came out of its shell and started spreading its radiance The day people call Mahasamadhi is actually the day of Sun's rise. Year by year the splendour was growing in intensity attracting people from far and wide. Nearly eighteen years after Mahasamadhi, this Power, called Sai Baba, drew to its Samadhi a fiery, resourceful spiritual sadhaka from Tamil Nadu, bestowed on him the 'gem' he sought, 'self-realisation', and charged him with the mission of spreading Sai Bhakti and Sai's teachings throughout the county and beyond. Fully charged with the 'Sai' power, this chosen Apostle, Sri Narasimhaswamiji carried on the Sai Mission for two decades in such a remarkable way that today the name of Sri Sai Baba is as familiar as that of Sri Rama and Krishna to people everywhere.

Baba's giving up his body, attaining Mahasamadhi, in 1918 marks an epoch according to Sri Narasimhaswamiji. In the editorial of Sai Sudha, September 1955 (before Mahasamadhi Day) Swamiji writes: "In 1918 the year of Baba's Mahasamadhi, his reputation was no doubt remarkable, but still it was only in a particular province and with particular sets of people. There were many persons closely moving with him at that time who could not imagine that Baba was anything more than an Ahmednagar resident or a resident of Maharashtra seeking to promote the interests of those connected with him by *rinanubandha*. It never struck such people that Baba's reputation could cross the borders of Maharashtra or Bombay State, and that he could become a great national asset useful especially for solving national problems, and it would have struck them much less that Baba would be a world factor. But what have been set out in Volume I (*Life of Sai Baba*) would suffice to show that *Baba has become a national asset and a world asset*, and these have become possible by Baba's laying down his fleshy body. Hence the Mahasamadhi of 1918 in Baba's case might well be considered as marking an epoch." Swamiji concludes saying "in the case of saints with *vibhutis* like Sri Sai Baba, the so-called death is really an epoch in the life, the postmortem life being the more important portion of the life of that personality."

Before Mahasamadhi, when Baba was in flesh, staying at Shirdi mosque, people had to go there to have his darshan and obtain his blessings. After Mahasamadhi, he has become all-pervasive and his presence can be felt at any place in the Earth by an ardent devotee. A divine manifestation like Sri Sai Baba moves everywhere at will with an astral body after giving up the physical body. Sri Ramakrishna Paramahamsa says about such divine manifestations thus: "Generally the body does not remain alive after the attainment of Samadhi. The only exceptions are such sages as Narada, who keep their bodies alive in order to bring spiritual light to others. It is also true of Divine Incarnations like Chaitanya. After the well is dug, one generally throws away the spade and the basket. But some keep them in order to help their neighbours. The great souls who retain their bodies after Samadhi feel compassion for the suffering of others…"

Those fortunate devotees who had earned enough merit to be in the company of Sri Sai in Shirdi Dwarakamayee before 1918, though were assured of the Master's continuous presence even after Mahasamadhi, were crestfallen; they missed his physical presence, naturally, to a great extent. One such privileged devotee, Mrs. Tarabai Sadashiv Tarkhad writes in her "Experience": "Now that he has passed away, I feel what a terrible loss it is, as I can no longer pass hours together in blissful unconsciousness of time and affairs at his feet. We feel we have lost our soul; our bodies alone are left to us now. Yet it would not be true to say that he has altogether vanished. *He is still living now and we have ample proof of his powers and providing care in many matters off and on .....*" Damodar Savalram Rasane, who got children by Baba's blessings, an ankita devotee, says, "After 1918 I still consult him by chits, etc. and he guides me still".

While Sai Mandirs, Samajas and institutions celebrate Baba's Mahasamadhi as a grand festival, on the Mahasamadhi day at least all Sai devotees will do well to spend some time in silent contemplation on Baba, his grace and his assurances of succour. Each one of us should contemplate on the divine purpose of Baba's advent. Let us recall the concluding exhortation of Sri Narasimhaswamiji in his Mahasamadhi Message given in 1944:

"Let us remember on this day of his Ascension, this central truth of his life, viz. that a life spent in sacrifice and loving service is Life; and that a life spent in indulgence and other ways is *Death –paropakaraartham idam sareeram paropakaraya sataam vibhootayah. Yate satpurushaah paraartha ghatakaah, swaarthanparityajya yeheh.*

If all of us do but strive to reach this ideal, our individual and national goals are sure to be achieved. 'Deserve and you will get it', so said Sai.

MAHASAMADHI - VII

(Sai Sudha – October 2009)

"Mahasamadhi is the casting off of the fleshy sheath. In the case of ordinary men, such a day is called the date of death or the anniversary of death. For recently departed souls, it is a day of mourning. But when time breaks off the edges of sorrow, pious and loving memories are recalled that day, and lead to acts that would please and benefit the departed souls. In the case of saints, the anniversary of their escape from the flesh is a day of rejoicing. From beyond the veil they are more clearly discerned as God or fragments of God that will continue to guard, guide and save their loving devotee and answer prayers. It is best to spend this day, the Dasara Ekadasi day on which Sri Sai Baba attained his Mahasamadhi with thoughts and actions that he would commend."

This is what Sri Narasimhaswamiji has written in one of his Mahasamadhi Day Messages (1944). He categorically states that the Dasara Ekadasi day was the day on which Sri Sai Baba attained his Mahasamadhi and that the ninth day of the ninth Islamic month, as the day of Baba's Ascension and that is observed by them as Mahasamadhi day.

Among Hindus, especially in the South, the day of death is observed every year on the particular thithi on which the person concerned died. In the case of ordinary people they call this ceremony as *Shraddha* or *thithi*. In the case of saints that day is called *Aradhana*. Saint Thyagaraja's nirvana day is *bahula Panchami thithi* in the month of *paush* and his aradhana is done on that day.

Sri Narasimhaswamiji, conforming to the above tradition, decided to do aradhana on the day of his Gurudev Sri Sai Baba's Mahasamadhi *thithi*, that *thithi* being *Sukla Ekadasi*, the next day to Vijayadasami. On the aradhana day, puja is being done invoking the blessings of the Guru and Guru parampara.

A question is raised, 'When Baba's Mahasamadhi is observed at Shirdi on Vijayadasami Day, why is it done the next day at All India Sai Samaj? It is hoped that the necessary explanation has been given. Sri Narasimhaswamiji, a realized soul, the apostle who spearheaded the Sai Movement, with all his erudition in scriptures, took the decision to observe Ekadasi Thithi as Baba's Mahasamadhi Day and it is being celebrated so for nearly six decades.

As the Mahasamadhi Day is preceded by *navarathri*, the period when Devi, the source of all powers, is worshipped, Swamiji in his wisdom decided on commencement of the Mahasamadhi festival with Kalasa Sthapana on Mahalaya Amavasya Day and Puja to Devi, in the mornings and evenings, with Lalitha Sahasranama Archana. Correspondingly, Laksharchana of Sri Sai Baba was introduced during the festival.

When the All India Sai Samaj was brought into existence by the Founder President Sri Narasimhaswamiji, with absolute foresight and sound reasoning, he incorporated in the byelaws that only a picture of Sri Sai Baba shall be worshipped. Nearly three decades after Swamiji passed away, this rule was ignored and a statue was installed.

If changes are brought about in the systems and procedures introduced by the great Swamiji, it can only be construed that those who bring out such changes are either unaware of Sri Swamiji's forethoughts or they may perhaps be wiser than Sri Swamiji.

MAHASAMADHI - VIII

(Sai Sudha – October 2012)

October 15, 1918. Vijayadasami Day. The abode for Sriman Narayana, Sri Vaikunta, shone with an extraordinary vibrant festive look. The inhabitants, Hari Bhaktas, nityasuris, were in a very jubilant mood; they were eagerly waiting to receive an emissary of the Lord, expected to return to Vaikunta from the Earth, Bhooloka. Yes, the one who appeared in the Earth as Sai Baba was coming back to Sri Vaikunta after eight decades. As he was crossing the border of Bhooloka, *silongan*, Sri Rama Himself came and took him to Vaikunta.

Just as when Sanaka, Sanandana, Prahlada, Dhruva, Vibhishana, Narada, Thumburu and Maruthi the son of Anjani and Vayu, Sabari, Sugreeva, King Shriyal, Nandagopa and his wife Yasoda, Bhima and Arjuna, Dharmaraja and Ajatasatru, and Madhva, Machindaranath, Goraknath, Gnaneswara, Nivritee- Sopana-Mukta Bai. Chant Dev, Namdev, Gorakumbhar, Damaji Panth, Tulsidas, Rohidas, Eknath. Savath Mali, Bodhala and Samarta Ramadas of Sajjangad, Tukaram-Dehukar, Sajjan Kasayee, Choka Mahar, Narsidas Mehta, Nagar, Kamal and other great saints and sages were given sakshatkar by Sriman Narayana, so also was Sai Baba was received by the Lord.

Kamal came forward and asked Sai Baba, "Where did you go for such a long time leaving me? My dear father, because of you I was much troubled and worried". The other saints told him, "Kamal, do not grieve any longer; your father Kabir has come back to see you. Till now he was at Shirdi having gone to the Earth to lead humans on the path of virtue and goodness. Henceforward he will not leave you".

The meeting between Sai Baba and other saints in Vaikunta was full of rejoicings. They all welcome him shouting "Jaya Jaya!" Yakshas, Gandharvas and Apsaras were present who sang in sonorous tones.

Baba sat in a seat next to Sri Hari.

(Sri Das Ganu Maharaj says that this was a scene in Vaikunta when Baba attained Mahasamadhi, which he saw in a dream and has narrated in his Bhakti Saramrita).

From what has happened later and what is happening now, one can infer what would have transpired in Sri Vaikunta after return of Sai Baba.

The sages asked Baba: You have come back. Poor people, devotees who have been depending on you and looking to you for their welfare, are feeling forlorn and miserable. They feel they have suddenly become orphans.

Baba: I have left my *sthula sareera* (physical body) entombed in the beautiful wada built by my loving devotee Buty. From this Samadhi, my spirit will radiate light of love and succour. People who visit my Samadhi will get joy and peace.

"My *sookshma sarira* (astral body) is pervading the whole universe and earnest devotees will feel my presence everywhere and get their earnest prayers answered.

"By the remarkable work done by Das Ganu, thousands of people in Maharashtra and the neighbouring States have come to know about me and are approaching me to get their problems solved. Through Upasani who has established an ashram at Sakori, many people are attracted to me.

"Fifteen years from now my chosen apostle will come to Shirdi in the course of his spiritual quest. He will get atmanubhava (self-realization) in my Samadhi Mandir. Mandated by me, he will take up Sai prachara very vigorously and convert millions and millions of people to look to me, worship me and reap enormous benefits both material and spiritual."

Just as Baba predicted Sri Narasimhaswamiji who did arduous tapasya at the feet of Sri Ramana Maharshi at Tiruvannamalai, pushed by the

Maharshi travelled North and finally reached the end of his quest at Shirdi Sai Mandir. He saw Rama, Krishna, Siva, Maruthi – all the forms of Lord in Sri Sai Baba. He realized that Baba was a wonderful Samartha Sadguru. For two decades he relentlessly carried on the mission of spreading the life and message of Sri Sai Baba throughout our country. The seeds which were sown by him then have sprouted and grown gradually into gigantic trees, in the form of Sai Mandirs, temples and other institutions in the name of Sai throughout the world.

Let us all offer our humble prayers to Sai Samartha and Sadguru Narasimhaswamiji on the eve of Baba's Mahasamadhi and Swamiji's Punyathithi.

BABA'S TEACHINGS - I
Peculiar method of Teaching

(February 2011 edition of Sai Sudha)

When someone is very intimate to a great saint like Sri Sai Baba, the intimacy generally results in that person totally becoming oblivious about the divine nature of the saint; if that person is asked by the Guru to fulfil his needs, he may become egoistic to think that he is the main provider for the Guru. About such a person Sri Narasimhaswamiji says that 'he is too close to the tree to see the forest'. Nana Chandorkar was a very intimate devotee of Baba, being the only privileged person to be drawn to Baba by Baba himself on account of rinanu–bandha. He was so close to Baba that when all others remained standing at the time of arati only Nana sat by Baba's side. Baba was imparting valuable lessons to Nana, and through him to all Sai devotees in general, on various aspects of leading a dharmic way of life, in keeping the six internal enemies like Kama, Krodha, etc. under control, in reining in ahambhava (ego) etc. We all know that Baba gave a blow to Chandorkar's pride of learning, his Sanskrit knowledge, by asking him to expound the meaning of a Bhagavad Gita sloka. Once Baba sent his young favourite devotee to Nana Chandorkar to get some money from him for paying dakshina. Rege went to Chandorkar who was seated in Khandoba Temple with Upasani Baba. Rege was sent to him because he had exhausted all the funds he had brought by being called upon Baba repeatedly to give Dakshina. The very worldly-wise Chandorkar told Rege how cleverly he managed to wriggle out of such situations. He would bring a lump sum, leave half of it at Kopergaon, and with the remaining half proceed to Shirdi, go on giving Dakshina to Baba whenever he was called upon, and at the opportune moment sent for the reserve left at Kopergaon. 'You must also act like that' he advised Rege. Rege reported this to Baba. Baba sent for Nana Chandorkar and asked for Rs.40, again for Rs.40 and again for the balance of Rs.20 he had. Before Nana could send for replenishment from Kopergaon, Baba asked him for further Dakshina. Thus Nana was taught a lesson that it was presumptuous to suppose that he was the great providence supplying the needs of Baba, which was the impression he had.

Earlier, Rege was sent to Hari Sitaram Dixit, and from this most worthy devotee of Baba Rege learnt a valuable lesson. Rege was taught different lessons first from Shama, then Dixit and finally through Chandorkar. Dixit was humility personified; he told Rege that Baba's direction must be understood as a lesson. Rege should not feel being poor or begging for money or asking for anything else to be a humiliation.

Many of us have some special attachment to certain things in the world and when we come upon such a thing instinctively we get a longing to have that. Baba wanted to see that his devotees were not subject to raga–dwesha. An incident where Rege was taught a valuable lesson by Baba is narrated by Sri Swamiji in Life of Sai Baba (Part III, Chapter V) which is reproduced below.

As Rege sat near Baba at the Mosque once, bunches of red plantains were brought by someone. Rege was fond of them, and he thought that he was going to have a good time of it, because Baba would have so much of it to give him. Baba of course knew what passed in his heart. So, when the fruits came, Baba took up one fruit, peeled it off, and gave the pulp to others, and the skin was thrown to Rege with the word 'khav' for him to eat (for it was the red skin that attracted him). The same thing was done a second time and a third time. All the three skins were quietly swallowed up by Rege on account of his powerful bhakti to his Guru. At last, Baba took up one plantain and turning to him said, 'Have I given you nothing'. Then, after peeling off the skin of one plantain, he bit off a portion and said it was nice. He presented it to the mouth of Rege for him to bite off. Rege bit off a portion and Baba bit off the next portion, so that between the two, that fruit was finished. So Baba gave Rege a very well remembered and impressive lesson on greed in the matter of eating. The skin of red

plantains would be very bitter; Rege was made to eat them first and then the Master's love fed Rege with the sweet portion.

Rege says that Baba had different methods of communication. He gives three main methods he was aware of. The first is in the active waking state. When the sishya is in difficulties or Baba wants his sishya to take a particular course, the sishya gets an inspiration as to what course should be adopted and the feeling that that is Baba's inspiration. That is quite enough; and is verified by the events in his own case. When he was at the Ayi's house, he would feel that Baba called him, and would go up to the Mosque and find that Baba was actually waiting for him there. So, the inspiration really came from Baba. Baba would give him some songs to sing or some tunes, because both Baba and Rege knew music. The second relates to the sleeping or trance state. Baba would appear in dreams or trances. This would be called Sakshatkara and is considered most impressive and unmistakable. Of course Rege had Baba's Sakshatkaras. In the third method Baba directed the sishya to go to some other person, who did not even know why the sishya was sent, but who nevertheless benefited the sishya in accordance with Baba's internal and unperceived guidance. Sometimes the person to whom Baba sends a devotee is totally unfit to give any reply, for instance the rustic girl, to whom Das Ganu was sent for interpreting *Isavasya Upanishad*.

BABA'S TEACHINGS - II

(Sai Sudha – December 2010)

Most of the people who came to Shirdi to see Sai Baba did so to get some material benefit or other. There were a few whose minds were disturbed and needed relief. They had to be imparted some valuable teaching that would offer them solace and mental calm. The channel through which Baba accomplished this is unique and remarkable.

Some devotees were directed to go to Shama (Madhava Rao Deshpande) and have a chat with him. Shama was a teacher in the primary school. He was a rustic and was a person not credited with any appreciable knowledge on religious or spiritual matters. His close proximity to Baba and acting as an aide earned him respect from all Sai devotees. Otherwise he was in no way qualified to offer any sort of advice to others. However it is Baba's sweet will to make him an instrument for conveying his message to the devotees in need.

Let us first take Anna Saheb Dabholkar who had the privilege of being called by Baba Himself as the famous Hemad Pant. On the occasion even this great devotee, the author of Sri Sai Satcharitra, felt that he was not considered fit enough to get Baba's grace in full measure. One gentleman by name Sathe incurred heavy losses in business and was disheartened. He came to Shirdi, had Baba's darshan and did Parayana of Guru Charitra in seven days with a heart full of devotion. Sathe then got a dream vision in which Baba appeared holding in his hand the Guru Charitra book and explaining its meaning and significance to him. When Baba was asked through Kaka Saheb Dixit what Baba wanted to convey to Sathe through this vision, Baba said "Let this book be read repeatedly. Then one will get God's blessings and get released from worldly shackles." Anna Saheb Dabholkar who was present at that time had a passing thought. "Here is a man who gets Baba's favour in just seven days! I am here for the last seven years and was not fortunate to receive Baba's grace." The all-knowing Sai directed Dabholkar to go immediately to Shama, get from him on his behalf a dakshina of Rs.15 and also chat with him for some time. It was on that occasion Shama narrated to Dabholkar the incident concerning the lady devotee Radhabai Deshmukin who ventured on satyagraha to get upadesa from Baba somehow and Baba, at the intervention of Shama, narrated to this lady how he received his Guru's grace. Baba emphasized the need for absolute surrender to the Guru with nishta and saburi. This most important lesson of Baba was conveyed by Shama to Dabholkar and through him to the whole of mankind.

In one of his visits to Shirdi, Ramachandra Atmaram Tarkhad was accosted by a Sadhu in Sathe Wada and was asked why educated people like him should come frequently to Shirdi because of which many ordinary people also were flocking there for no good reason. Later, another Sadhu came and enquired Tarkhad about the meaning of the epithet 'Stithaprajna' (a man of serene wisdom). Tarkhad's mind got disturbed and he decided to return to Bombay after having Baba's darshan. Sensing his mood, Baba asked Shama to take him along and tell him something. Shama took him for a walk and told him, "This is Baba's leela. There is a lesson in everything. That is, even in the midst of trials and tribulations, pressure of work, ups and downs of family life, one should not lose one's balance and direct the mind toward God". Tarkhad took the advice, followed it religiously and never again lost his mental poise.

Similarly, one Prarthana Samajist devotee during his visit to Shirdi chanced to meet someone who raised a doubt whether Sai was really a 'Stithaprajna' and whether there would be any good in going to him; this upset his faith. When he went to Baba with this irritant in his mind, Baba asked Shama to take that devotee aside and tell him something. Shama took him aside and told him, "Outsider's talk and your faith being affected by it is all Baba's leela. Do not mind what others say and its consequent troubles. Keep your mind at Baba's feet and Baba will give you peace." Later when the devotee went to Baba, Baba advised him to follow Shama's advice.

Once Baba repeatedly asked for Dakshina from Rege and even after Rege parted with the entire money he had, Baba asked him for more. When Rege pleaded that he had no more money left, Baba advised him to borrow it from others and give. The first person to whom Baba sent him was Shama. Shama who had no money told Rege, "You have not understood Baba. He cares a rap for your rupees. What he wants is your mind and heart, your time and soul to be devoted to him."

When Das Ganu Maharaj sought Baba's help in understanding the true meaning of *Isavasyopanishad* for writing a commentary in Marathi, Baba said Das Ganu would learn it from the servant maid at Dixit's house in Vile Parle. Das Ganu Maharaj did get the message of the Upanishad from the way the girl conducted herself while discharging her duties as a maid.

Baba sent Rege to a wada where some pandits were engaged in a heated discussion about the correct *patanthara* (passage) in Jnaneshwari; there he learnt that too much bookish knowledge leads one to *Bhrama* (confusion) only and not to God.

A devotee by name Shamrao Shrotrie went to Sai Baba and in Baba's presence, his mind sought an answer to a particular question. Baba told him to go to a lady called Bua reading some purana in the temple. Shrotrie went there and listened to what the elderly lady was reading. In what she read Shrotrie found the answer to the question that cropped up in his mind.

One devotee Madhava Bua was interested in learning about the nature of saints called 'Hamsas' and 'Paramahamsas' and with this thought he went to Baba. Baba directed him to go to Dixit wada where Dixit was reading a Pothi. When Madhava Bua went there, he found Kaka Saheb Dixit reading the chapter in Eknath Bhagavat, Ekadasa Skanda of Srimad Bhagavatha, in which description about 'Hamsas' and 'Paramahamsas' has been given.

Even after Baba's Mahasamadhi when an earnest devotee prays to Baba for some guidance in spiritual Sadhana, Baba sees to it that the devotee gets help in some peculiar way.

BABA'S TEACHINGS - III

(Sai Sudha – July 2011)

The Lord, in His avatar as Sri Krishna, took the position of a World Teacher, (*Krishnam Vande Jagadgurum*) and bequeathed to humanity through Arjuna Srimad Bhagavad-Gita, the quintessence of all moral and spiritual teachings contained in the Vedas and the Upanishads. Again, in Srimad Bhagavata, we get the Lord's discourse to His devotee Uddhava in Skanda XI, which is called Uddhava Gita, which expounds succinctly what is dharma and how to lead a dharmic way of life. The Lord has also given us through Bhishma the soul – uplifting Vishnu Sahasranama, the regular chanting of which is prescribed for obtaining all spiritual and material benefits by all classes of people. The great Acharya Sri Sankara says *geyam gita namasahasram, dhyeyam sripati roopam ajasram* – one should recite the Gita and Vishnu Sahasranamam, always meditating on the wonderful form of Lord Vishnu (Sripathi).

Sri Sai Baba, who identified himself with Sri Krishna, who named his residence, the mosque, *Dwarakamayi*, exhorted many of his devotees to do parayana of Vishnu Sahasranama and Bhagavad Gita. A person reciting Sahasranama is expected to be free from ahankara, ego and other tendencies that take one away from God. Baba in his own characteristic way decided to teach two valuable lessons, (1) the efficacy of Vishnu Sahasranama parayana and (2) the need to give up ego, pride of learning, etc. The lessons were imparted to Shama and Ramdasi Bua (through them to all of us) as narrated in detail in Chapter 27 of Sri Sai Satcharithra. Shama was an ardent devotee of Baba, but he did nothing to progress spiritually. Baba wanted to initiate him on some spiritual practice. One Ramadasi Bua was regularly reading Vishnu Sahasranama and Adhyatma Ramayana, and he knew Sahasranama by heart. He always carried these two books with him, as valuable possessions. His mind was gripped by a sense of pride in chanting Sahasranama and doing parayana of Ramayana and by a sense of possession. Baba thought it fit to teach a lesson to the Ramdasi.

One day Baba called the Ramdasi Bua, told him that he had a splitting stomach pain and bade him to go and get some herbal medicine. As soon as the Ramdasi left the mosque, Baba took the books left by him, picked up the Vishnu Sahasranama book and offered it to Shama, elaborately telling him the efficacy of Sahasranama Parayana. Knowing the temperament of Ramdasi well and not being much keen in doing Sahasranama Parayana, Shama declined the offer. But Baba forced it on him. He said: "Once I suffered intensely. My heart began to palpitate and I was restless. I hugged the Sahasranama book to my heart and instantly felt relief. It seemed Allah (Hari) Himself had descended from the book into my heart and my life was saved." Baba further declared, "My Shama may be mad, but I am fond of him. He has a special affection for me. I am very much concerned about his welfare and I shall tie the necklace of Vishnu Sahasranama around his neck with my hands and free him from the miseries of the worldly existence by infusing in him a fondness for reciting it." Baba then expounded in detail the greatness and unique value of Bhagavan Nama and thrust the book in Shama's hands.

When the Ramdasi Bua returned, finding that one of his valuable possessions, Vishnu Sahasranama book, in the hands of Shama, flared up and showered a volley of abuses on him for taking away his book by playing a trick of having him sent out by Baba on some pretext. Baba now intervened and imparted a valuable lesson to the Ramdasi.

"Why are you always ready to fight? Can you not speak soft and sweet words? Though you read these books regularly, your mind is still impure. Every day you read the Adhyatma Ramayana and recite the Sahasranama. Yet you have not discarded your passions which remain uncontrolled. And you call yourself a Ramdasi! What kind of Ramdasi are you? You should be absolutely detached, but you are not able to overcome your intense desire to possess the book. What a behaviour! A true Ramdasi should have no attachment and look at the young and old with equality. You are harbouring enmity for this lad and coming to blows for this book! Go and sit in your place. Books can be had in plenty for money but not men, till the end of time. Remember this well." About this incident Sri Anna Saheb Dabholkar writes:

"That book which was the cause of such a big quarrel was also the reliever of Baba's pain. It is also now the cause of my well–being. Invaluable is Sai's gift! If this great effort had not been made, Madhavarao would not have faith in it. Truly, he would not have been able to recite it. This Sainath, how loving he was! A rare teacher of spirituality with pranks! No one can understand how and when he would practise this art. His ways are incomprehensible. Later on, Shama's faith was developed. Dixit and Narke taught him to pronounce the words correctly by repeating and conning them over and over again to know their meanings. He learnt it by heart."

Dabholkar had his own notion about the necessity or usefulness of a Guru. Dixit's young daughter Vatsali died even in the proximity of a Samartha like Sai Baba. "If a Guru cannot save the child of his own intimate devotee, what good of having such a Guru?" One day Dabholkar had a heated argument on the subject with Bhate during his first visit to Shirdi. Dabholkar was vehemently of the view that a Guru was unnecessary and that it was a question of free will of everyone to follow his own course. But Bhate totally differed; he said that there was no such thing as free will and that the only thing was destiny; he further held the view that a Guru is absolutely essential. No conclusion was arrived at and with a disturbed mind Dabholkar went to the mosque and prostrated before Baba. Dabholkar's view on Guru was more or less similar to the view of one of the three fellow sadhakas of Baba when they embarked on their spiritual quest. The all–knowing Baba pointing his finger at Dabholkar asked, 'What talk was going on in the Wada? And what did this Hemad Pant say?' Hemad Pant was a great scholar, well read and informed; by calling Dabholkar as 'Hemad Pant'. Baba made Dabholkar realise that he was before a great Sadguru who gave a blow to his pride of learning and dialectical skill. This influenced his mind to accept Baba as his chosen Guru and ultimately Baba choosing him as the fit person to write about his leelas, which resulted in Sai devotees having got the wonderful Sai Satcharithra.

Eka swadu na bhunjita, one should not eat without sharing with others, is a rule which Baba wanted his devotees to follow. Sai devotees, before eating any sweet dish, must offer it to Sri Sai mentally from their heart. Baba's charter is, "*If one ever dwells on me in his mind and will not even taste food before offering it to me, I am his slave.*" Baba wanted to impress on his devotees the significance of this role and chose Dabholkar as the instrument. This has been narrated in Part IV of Life of Sai Baba which reads as follows:

"On one occasion when Anna Dabholkar came to Baba, there was in the fold of his coat some channa, that is, fried grain, and it fell from his coat; and people were joking at him. That was the day of the fair at Shirdi, and Dabholkar had perhaps been to the fair. Baba, wanting to have a joke at him, said, 'Oh! This channa shows that he is in the habit of eating things all by himself without sharing it with others.' Dabholkar was much upset and he protested that he had no such habit. But how the channa got into his dress, he could not explain. Then Baba made further use of the occasion, and told him, 'When you eat, do you give things to me? Am I not always by your side?' thus impressing on him a very valuable lesson that Baba was present everywhere and that devotees should first offer their food to him as their Gurudeva, before taking it. This is a sacred lesson, and this teaching is divine. But it comes out of Baba's humour, and fun poked at Anna Saheb Dabholkar."

BABA'S TEACHINGS - IV

(Sai Sudha – November 2011)

Jaya mani jaisa bhava; Taya taisa anubhava Davisi dayaghana; Aisi tujee hi mava

(Baba's Arati Song)

You grant experiences to everyone in a way best suited to the individual's faith and devotion; that is your special way, O Merciful One!

Each one that approaches Sai gets His grace in a degree and manner the particular devotee deserves or is capable of receiving. Baba's teachings also would vary from individual to individual. Baba's guidance would be on a path that would be best suited to the individual concerned, it may be bhakti marga, jnana marga or karma marga depending upon the particular individual's capability and receptivity.

Anantrao Patankar was a well–read person conversant with various facets of Sastras. Yet peace of mind evaded him; he was in a distressed mood. He approached Baba, having heard that Baba would put him on the right track. Baba spoke to him in a quizzical manner.

"Once a merchant came here; in his presence a quadruped passed its stomata, in the form of nine balls of stools. The merchant, anxious to succeed in his quest, spread his cloth beneath its tail, gathered all the nine balls and took them away. He then got concentration and peace of mind."

Whenever Baba thus speaks in riddles, there would always be someone who could understand Baba's message and explain same to the person concerned. In this instance it was Dada Kelkar who was chosen by Baba to clarify to Patankar, He said:

"God's grace is the quadruped. The nine balls excreted are the nine forms of bhakti. You are to be in the position of the merchant. If you acquire navavidha bhakti (nine forms of devotion), you will attain peace".

When Anantrao went to Baba with this clarification, Baba asked him whether he had gathered the nine balls. The devotee answered that to do so he should have Baba's grace. Baba blessed him.

When some devotee asked Bhagavan Ramana whether he had Bhagavan's grace, Bhagavan answered him that it was only because he had the grace he was then in Bhagavan's presence. Thus, not only Patankar, but each one of the devotees who comes to Baba for some reason or other has definitely Baba's grace, that is why he has developed devotion to Baba.

To a large majority of devotees Baba prescribed only bhakti marga. The navavidha bhakti was a concept expounded by the greatest of Hari bhaktas Prahlada to his father. Navavidha bhakti is thus defined:

Sravanam keerthanam Vishno: Smaranam padasevanam!
Archanam vandanam dasyam Sakhyam atmanivedanam!!

The nine steps of bhakti are (1) listening, (2) reciting, (3) remembrance and meditation (4) prostration at the feet of God, (5) worship, (6) paying obeisance, (7) serving, (8) friendship and (9) surrendering the Self.

According to Sri Narasimhaswamiji these modes of bhakti are not only to God but to the Guru, saints and sages and Mahatmas. The ultimate is Self-realisation.

Baba not merely preached; he had been a role model to his bhaktas. This can be seen from the narration he gave about his devotion and total surrender and blemishless love towards his Guru. Baba repeatedly emphasized the need to have *nishta* (total faith) and *saburi* (patient perseverance). This may be called *prapatti marga*.

Baba stressed on the need to have full-fledged devotion in and absolute faith towards one's Guru for spiritual advancement. He told a devotee, "Stick to your own Guru with unabated faith, howsoever great the merits of other Gurus may be; one must not give up loyalty to one's own Guru but must be firm in faith towards him and him alone".

To a lady who approached Baba requesting him to be her Guru and give her upadesa, Baba's advice was:- "It is not the Guru that makes himself your Guru. It is you who must regard him as Guru. Take a potsherd and regard it as your Guru and see if your goal or aim is reached or not".

BABA'S TEACHINGS - V

(Sai Sudha – January 2012)

Sri Sai once told Chandrabai Borkar, 'we should not harbour envy, rivalry, or combative disposition towards others. If others hate us, simply take to Nama Japa and avoid the company'.

Baba's advice: 'As God places us let us remain. Take what comes. Be contented and cheerful. Never worry. Not a leaf moves but by His consent and will. We should be honest, upright and virtuous. We must distinguish right from wrong. We must each attend to one's own duty. But we must not be obsessed by egotism and fancy that we are independent causes of action. God is that Actor. We must recognize His independence and our dependence on Him, and see all acts as His. If we do so, we shall be unattached and free from Karmic bondage'. Sri Narasimhaswamiji writes that this is the most important doctrine, the doctrine of submission and surrender. This is the essence of Srimad Bhagavad Gita.

Young and old, men and women, rich and poor, whoever that came to Baba was exhorted by him to lead a moral life, a noble life, a life exuding love, sympathy and kindness to all. People who were straying from the path of dharma were being warned by Baba. How much did Baba succeed? Sri Narasimha swamiji writes. "Baba was dealing with large numbers of devotees. It was not possible to make the entire lot moral and properly behaved, in spite of all the efforts of Baba to correct them. Baba once said, 'I have been considering long and thinking day and night. All are thieves. But we have to deal with them. I prayed to God day and night for their improvement. God delays and does not approve my attitude and grant the prayer. I will wait for a month or two and then see. But living or dead, I will have what I have been praying for. I will not go to Teli or Vani nor beg of them. People are not good and devoted. They are unsettled in mind. A few friends will gather and talk divine wisdom, and sit and contemplate'. Again in 1918, he said, 'People have got bad and give trouble. They are pestering me for money. Moreover, they become shameless. Now I am disgusted'. He was so distressed that he expressed a desire to leave Shirdi forever".

Baba's advice to ascetics like Devadas:

1. Adhere to *vairagya*; 2. Women are great danger to ascetics; 3. Avoid the *upadhis* – *moha* (delusion) and pomp; and 4. Think of God and annihilate the ego.

Devotees of Baba should remember Baba's other important instructions while living in the world.

1. Never accept gratis the labour of others. (Baba himself paid Rs. 2/- to a man who brought him a ladder to get down from the top of a house).

2. None who has firm faith in God is left in want for anything.

3. Do not be idle. Work, utter God's name, read scriptures.

4. Have as friends those who will stick to you till the end through thick and thin.

5. Eat very little. Do not go in for a variety of dishes. A single sort will suffice. Do not sleep much. Have dhyan on what is read. Think of Allah (God)

6. You should not stop even one second at a place where anybody talks ill of a saint.

7. If anyone begs for something, if that be in your hands, give; do not say 'no'. If you have nothing to give, give suave negative reply. Do not mock at or ridicule the person and do not get angry. If you do not like to part with what you have, do not utter falsehood saying that you have nothing. Decline to give it in polite terms.

8. What you sow, you reap. What you give, you get.

9. When you undertake to do something, carry it out thoroughly; or do not undertake it.

10. This world is funny. All are my subjects. I look upon all with equal eye. But some were thieves. What can I do for them? People at death's door plot against the lives of others. These offend and hurt me much. But I am quiet, saying nothing. God is great. He has his officers everywhere who are allpowerful. One must rest content with one's lot.

11. Do not borrow for celebrating a feast or festival, or for a pilgrimage or other journey.

12. Always take your meal before you start on a journey.

BABA'S TEACHINGS - VI

(Sai Sudha – February 2012)

Did Baba follow or preach Advaita? This is a very ticklish question. When one goes through the enormous literature generated on the life and teachings of Sri Sai, one can see that Baba was on Advaitic plane at times and now and then he prescribed the Advaitic path to some select devotees. The vast majority of the people who approached Baba considered that he was a Godman, a God-incarnate, Dattaavatara or a *Chalthe-bolthe* deva (moving and talking God), a Pratyaksha-daiva who was both capable and ready to alleviate all their woes. As hailed in Sai Ashtotra he is both *Bhaktavana-samartha* and *bhaktavana-pradijna* – capable of protecting devotees and also one who solemnly vowed that he would protect his devotees. Responding to this mental attitude of the large number of devotees, whose plank was devotion to the Guru-God, Baba confirmed them in their implicit faith. In an effort to put them on the spiritual path, he advised his devotees to take to nama-japa, reading of pothis, recital of Vishnu Sahasranama, doing Bhagavata saptaha parayana, etc. This was perhaps Baba's way of preparing the field with proper manure before sowing the seed of spiritual education. The highest form of bhakti goes with absolute, unconditional, bargainless surrender - *prapatti*. Baba's advice to devotees in general is to surrender to the Guru-God totally, have firm faith in him and serve him with Saburi (patient perseverance); he said no other Sadhana was necessary. This gave many an impression that Baba was a protagonist of bhakti marga.

While on the subject, let us look into the life of the foremost apostle of Sri Sai Baba, Sri B.V. Narasimha Swami. Sri Narasimha Iyer of Salem decided to leave home and grihastasrama and take to spiritual Sadhana. He proceeded to seek the direction of his family Acharya and other Gurus and elders. Being advised to resort to the Sage of Arunachala, Sri Ramana Maharishi, he spent three years at Tiruvannamalai, leading a life of cloistral seclusion concentrating all his efforts on the study of Vedanta works and the adoption of the necessary consequential steps. Narasimhaswamiji learnt all the intricacies of Vedanta at the feet of the Sage and he produced the monumental work "Self Realization" depicting the life and teachings of Bhagavan Ramana. This was the first ever detailed biography (in English) of Sri Ramana and was instrumental to draw spiritual aspirants form all over the world to the feet of Sri Ramana. Unless Sri Narasimhaswamiji was thorough with the Advaita Vedanta propounded by Sri Ramana, it would not have been possible for him to write a biography presenting the Divine personality and his essential universal teaching to yearning spiritual sadhakas. He got a powerful push from Bhagavan Ramana and an equally powerful pull from another Great Master who lived in Shirdi. Swamiji writes, "At the close of three years he discovered that he had lost the bhakti in which he had made good progress before leaving Salem and approaching Ramanashram. Hence in 1930-31, he resumed his efforts at re-adoption of the Bhakti Marga and in quest thereof was going to temples, shrines and holy places such as Pandharpur, Nasik, etc." Ultimately, Sri Sai Baba, in the apantaratma form, took Swamiji into his fold, enabled him to attain his spiritual goal and entrusted to him the onerous task of spreading his life, mission and message to humanity at large. This happened when Swamiji was seated in meditation in the Samadhi Mandir at Shirdi, where the mortal frame is enshrined radiating rays of love and life.

Swamiji, an adherent of Bhakti Marga, graduated in Advaita after a three-year course at the feet of Bhagavan Ramana. Sri Ramana himself, it is reported, once remarked that it took several years for a student to learn about Vedanta but for Narasimha Swami, a person of sharpened intellect, it took just a week to learn the intricacies of Advaita Vedanta. Thus Swamiji was fully equipped to discuss and elucidate on what paths Sri Sai followed and what he preached. Based on the material he collected from several devotees who had direct personal contact with the Master while he was in the flesh at Shirdi, Swamiji has given an analytical commentary on the path taught by Sri Sai.

Sri Ramana says: "Jnana Marga and Bhakti Marga (prapatti) are one and the same. Self-surrender leads to realization just as enquiry does. Complete Self-surrender means that you have no further thought of 'I'. He, also says, "Bhakti is the mother of Jnana". Baba laid great stress on self-surrender – prapatti, to get over thoughts of 'I' and 'mine'. On occasions Baba spoke of Vichara Marga, path of enquiry, as Ramana did – "Who am I? Who are we? Night and day think on this". To a Bombay lady who prayed to Baba to free her from the whirl of births and deaths, Baba prescribed the path of enquiry, "Who am I?" Baba enabled the lady to learn this through a dialogue with her husband (Charters and Sayings, Para 121).

When the thought of 'I' and 'mine' is got rid of there is no difference between one and the other. Baba wants his devotees to bury all differences by realizing one's true nature. He told Purandhare, "People differentiate between themselves and others, their properties and others' properties. This is wrong, I am in you and you are in me". He also said, "This is the Teli's wall that parts you from me; pull down this wall, and then we see each other clearly face to face".

"Saints do not recognize this differentiation. To serve me, remove this differentiation. Continue to think in this way and then you will realize it… Search the scriptures, see if Atma is one or many".

In explaining to Chandorkar the real import of Sri Krishna's instruction to Arjuna in the Gita (Chapter IV, Verse 34), Sri Sai says, "The root cause of ajnana – ignorance is the thought 'God is one. The devotee is another'. Remove it. Jnana remains. Ignorance finds a snake in the rope. Remove the ignorance; then the rope is known as it is".

Again by the incident where Nana Chandorkar was asked to prepare for him Puran Polis, Baba revealed that he was not the physical body seen in Shirdi but the universal Spirit dwelling in all forms, ants, flies. He was sarvantaryami. Baba admonished Mrs. Khaparde for throwing a burning faggot on a dog and told her that it was he who took that form. Baba was pleased with Mrs. Tarkhad when she gave bread to a dog and a pig and said that being the antaryami of these creatures also, he was fully satisfied.

When the boys from Bombay tried to take a photo of Sri Sai, he told Shama, “Tell the boys that no photo should be taken, (If they want a real likeness of mine), the wall (of difference) is to be pulled down”. According to Baba, if the wall (body) is pulled down, you get at the real likeness, i.e. Brahman.

In his efforts to mould Upasani Baba into a Samartha, Baba adopted various means to remove the ‘I-am the-body’ notion from Upasani’s mind. Sri Ramana said that silence is the most eloquent form of Upadesa. Likewise, Baba instructed Upasani to stay aloof in Khandoba’s temple doing nothing, just to keep quiet. By appearing at Khandoba temple in the form of a lowly sudra and a dog, he taught Upasani how to see his Guru-God in all forms. By giving visions of Papa purusha and punya purusha, Upasani was made to raise a question as to what his real self was. Baba gave the explanation, “You are neither the one nor the other. That which constitutes me, constitutes you”.

Sri Narasimhaswamiji writes: “According to true Advaita of Sankara, the jiva talked of as ‘I’ by Kasinath Upasani was in essence the same as Parabrahman, the one underlying Reality which ought to be seen in all manifest things and which people call Brahman or God. Many years later Upasani Baba understood how the jiva also merges in the Purna Parabrahman, and how real moksha or liberation consists in the jiva losing its separate identity and imaginary independence and sinking itself into the one absolute, undifferentiated Real”. Sri Krishna tells Arjuna, “He who sees Me in all beings, and all beings in me - to him I am never lost, nor is he to Me. Established in the unity of all existence, a Yogin who serves Me present in all beings, verily abides in Me, whatever be his mode of life” (*Bhagavad Gita, Chapter VI, verses 30 & 31*). Baba was teaching this all-important lesson to several devotees in various ways.

Baba once proclaimed, “This body is but my house. My Guru Mourshad has long ago taken me away from this”. Thus he promised Rege “I shall be with you, inside you and outside you, whatever you may be or do”. Rege sums up Baba’s real nature and valuable message in these words:

“To me he is not gone. He is even now. To me he had no limitations. Of course, when he was with us, there was the fleshy tabernacle. That was prominently brought to our notice at times. But mostly the infinite aspect of his was what remained before me. I thought of him as a mental or spiritual image in which the finite and infinite blended very perfectly – yet allowing the finite to appear before us at times. Now that the body has been cast off, the infinite alone remains as Sai Baba".

These are not words of exaggeration. The writer had the rare privilege of enjoying the company of Sri Rege, the pet child of Sri Sai, frequently for six years hearing from him directly about the greatness of his master; one could see that Baba was 'inside' and 'outside' this great devotee of his and feel the presence of the Master himself while in the company of this jewel of a devotee, who was the inspiring force behind Sri Narasimhaswamiji's Sai Prachar.

BABA'S TEACHINGS - VII

(Sai Sudha – August 2012)

In previous chapters some of the valuable teachings imparted by Sri Sai Baba to his devotees in his own unique and characteristic way were discussed. Let us now take perhaps the most important and most valuable lesson which Baba conveyed by practice, by parables and at times by enigmatic talks.

On several occasions Baba pointed out that everything in the world is evanescent and nothing is permanent. He wanted his devotees to eschew attachment to wealth, property and material things to which no one can claim eternal ownership.

We read that Das Ganu Maharaj wanted to write a commentary on Isavasya Upanishad and when he sought Baba's help to interpret the real purport he was advised that a maid in Dixit's bungalow would throw light. Baba's whole life was a practical illustration of the message this very valuable Upanishad conveyed. Baba's peculiar way of conveying this is seen here; Das Ganu and the maid servant were instruments. Sri Narasimhaswamiji writes: The first verse of the Upanishad says 'All this world is covered by the Maya of Iswara. So enjoy bliss, not by having the external but by rejecting the externals. *Tena tyaktena* means renouncing; it might also mean being content with what God gives'.

When the Marwadi who incurred loss when his hay stack was burnt due to catching of fire mourned, Baba said: "This Marwadi Bagchand whose stack caught fire begged for help to avoid loss. But how blindly do these people forget God? Gain and loss, birth and death, are in the hands of God. But how blindly do these people forget God? If profit comes they rejoice. If loss, they weep. Why? Why say 'This is mine?' The stack is not the Marwadi's. It grew from seeds on the earth and was fed by rains from the clouds and by sunlight. Earth, clouds and sun are the real owners. This fellow's claim is ungrounded. Fire is in all these three and it consumed the stack. We are not the owners. God gives with one hand and takes away with another'.

When Dixit got a cow, Baba said, 'This cow was formerly a Jalna man's, before that an Aurangabad man's and before that Mahlsapathy's. God knows whose property it is'. Sri Narasimhaswamiji says that Baba's statement was an exposition of the Isavasya Upanishad.

Sri Swamiji writes that both by example and precept Baba showed Dixit (to all devotees also) the absurdity of the worldly man's desire for much wealth and how little was necessary even to an ordinary sadhaka. Dixit imbibed this teaching totally. On the occasion when Dixit came to Shirdi, he came along with a trunkful of rupees (may be Rs 1000/-), which he earned in a Native State. He came to Baba, placed the trunk before him, showed him the rupees, and said, 'Baba, all this is yours'. Baba at once said, 'Is that so?' and plunged both his hands in the box, gathered the rupees therein and distributed same to people crowded around him like bees for honey. In a few minutes the trunk became empty. A Sub Judge friend of Dixit, one Mr. Garde, who was present then, narrated this incident; there was absolutely no reaction on the face of Dixit when the money earned by him was frittered away in quick time.

Mahlsapathy was another devotee who reached perfection in his vairagya. According to Sri Narasimhaswamiji, he strongly reminds us of the holy poverty of St. Francis of Assissi, the *akinchanya*, which is so highly praised in scriptures.

The rich man who wanted to realize Brahman was shown by Baba how difficult it is even to take up a sadhana for realizing Brahman with attachment to wealth in the mind remaining undiminished. Baba taught another devotee who wanted to be shown God that one should deserve before desiring. Unless one gives up attachment to worldly objects, seeing or realizing God cannot even be thought of.

Once Baba proclaimed: 'Poverty is highest riches and is a thousand times superior to a lord's position. God is the brother of the poor. Fakir is the real emperor. Fakirship does not perish, but empire is soon lost'.

Baba's collecting money as dakshina from devotees was also a device to impress upon them that money will not be with one person forever and it will always be changing hands and that one should not feel remorse in parting with money. It should be noted that Baba never kept with him the money that he collected by way of dakshina and was distributing same to several persons. Baba strictly followed the principle laid down in Srimad Bhagavata, Ekadasa Skanda (Chapter VIII, Verses 11 and 12) which stipulates: 'The Sage should not store what he obtains by begging for the evening or keep it for the next day. His vessels for receiving alms must be either the hand or the stomach. He should not hoard things like the bee. If he does, like the bee he will be killed.' Sri Narasimhaswamiji bemoans. 'If all sadhus had followed Baba's example, there would not be so much wreck in sadhus' lives that we notice'.

Sri Narasimhaswamiji clarifies: "Baba realizing himself as the Atman, had no fear of being tainted or tempted by touching money. See Srimad Bhagavata where in Bhikshu Gita it is stated "*Arthanjushan api hrishikapate na liptah, ye anye svatah parthritadapi bibhyatisma*" which means, "O Lord, of your senses you are unaffected by objects you enjoy, while others are afraid of them even in the absence of those objects".

Sri Sai's parables also reiterate his message on the need for detachment and renunciation bearing in mind that whatever one acquired is not permanent and will change hands sooner or later.

Parable 1: Once I was a little boy and I tried to earn my bread. I started in quest of employment. I went to Bid and got employed in weaving lace cloths. I was never wearied in my work. By my fakir's ways, there was no feeling of fatigue. Each day I turned out as much work as four boys together turned out. One boy produced Rs. 50/- worth cloth per diem, another Rs. 100/- and another Rs. 150/-. I produced Rs. 500/- worth. My employer was pleased. He loved me and praised me to others. He gave me nice dress, a pagota for my head and shawl for upper cloth. I did not use them, but gave them away to others. What Sircar (God) gives lasts forever, not what man gives.

Parable 2: My rich father had much buried wealth. I sat on one and became a big cobra. After a time, I left the treasure and regained human form. (Baba points out the result of clinging to wealth and the effect of renouncing it).

Parable 3: I had brought numerous asses laden with gold. Robbers looted all that on the road. So it is very hard to live in the house (or proximity) of thieves. You (Bhav Saheb Pradhan, Sub-Registrar) have been sent to me so that I may teach you this. It is very difficult to remain in this sapless world. That is what I was taught. Convey this much to my brother Madhav Nath (Maharaj).

SADHANA PRESCRIBED BY BABA

(Sai Sudha – September 2010)

Guru's grace is our only Sadhana. Jnana comes (in its wake) as experience.

Making the Guru the sole object of one's thoughts and aims, one attains Paramartha, the Supreme Goal. This is the only truth the Guru taught me. The four sadhanas and six sastras are not necessary. *Trusting in the Guru fully is enough.*

Thus spake Sri Sai. In Baba's school, there is only one course – surrender to the Guru. Like Kabir, he asserts, 'without a Guru, where is a way?'

Asked by Kaka Saheb Dixit what was the way to go up in spiritual sadhanas, Baba says, "There are plenty of ways proceeding from each place. For you (for Sai devotees), here is this way, leading hence. But the way is rugged. There are tigers and bears on the route. If one has a guide with him, then there is no difficulty. Then, the tigers and bears move aside. If there is no guide, there is a deep yawning pit on the way and there is a danger of falling into it'. The 'Guide' referred to by Baba is the Guru.

Baba says that he reached the pinnacle of spiritual Sadhana, the stature of Maha Yogi, a Samartha Sadguru, simply by serving his Guru for twelve years with burning love, total dedication and absolute surrender; just by the gracious look of his Guru, with no spoken words or any other mode of Upadesa. The Guru transformed him unto his likeness. All the powers the Guru had, the disciple got in full measure.

What should be the attitude of the disciple in serving the Guru? What is the proper approach? In elucidating the actual meaning of Sloka 34, Chapter 4 of Srimad Bhagavad Gita to Nana Saheb Chandorkar, Baba spells out the proper approach. Sri Krishna, in this Sloka, exhorts Arjuna to approach the 'Seers', serve them, enquire again and again, when the Seers would impart 'Jnana'. What Sri Krishna meant could not have been elucidated in any manner better than what Baba did.

"This sloka refers to how a sishya should approach his Guru to obtain realization of the Real. The disciple must approach the Guru, completely surrendering the body, mind, soul and possessions to the Guru. The Pranipata or Prostration must be one accompanied by that attitude. As for Pariprasna, the request for knowledge must be repeated and must not be mere idle questions or merely out of curiosity or with any improper motive, or attitude, e.g. to trap the Guru into a mistake and catch him. The object must be pure desire to attain progress and liberation and the questions must be humbly repeated till full light is gained. As for Seva, mere service, e.g. massage etc. is not enough. To be effective, there must be no lingering idea that one is free to yield the service or refuse it. One must feel that one is not the master of the body – which has become the Guru's and exists merely to render him service."

"Jnana is to be realized and is not a matter of direct upadesa. Salutation, questioning and service are sadhanas for obtaining the Guru's grace".

The qualifications of Guru and sishya are elaborately dealt with by Sri Narasimha Swamiji in his wonderful book "The Life of Sai Baba – Part I".

Baba once told a lady devotee who came with a prayer that Baba should be her Guru: "It is not the Guru that makes himself your Guru. It is you who must regard him as Guru, i.e. place faith in him.

Take a potsherd and regard it as your Guru and see if your goal or aim is achieved or not".

Baba lays great stress on the Bhava, attitude of the sadhaka. Baba exhorts his devotees to "stick to your own Guru with unabated faith, however great the merits of other Gurus are and however little the merits of your own". The result depends very much on the attitude of the disciple.

Unfortunately, among the thousands that approached Baba, there was hardly one that came with a thirst to receive in full measure the nectar that Baba was holding. Baba himself had to express once, 'Is there anyone who is prepared to serve his Guru as I did?'

Balakram Manker was one devotee who, according to Sri Swamiji, was one who was able to dissociate himself from family, to give up highly lucrative position in business, and even lead a life in solitude on Machendragad Hill by Baba's order, and was deriving great benefit from Baba's contact and guidance. In fact, many hoped that he would be Baba's successor on Baba's gadi. But his premature death in 1913 destroyed that hope.

Baba had great hopes in Upasani Baba, and was taking special efforts in moulding him to be a fit person to be his successor. Seeing the special attention bestowed on Upasani by Baba, one devotee asked Baba, "What Baba, we have been attending upon you for years, and you seem to be conferring a copper plate grant of all your powers to this stranger, and are we all, therefore, to be neglected?" "Yes", asserted Baba. "I speak only the truth sitting as I do in this Masjid. What I have spoken, I have spoken. I have given everything to this person. Whether he be good or bad, he is my own. I am fully responsible for him, and, as for sasana or a grant, why a copper plate grant? I have given him a gold plate grant!" Unfortunately Upasani Baba lacked the saburi required and failed in Baba's expectations.

Rege was a wonderful devotee who came to Baba not for any material gain. To him Baba, who endearingly was called Gurudev, was everything. He extracted a promise from Baba that in all his future births, as in this birth, Baba would always be with him. Thus Rege, a perfect devotee though, had a few more births to attain the Supreme.

Baba revealed on many occasions, covertly and overtly his divine nature, that he has come to lead people in the subra marga, that he is a Samartha ready to give the best. Let us see Baba's Charters & Sayings, 44 and 45:

44. Come, Sirs, carry away bags of Udhi. Come, cart away the treasures of your mother. Look here. People come and say, 'Baba, give'. I tell them to take. No one takes.

45. My master told me to give bounteously to all that ask. No one listens to me or wisdom. My treasury is open. None brings carts to take from it. I say dig, none will take any pains. I said, 'dig out the treasure and cart it away'. Be the real and true sons of the mother and fully stock your magazine. What is to become of us, i.e. this bodily life? Earth will return to the Earth, and the Air (Breath) will return to the Air. This opportunity will not return.

Samartha Sai is still waiting with outstretched hands to receive earnest devotees keen on spiritual pursuit and lead them to their cherished goal.

DANA – GIVING

(Sai Sudha – January 2013)

In Sai Sahasranamavali the importance which Sai attached to dana is revealed in the following namavalis:

Annadana sada nishtaha: Always keen in offering annadana – food to the hungry. *Atithibhukta seshabhujah*: One who ate what remained after feeding the guests. *Dana soundah:* An adept in giving (dana).

Danaischa anyan vasamnayah: By giving (dana), he drew people to him.

Being a very poor fakir how can Baba give? Wherefrom to give? He cherished living poor. He said, 'Poverty is the highest riches'. He wanted to give and he gave bounteously to all who came to him with need, not for accumulating any merit (punya) for himself but to set an example to all devotees who came to him. Baba never preached anything that he himself did not practise; for him practice is more important than precept. Baba wanted his devotees to give dana; many may listen to his words but may not put them to practice. That was the reason why he devised the means of collecting dakshina from his devotees. He demanded dakshina from everyone he favoured; the demand would depend on the concerned individual's capacity to give. The amounts so collected as dakshina from the devotees were liberally given to hundreds of deserving people by Baba. Baba thus secured for his devotees the benefit of giving. Baba acted as a conduit. Baba is hailed as *dakshina prarthana dwara subhakrit tattwa bodhakah* – by means of asking for dakshina from devotees Baba earned for them merit and thus did good and also imparted valuable instruction on the importance of giving. Baba was *yatheshta dana dharmakrit*, one who gave dana and dharma abundantly – all for the benefit of his devotees.

Through Nana Saheb Chandorkar, Baba taught what the attitude of the giver should be in giving dana to others. Baba is hailed as *danamargaskhalatpada nanachandorkaravanah* – one who protected his devotee Nana Chandorkar by correcting him when he did not have the proper attitude in giving dana. Baba said, "If anyone comes and begs for something, give him whatever you can, and if that person be not satisfied and asks for more, answer him suavely in the negative. Do not pour out your wrath or display all your official authority against that person."

Karmanyeva adhikaraste na phalesha kadachana – "Your duty is only to act, you never have any claim for the fruits" - This is what Sri Krishna said. Baba made Nana Chandorkar realize this and that he should not arrogate to himself a sense that he was the provider. In chapter II in Part II of *Life of Sri Baba*, titled Narayana Govind Chandorkar, Sri Narasimha Swamiji says that Baba used '*dana*' in the case of Nana Chandorkar as an antidote for the venom called attachment or greed, '*lobha*'. Let as read what Swamiji writes.

"*Lobha* is only an exaggeration of one's attachment to moneys and goods. Baba took very good care to see that Nana's attachment did not reach excessive heights. Baba adopted his usual methods for this purpose. It is '*Dana*' that is the exact opposite of, and therefore, the antidote for, the venom called attachment or greed. This truth comes from even the date of the *Brihadaranyaka Upanishad* (V2). Prajapati was approached by his three sets of children, the Devas, the Naras and the Asuras. Each of them came and said, 'please give us instruction as to what we should do'. Prajapati answered, '*Da, Da, Da*', to each of these. In the case of the gods, the '*Da*' required for them was '*Dama*', i.e. self-control, moderation. In the case of the asuras, the '*Da*' required was '*daya*' i.e. mercy. Their excessive cruel nature had to be met by the spirit of compassion, which was the antidote for their cruelty. In the case of men, the '*Da*' was '*Dana*', i.e. charity. Man's natural instinct is to grasp, to be greedy, and to get more and more and the best way of checking this greed is by making man give up all that he has got. *Dana* forces a man to part with his money, etc., and by constant parting he will get accustomed to feel quite nonchalant, quite unaffected while parting with moneys or when moneys are lost. Thus '*Da*' *(Dana)* is the recipe given to men as the rule of their life by Prajapati."

The craze to possess all modern amenities, to lead a luxurious life, is seen to be reaching its peak now. This requires accumulating money by whatever means possible. Man is being possessed by the ghost 'greed' even without his knowledge. Let us pray to Baba, to give us the will to resist this greed, to give us the heart to spend a portion of what we earn in 'Dana' and lead a peaceful life.

BEHAVE PROPERLY

(Sai Sudha – March 2001)

In Volume IV of *Life of Sai Baba* – Pujyasri Narasimhaswamiji has devoted an entire chapter to "Baba's Moral Teachings". This is a chapter which has to be read over and over by all Sai devotees, those devotee-sevaks who want to serve in Sai institutions in particular, as that will definitely bring about a thorough transformation in their hearts. This will do a world of good to them and also to those who come in contact with them. More than doing puja, more than doing bhajans, this will please Baba immensely. The best thing a devotee can do is to conduct himself in word, deed and thought in such a way that Baba will mark him as his own or ankita and that is the aim of being a Sai devotee.

Swamiji writes: We may sum up the whole in the way which Baba Himself, put it to Shama, namely 'Behave properly', and the way in which he put it to Rao Sahib Galwankar, 'Behave with integrity and probity', This advice is represented by the Sanskrit stanza:-

slokardhena pravakshyami yad uktam granthakotibhih
paropakarah punyaya papaya parapeedanam

This means, "In half a stanza I shall tell you the teaching which has been set forth in crores of moral books. That is benefiting humanity is *punya* (merit) 'Hurting others is sinful'. This is a teaching that even children and sometimes creatures like dogs also, can understand. Baba expected people to act up to this teaching."

Sri Swamiji himself feels that it was not possible to make the entire lot moral and properly behaved, in spite of all the efforts of Baba to correct them. Baba laments: "I have been considering long and thinking day and night. All are thieves. But we have to deal with them. I prayed to God night and day for improvement or removal but God delays and does not approve of my attitude or grant the prayer. I will wait for a month or two and then see. But living or dead, I will have what I have been praying for. I will not go to Teli or Vani nor beg of them. People are not good and devoted. They are unsettled in mind. A few friends will gather and talk divine wisdom, and sit and contemplate". Again in 1918, Baba said, "People have got bad and give trouble. They are pestering me for money. Moreover they become shameless. Now I am disgusted". Swamiji writes that once in such disgusted mood Baba went to Nimgam and told the zamindar of the disgusting way in which devotees behaved at Shirdi, and added that he wanted to leave Shirdi.

We can thus see that Baba is so disgusted when devotees do not behave properly that he even contemplates leaving Shirdi. Here Shirdi means all places where He abides, including the one in Mylapore, Chennai, founded by His Apostle Pujyasri Narasimha-swamiji. If Baba is forced to leave, will Swamiji stay? It is time that each one contemplates, meditates, takes stock of the situation and does what Baba expect him or her to do.

NISHTA AND SABURI

(Sai Sudha – April 2003)

Devotees of Sri Sai Baba who read and hear the life and teachings of the Great Master come across the two words '*Nishta*' and '*Saburi*'. What do they connote actually? Have we grasped their full import? Are they within our reach?

If we read carefully over and over again the narration about Mrs. Radhabai Deshmukh in Shri Sai Satcharitra (Chapters XVIII and XIX), we get a ray of light. Baba tells this lady that his Guru, a great merciful saint, whom he served very long, asked him to give two pice as dakshina. His two pice were (1) *Nishta* – firm faith and (2) *Saburi* – patient perseverance. Baba says that he readily gave these two 'pice' and the Guru was pleased. The value, the merit, of the two objects which Baba submitted to his Guru is beyond description in words. Let us see how Baba narrated.

"I resorted to my Guru for 12 years. He brought me up. There was no dearth of food and clothing. He was full of love, nay, he was love incarnate. How can I describe it? He loved me the most. Rare is a Guru like him. When I looked at him he seemed as if he was in a deep meditation and then we both were filled with bliss. Night and day I gazed at him with no thought of hunger and thirst. Without him I felt restless. I had no other object to meditate, nor any other thing than my Guru to attend. He was my sole refuge. My mind was always fixed on him. This is one pice of dakshina *(Nishta)*. *Saburi* (Patience or perseverance) is the other pice. I waited patiently and very long on my Guru and served him. This *Saburi* will ferry you across the sea of this mundane existence. *Saburi* is manliness; it removes all sins and affections, gets rid of calamities in various ways and casts aside all fear, and ultimately gives you success. *Saburi* is the mine of virtues, consort of good thought. *Nishta* and *Saburi* are like twin sisters loving each other very intimately".

Now we have a broad idea about what is meant by *Nishta* and *Saburi*, i.e. Faith and Perseverance. Each of these two coins have two sides, obverse and reverse. One side of *nishta* is Faith, absolute faith, total faith unquestioning faith, unwavering faith; the other side is Love, Pure Love, Perfect Love, Bargainfree Love. Of *Saburi*, one side is unrelenting, obdurate, perseverance in our efforts with unflinching patience, not to be moved a bit by any disappointment or hindrance, totally free from fear or cares – Baba calls this 'manliness'; the other side is dedicated service, loving service, with readiness to sacrifice anything and everything. *Nishta* and *Saburi* mean *prapatti, saranagati*, total surrender. They are the derivatives from Sri Krishna's charter in Gita, "*sarvadharman parityajya maamekam saranam vraja, aham tva sarvapaapebhyo mokshayishyaami ma scucha'*; i.e. "Giving up your dependence on all other sadhanas, take Me as your Sole Refuge. Grieve not; I shall deliver you from all sins (and their effects)".

It seems easy to place faith on someone, a Divine Person, a saint, an Acharya, etc. But in practice it is seen that it is a difficult path to tread. Obstructions come in the form of our ego, our vasanas, influences of the people whose company we keep with, events taking place around us, etc. At various places in the great book "*Life of Sai Baba*", Sri Narasimhaswamiji has given valuable hints and guidelines for cultivating faith. These have been extracted and published in January 2003, issue of Sai Sudha in the article Sai Seva. This faith has Love linked to it. A love which endures all things, love that does not blame, love that does not find fault. Baba had this absolute, pure, perfect love for his Guru. Sri Swamiji writes: "For Baba's Guruparampara, the sishya has to absorb the Gurudeva's soul into himself by concentrated love forgetting the entire world beside. This was possible for Sai at his early age of five when he contacted his Gurudeva and continued to serve him for 10 or 12 years with concentrated love. Baba says that he loved nothing in the world except the Guru and if the Guru was not there, he wondered what his eyes were for. That is a romantic attachment to the Guru and an ability to banish all worldly thought unconnected with the Guru. But this was not possible for any person other

than Baba, and especially for persons who have already dipped themselves into the world deep enough".

Now, armed with *nishta*, we aim at saburi – patience, perseverance. Here we must go through carefully the narration of Baba with regard to quest for realization, along with three other sadhakas. All four had enough of bookish knowledge and discussed how they were to get realization. Each expounded his own views, except Baba who was practical and noted that. surrender and love to the Guru were the only solutions. Having entered a trackless dense forest and lost the way, only Baba accepted the help offered by the Vanajari, the guide – Guru. Somehow Baba reposed faith in him and before accepting Baba as his chela, the Guru wanted to test his strength of perseverance, patience, i.e. *saburi*. Baba says, 'he took me to a well, tied up my legs with a rope and suspended me head downwards from a tree by the side of the well. My head was about three feet off the water, which I could not reach. And the Guru left me there and went away – God knows where. He returned after 4 or 5 hours and asked how I fared'. 'In great bliss was my time passed' I answered. The Guru, mightily pleased with me, drew me near him, placed his palm over my head and body and spoke to me tender words dripping with love, and he put me into his school – where I entirely forgot my father and mother and all attachments and desires'. What Baba went in search of was realization. The Guru did not give any upadesa or instruction in that direction. For a long period Baba served his Guru. He was persevering in his loving service to the Guru and exhibited enormous patience, with the firm determination to stop not till the goal was reached. One may have to pass through innumerable adverse circumstances with powerful resistance.

In Baba's dialogue with Nana Chandorkar regarding the meaning of the message conveyed in *Bhagavad Gita* (IV-34), Baba tells that by 'seva' the Lord does not mean mere service. The service should be with total humility and there must be no lingering idea that one is free to yield the service or refuse it. One must feel that he is not the master of the body, which has become the Guru's and exists merely to render him service. Sri Narasimhaswamiji writes, "In Baba's course, the Guru must be everything to the sishya, the giver of bread, the giver of life and light and the giver of all that life is worth living for, and at one stroke. This alone is the tyaga of *tan, man, dhan* – body, mind and possessions. This Baba himself has fully described in setting out his relations with his own Guru. Baba expected that others who came as pupils to him should adopt the same course. But none of the persons that came to Baba could adopt the entire course, Baba himself said on one occasion, 'Is there anyone who will serve me as I served my Master, that is with perfect *nishta* and with absolute surrender?' There was none". A service with humility, with *daasabhava*.

Nishta – Saburi is the essence of Baba's teaching. Once when Swami Vivekananda was asked by an eminent scholarly gentleman to explain the message of Bhagavad Gita in two words he shot back promptly '*pravritti and nivritti*'. Only another Swami Vivekananda can expound its full meaning. Similarly Baba's message can be summed up in two words 'nishta and saburi'. Only the Grace of the Master can reveal to us the full meaning. It is a subject as vast as an ocean. In fact, a large portion of *Life of Sai Baba* written by Sri Narasimhaswamiji revolves around this subject only. By reading it over and over again, we can get some idea – the reading should be with faith and patient perseverance.

BABA'S MESSAGE TO THE WORLD OF TODAY

(Sai Sudha – November 2001)

Right from the beginning of the last century terrorism has grown steadily and has today assumed alarming proportions. The root cause for the terrorism witnessed today can be traced to religious bigotry and absolute intolerance on the part of a group of individuals. Terrorism flourished because of rivalry between one nation and the other; terrorism was also used by one political party to get even with another party. At last when one mighty nation became a victim to terrorism, concerted action is being taken to put it down. A war is waged against Afghanistan which is considered to be the country where terrorism is being nurtured to grow as a huge monster to devour the whole civilisation.

Terrorism cannot be fought by ahimsa. Ahimsa can be effective when one fights with people with hearts, people who are essentially human. One becomes a terrorist only when the last trace of love, the human trait, is totally removed from his heart. Every action of his is motivated by most poisonous hatred. Therefore, terrorism can be eliminated only by force and with a firm hand and every individual, organisation or nation interested in the survival of civilisation should join together burying all their differences in this effort.

Because terrorists by and large belong to particular religion, it is not just and correct to condemn all the people practising that religion. Terrorism is not sanctioned by any of the world religions. Ours is a nation where people belonging to different religions coexist with mutual love for the last five or six centuries.

Our nation is committed to secularism. Secularism means total freedom to people belonging to various religions and faiths to practise their own religion or faith. While each religious group has the right to practise its own faith, it does not have the right to encroach upon the rights of other religious groups. If and when an organisation belonging to any particular religion is found to be helping people engaged in anti-national and terrorist activities, it is the duty of the Government to ban such an organisation and initiate action. When such an action is taken, it is absurd and unfortunate that people in opposition parties call it foul and criticise. They issue statements to make people believe that vindictive action is taken against a particular religious group while it is actually against an act of terrorism or anti-national activity. Thus they indirectly help people engaged in or promoting terrorist activities.

Ever since Moslems set foot in India, history is replete with instances where Hindu temples were destroyed, rummaged and plundered. People in the country, by and large, have forgotten all the past and are learning to live together peacefully. However, the fact that there continues to be mutual distrust among certain sections of Hindus and Moslems cannot be refuted. Sri Narasimhaswamiji traces the reason for this "to a strong feeling on the part of the Hindus that they should not go near a Muslim whose views run counter to their cherished ideas, and who should destroy their religious emblems and idols. Similar is the repugnance on the part of the Muslims to accept purely Hindu traditions which they consider too idolatrous and unholy".

The mission of Sri Sai Baba, whose antecedents are shrouded in mystery and whose ancestry - Hindu or Moslem – is still to be established beyond any reasonable doubt, is to bring together these two religious groups. To do this, he practised Love and preached Love. Sri Swamiji writes, "to those who considered him a Muslim, he responded as a Muslim and to those who cared to treat him as a Hindu, he responded as a Hindu; and he expounded the Koran to the former and the Sastras to the latter".

In introducing Sri Sai Baba to the world in the early 'forties of the last century through a small booklet, "Who is Sri Sai Baba of Shirdi", Sri

Narasimhaswamiji summed up the mission and teachings of Sri Sai Baba in the following words:

"Beyond the miracles of Baba, there is one bright, marvellous fact, worthy of people's adoration and that is his golden heart of love with its message of universal love."

"Baba declared that if people hated one another, his heart was smarting with pain and sorrow and if persons forgave enemies and endured the ill-treatment, he was highly pleased. This is the most valuable lesson for this day and for all time. A story is told in Bhagavata of the world going as a cow to Brahma, groaning under the weight of the cruel Asuras harassing innocent people. That is just the spectacle all over the world today. Hatred, destruction, plunder, and absolute disregard for truth and virtue, are the predominant features in the daily history of the world today. Man's claws and teeth are red with the gore of brother man; and the criminal is not apologetic but blatant. Civilisation is in imminent danger of being submerged in pools of human blood and devastating fire leaving the human form a fossil to be discovered within some rocks by some later race. The only thing that can avert this gloom is LOVE, a revival of the very ancient message to Asuras from God, '*Dayadhwan*', i.e, 'Be merciful'."

Swamiji's message was to the world that existed six decades back. That was the time when the whole world was in a stupor because of World War II and nuclear assaults. The gloom is deeper and acts of asuric nature are at the peak today. Let us now ponder over the message of Sri Sai and Swamiji seriously.

ALL INDIA SAI DEVOTEES' CONVENTION

The main objective behind organizing a convention of Sai devotees all over the country, as commonly understood, is to bring together all devotees of Sri Sai Baba in one place periodically and give them an opportunity to exchange their experiences and views. Pujyasri Narasimhaswamiji, our Gurudev, who set in motion the Sai Mission, the Sai prachar work in the Thirties of the Twentieth Century went about his work methodically. First, he travelled extensively throughout the country and in several cities, towns and villages he introduced his Master to the masses. This he did through lectures, bhajans, pujas and distribution of small booklets. A unique way! Taking the Master to the masses and not bringing them to the Master! By 1940 pictures of Sri Sai Baba adorned the puja rooms of thousands of devotees.

Sri Swamiji who was writing articles on Sri Sai Baba in some magazines and newspapers like The Sunday Times, started publishing a magazine 'Sai Sudha' with articles in English, Tamil and Telugu in 1940. This was the second step he took.

In 1941 Sri Swamiji founded the All India Sai Samaj in Chennai to serve as the nucleus for spreading the life of Sri Sai Baba, his mission and teachings systematically. He published several books like "Who is Sai Baba?", "The Wonderous Saint Sai Baba", "Introduction to Sai Baba" and others and these books were made available to public at cost price; they were sometimes distributed free also. Simultaneously, Sai Samajams and institutions were started in various other places like Bangalore, Nellore, Omalur, Madurai, etc. This was Sri Swamiji's Third Step.

In the next five years the number of Sai devotees in the country grew sufficiently and several organizations in the name of Sai were also coming up. With a view to consolidate the work done over a decade and to step up the momentum gained, Sri Swamiji introduced the next, that is the fourth step – holding of All India Sai Devotees' convention. The first such convention was organized by Sri Swamiji himself in Madras (now Chennai) in 1946. What was the purpose? Leaving aside all guesses, let us read what Sri Swamiji himself said in his appeal to devotees on the eve of this first convention:

"It is by united action that anything is achieved by society. Division on the other hand weakens and finally kills our life. This patent truth, though sometimes forgotten by frenzied people is always proven by the course of events. The truth was pressed by Sai on his devotees time and again. Said he, "If you fight between yourselves, my heart aches within me. But if you put up with each other's faults and wrongs, I feel glad...... "most movements have found an annual convention not merely useful but almost a necessity...... The need for a Sai convention is specially noticeable in view of the numerous ramifications and forms of activity that are in evidence.

"Amongst Christians, the Christmas Day is considered a special occasion when Christians meet together, bury their differences and start a fresh life of harmony and peace under the inspiration of their common saviour. Similarly Sai devotees who may have had mutual misunderstandings and even differences would use this and other similar conventions for forgetting their differences and extending the right hand of fellowship and friendship to each other under the wings of their common MOTHER Sri Sai".

Thus, in the first convention Sri Swamiji exhorted all Sai Sevaks to draw up a common agenda and work as an integrated whole in carrying on the Sai Mission. He also stressed on the need for developing a feeling of love among all Sai devotees. Sri Swamiji believed that conventions will be ideal to achieve these aims. In Sri Swamiji's life time eight conventions were organized in different towns, spread over a period of nine years. By that time the name of Sai Baba became a household word and the number of Sai devotees grew to millions from thousands. Now Swamiji should have felt that it would not suffice if the number of people worshipping

Sai Baba multiplied; a large number, as many as possible, should grasp the significance of Sri Sai Baba's advent and the essence of his mission. People should strive to derive the highest benefit that a Samartha Sadguru could confer, is waiting to confer. Let us see what Sri Swamiji said in his message for the eighth convention:

"It is up to every hearer of this message to vigorously whip up his own attachment to Baba, improve his knowledge also of Baba's ways of working, get into contact with Baba's children, and develop himself by surrender and service to Baba into an 'Ankita' child. This is only part of the work of diffusion of knowledge about Baba. The work of this convention is to diffuse as much knowledge about Baba as possible to as many as possible. As already mentioned, literature is the chief means that we think about in this convention. Journals must be multiplied in various languages and books must be published or translated into various languages and gatherings and lectures and kirtans should be held all over the country."

The most valuable, authentic and authoritative commentary on the Life, Mission and Teachings of Sri Sai Baba is enshrined only in the number of books written by Sri Narasimhaswamiji. It is unfortunate that today several books are just not available. It should be the endeavour of every sincere Sai Sevak to do whatever possible to collect all the works of Swamiji from All India Sai Samaj and other possible sources, publish them again and have them translated into other Indian languages also. More and more Sai temples coming up is just not enough. People volunteering to carry on Sai prachar work should first read thoroughly various Sai literature and then share the knowledge gained with others through periodical study circles or groups. This writer has great hopes that a good and sound beginning will take place at this convention being held in Hubli since Hubli is a very significant place in the history of Sai prachar.

Many of us know the tragic circumstances which made the leading lawyer, patriot, B.V. Narasimha Iyer of Salem to renounce the material life and take up the spiritual quest. In Chapter II, 'Sri Upasani Baba', Part II of *Life of Sri Sai Baba*, Sri Narasimhaswamiji himself has given a brief narration about this phase of life. He stayed in Ramanashram at Tiruvannamalai, engaged in meditation, tapasya, in quest of the self. There he wrote the wonderful book 'Self Realisation' the first ever biography of Ramana Maharishi in English which was instrumental in making the

Maharishi known throughout not only in India but in Western countries also. But "at the close of three years he discovered that he had lost the Bhakti in which he had made good progress before leaving Salem and approaching Ramanashram. Hence, he resumed his efforts at readoption of the Bhakti marga and in quest thereof was going to visit various temples". During the sojourn he met Meher Baba and as advised by his followers he went to Sakori to meet Sri Upasani Baba, Guru of Meher Baba. "Sri Upasani Baba made him stick to the Bhakti Marga (without frittering away his powers in metaphysical speculation) and develop his knowledge and tendencies through well recognized methods such as japa, bhajan, parayana or pothi etc., and the leading of the akinchana's life, i.e. life of holy poverty or asceticism. When trying to progress on these lines with the help of Upasani Baba, he was startled to discover that there were elements in that Baba's teaching and methods which jarred very much against his previous opinions and expectations as to the correct religious life and so he left Sri Upasani about the beginning of 1933 with the idea of never returning to him". Thus though Swamiji was very near Shirdi he did not get contact with Sri Sai Baba in his first period of stay at Sakori.

Sri Narasimhaswamiji who returned to Madras once again started on a pilgrimage in his quest for God-realization. His first place of halt was Hubli where he stayed at Siddharudha's Mutt. While at Hubli the Great Master Sri Sai Baba decided to pull his chosen apostle to Shirdi through Sri Upasani Baba.

"Strangely enough his commiseration for a poor devotee in trouble at Hubli made him promise to help that devotee to get some place for a fixed habitation and adoption of a purely religious life of service". This is how Sri Sai worked on the mind of Swamiji. Swamiji took that devotee to Sakori to be left there. Since Upasani Baba would not allow that devotee to stay there unless the Swami also agreed to stay there, Sri Swamiji was forced to once again stay at Sakori. "Thereafter for a number of years, the author stayed at Sakori and went on studying both Upasani Baba and Sri Sai Baba, the latter being the Guru of Upasani and the latter's place being only three miles distant, an easy walk from Sakori. The author slowly gathered information and went on with his research about Sai Baba and noted that it was Sai Baba after all that was drawing him through Upasani Baba and that, in one form or another, he had been drawing him for decades, all unknown to him (the author)."

Baba had been drawing Swamiji to him for decades, but the final pull was from Hubli and thus pulled, Swamiji identified himself with the Great Master Sri Sai Baba and presented him to humanity at large. A convention was held in Hubli in 1951 itself with Sri Swamiji himself as the motivating force. It should be a thrill to participate in a convention at this historical place after 53 years. May be there are some old devotees in Hubli who can recall particulars about Sri Swamiji's visit in 1933. In May 1965 when the 10th All India Sai Devotees' Convention was held in Chennai, for the first time Sri Rege Maharaj kindly condescended to participate and address the devotees. It was the second convention after Swamiji's passing away, the first one being the one organized at Naga Sai Mandir, Coimbatore in May 1963. In both the conventions Saipadananda Radhakrishnaswamiji presided. The vaccum left by Sri Narasimhaswamiji was filled by him. In 1965 convention at Madras several elderly devotees who were with Sri Narasimhaswamiji participated recalling their memories about the yeoman service rendered by Swamiji. Those of us who, by the benign grace of the Great Master Sai Baba, had the privilege of being in the company of Sri Rege Maharaj and hearing from him first hand account of Baba's acts of love, felt ineffable joy and thought that they had been transported back by five decades to directly realise what it was to be in the company of Baba. Similarly, if we get an opportunity to mingle with and talk to the devotees who were fortunate to enjoy the company of Sri Narasimhaswamiji, there is every chance of our being taken back by five decades.

(Source: Souvenir published on the occasion of 28th All India Sai Devotees' Convention held at in Hubli on 15th and 16th May 2004. Keynote address delivered by Sri S. Seshadri on the occasion.)

EVERLASTING INHERITANCE – FROM SRI NARASIMHASWAMIJI

(Sai Sudha – April, 2010)

Today we come across a plethora of books on Sri Sai Baba of Shirdi. Sri Sai Baba shed his mortal coil in 1918 and till the middle of the twentieth century there was no authentic or cogent biography of Sri Sai Baba. Most of the people who had come in contact with Sai considered him to be a unique, incredible saint, a godman, an aulia, Dattatreya reincarnate and so on, each according to his or her perception. A divine personality or godman does not appear on earth without a mission. There should be a specific purpose behind a godman's advent in this world. Any book on a great saint should clearly reveal the mission and essence of his teachings, teachings that would elevate a reader to higher and higher human levels first and then lead on the spiritual path leading to Self-realisation or God-realisation which is the aim of a human birth.

Before Sri Narasimhaswamiji started writing the Life of Sai Baba exhaustively and analytically in four volumes, there was no noteworthy biography of Sri Sai Baba. The noteworthy one was Dabholkar's Sai Satcharitra in Marathi. "That is a brilliantly written poetical work extending to 53 chapters and over 1000 pages mostly narrating incidents connected with Sai Baba's life, and serving excellently the purpose of Puranic study and daily parayana", writes Sri Swamiji in Chapter I (introduction) of Life of Sai Baba, Part I. There were a few other small books in English and other languages, besides a few chapters in Bhakta Leelamrta, Santha

Kathamruta and Bhakti Saramrutha written by Das Ganu Maharaj. It should also be noted that in those days people who had heard of Sri Sai were only a few thousands; majority of the people who worshipped Sai and went to Shirdi were only with a view to obtain some material benefit or other since they had been hearing that Baba was like a wish-fulfilling tree. When Narasimha-swamiji was chosen as the Apostle of Sai Baba to carry on Sai Prachar by the Master himself, his first task was to make the name of Sai Baba known to as many people as possible throughout the country. Earlier Baba was largely known in Maharashtra and adjacent States only.

In a book, *Shirdi Sai Baba: The Divine Healer*, written in 2009 by a lady devotee Mrs. Raj Chopra, she has acknowledged that what inspired her to write the book was the books written by Sri Narasimhaswamiji. But she adds, "Nobody can underestimate their value but I found them too voluminous for an average reader. They are full of sermons and Sanskrit slokas. Frankly speaking, how many of us know that much Sanskrit as to appreciate them? For me, at least they did not serve any purpose'. But on going through the book one can see that Sri Swamiji's books had served this author a great purpose inasmuch as a large portion has been taken out from the Devotees Experiences of Sai Baba and other books written by Swamiji; they have been grouped under various interesting captions.

Besides this author, a few readers had also expressed to this writer some difficulty in reading the *Life of Sai Baba* by Swamiji since it contains several quotations from the Hindu Scriptures and Vedantic texts which are all in Sanskrit. The first few books written by Swamiji commencing 1937 like *Who is Sai Baba of Shirdi, Wondrous Saint Sai Baba, Introduction to Sai Baba, Devotees Experiences of Sai Baba etc.*, do not contain such quotations. At that time Swamiji's primary aim was to draw as many people as possible to Sri Sai. It was not an easy task. A large number of people among Hindus were still orthodox and conservative and it was not easy to make them accept a Muslim Fakir. The obstacles and objections to Sai worship Swamiji had to face in his Prachar work have been clearly described in Chapter XIV of *Life of Sai Baba*. When more and more literature is produced highlighting the miracles worked by Baba to help his devotees, a doubt arose whether such miracles and exhibition of Siddhis alone could make one Divine. Sri Swamiji was posed with this question by the President of Sri Ramakrishna Math himself. So it became necessary for Swamiji to write in detail a book substantiating his conviction that Baba was God Himself and he possessed all the powers that God as Sri Krishna had. For this, to convince even scoffers that Baba is Divine by nature, he had to quote pramanas, authorities from religious scriptures like Bhagavad Gita, Guru Gita, Srimad Bhagavata, Upanishads etc. To establish Sri Sai was a Samartha Sadguru, Swamiji had to quote passages from Guru Gita. Baba once said that he was a Brahmin, White Brahmin. This does not mean that by birth he was Brahmin. By virtue of his having realized Brahman, he is a Brahmin. To explain who is really a Brahmin, Swamiji had to quote from Mahabharata, Upanishads etc.

Siddhis or Powers – Omniscience, Omnipresence, Omnipotence and all-pervasiveness – were not attained by Baba as a result of any strenuous religious or spiritual sadhanas. These Siddhis or Divine Powers came in full measure to Sri Sai because he had attained Purna Laya (total merger) in God and all powers flowing from God are found in such a devotee who had got Purna Laya in God. Swamiji had to quote relevant portion of Sri Krishna's teaching to Uddhava in Eleventh Canto of Srimad Bhagavata to substantiate this fact.

The ultimate aim of Swamiji's spiritual quest is Self-realisation or God-realisation. He got a push in his progress by his stay with Sri Ramana Maharishi, whose first biography titled "*Self-Realisation*" was written by Sri Swamiji, to serve as an instrument to draw several Western seekers to the feet of Maharshi. Swamiji reached the end of his spiritual quest at Shirdi Sai Samadhi Mandir. By rinanubandha Baba pulled his chosen apostle to himself and anointed him as his Chief Pracharak. Swamiji, who was well-versed not only in Hindu scriptures but also in other religious scriptures like the Holy Bible had to convincingly establish, supported by relevant authorities, that Baba was an Avatara Purusha, who appeared in the world for the redemption and upliftment of humanity by promoting love and harmony. Sri Swamiji's work in recording the statements of several direct contemporary devotees of Sri Sai Baba and publishing it as Devotees' Experiences of Sai Baba is monumental. This formed the basis for all his other works.

Even in 1950's and 1960's a large section of orthodox Hindus was not visiting Sai Mandirs. Only after the various publications of Swamiji reached several educated people, the number of Sai devotees gradually increased from thousands to lakhs and today it is millions. All later writers had to rely on Swamiji's Sai literature for their books. It would, however, be better if more books are produced highlighting the mission and teachings of Baba rather than highlighting Baba's powers because a vast majority of religious-minded people know who Baba is. Emphasis should be on what Baba's mission was and on what Baba essentially taught so that at least a few can now venture on the spiritual path and make progress by the grace of Samartha Sadguru Sai.

Books on
SHIRDI SAI BABA

STERLING

NEW BOOKS

2021-2022

Sai Musings
Kabita Mohanty
ISBN 978 81 950824 5 2
Pages 192
Size 5.5×8.5"
Paperback
Price ₹ 300

Healing with Shirdi Sai Baba
Nandini Dhanani
ISBN 978 81 947772 7 4
Page 216 Size 5.5×8.5"
Paperback Price ₹300

DWARKAMAI: A Magical Trip
Sujay Khandelwal
English ISBN 978 93 93853 04 2
Hindi ISBN 978 93 93853 02 8
Paperback
Price ₹199 each

Prema Rathna Radhakrishnayee
Lakshmi Ramanan, Veena Jayatheertha Rao, Lakshmi Gambhira, Saraswati Risbud

ISBN 978 81 947772 0 5
Pages 80 Size 5.5×8.5"
Paperback Price ₹100

Aarati Sai Baba Rachanakar Madhavrao Vamanrao Adkar
Janardhan alias Balasaheb Ramchandra Adkar Translated by Mahesh Vasant Nene

ISBN 978 81 954046 1 2
Pages 104 Size 5.5×8.5"
Paperback Price ₹100

Life History of Sri Shirdi Sai Baba (Tamil)
Ammula Sambasiva Rao

ISBN 978 93 86245 77 9
Pages 319 Size 5.5×8.5"
Paperback Price ₹250

SHRI SAI GYANESHWARI BY RAKESH JUNEJA

Tamil
ISBN 978 81 947772 5 0
Page 211
Size 5.5×8.5"
Hardbound
Price ₹250

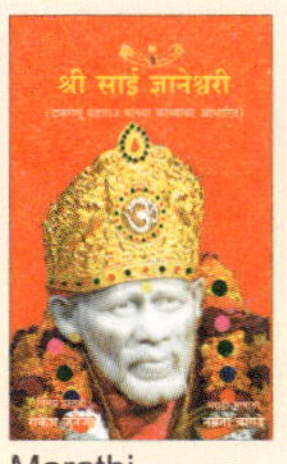

Marathi
ISBN 978 81 947772 2 9
Page 264
Size 5.5×8.5"
Hardbound
Price ₹250

Punjabi
ISBN 978 81 954046 3 6
Page 248
Size 5.5×8.5"
Hardbound
Price ₹250

Bengali
ISBN 978 81 954046 8 1
Pages 248
Size 5.5×8.5"
Hardbound
Price ₹250

Shri Shirdi Saibaba:
Gems From His Philosophical Teachings
Dr. Anitha D.
ISBN 978 81 944007 3 8 ₹300

Shri Sai Satcharita
The Life and Teachings of Shirdi Sai Baba
Translated by Indira Kher
ISBN 978 81 207 2211 8 ₹ 600(HB)
ISBN 978 81 207 2153 1 ₹ 500(PB)

New Findings on Shridi Sai Baba
Chandra Bhanu Satpathy
ISBN 978 93 86245 52 6
₹ 300

Shirdi : within & beyond
A collection of unseen & rare photographs
Dr. Rabinder Nath Kakarya
978 81 207 7806 1 ₹ 750

Shirdi Sai Baba: The Universal Master
Sri Kaleshwar
ISBN 978 81 207 9664 5
₹ 150

Shri Sai Ekam
Shri Sai is the One
Harjeet Yadav
978 93 86245 38 0
₹ 900

Shri Sai Baba
Teachings & Philosophy
Lt Col M B Nimbalkar
ISBN 978 81 207 2364 1
₹ 150

Shirdi Sai Baba
Anusuya Vasudevan
ISBN 978 93 86245 16 8
(64 pages plates)
₹ 200

Unravelling the Enigma: Shirdi Sai Baba in the light of Sufism
Marianne Warren
ISBN 978 81 207 2147 0
₹ 400

Sai Baba of Shirdi: A Biographical Investigation
Kevin R. D. Shepherd
ISBN 978 81 207 9901 1
₹ 450

The Eternal Sai Consciousness
A. R. Nanda
ISBN 978 81 207 9043 8
₹ 200

BABA:
The Devotees' Questions
Dr. C. B. Satpathy
ISBN 978 81 207 8966 1
₹ 150

The Loving God:
Story of Shirdi Sai Baba
Dr. G. R. Vijayakumar
ISBN 978 81 207 8079 8
₹ 200

Sai Samartha and Ramana Maharshi
S. Seshadri
ISBN 978 81 207 8986 9
₹150

Shri Sai Gyaneshwari
Rakesh Juneja
ISBN 978 81 950824 7 6
₹300

The Age of Shirdi Sai
Dr. C. B. Satpathy
ISBN 978 81 207 8700 1
₹ 300

Message of Shri Sai
Suresh Chandra Panda
ISBN 978 81 207 9512 9
₹ 150

A Divine Journey with Baba
Vinny Chitluri
ISBN 978 81 207 9859 5
₹ 300

Sai Baba: Faqir of Shirdi
Kevin R.D. Shepherd
ISBN 978 93 86245 06 9
₹ 350

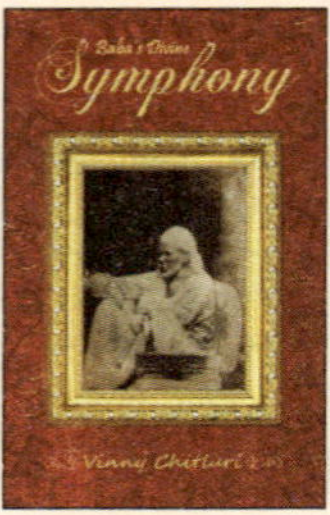

Baba's Divine Symphony
Vinny Chitluri
ISBN 978 81 207 8485 7
₹ 300

Sai Baba an Incarnation
Bela Sharma
ISBN 978 81 207 8833 6
₹ 200

Shirdi Sai Baba: The Perfect Master
Suresh Chandra Panda & Smita Panda
ISBN 978 81 207 8113 9
₹ 200

The Eternal Sai Phenomenon
A R Nanda
ISBN 978 81 207 6086 8
₹ 200

Baba's Rinanubandh Leelas during His Sojourn in Shirdi
Compiled by Vinny Chitluri
ISBN 978 81 207 3403 6
₹ 300

Baba's Gurukul Shirdi
Vinny Chitluri
ISBN 978 81 207 4770 8
₹ 250

Baba's Anurag Love for His Devotees
Compiled by Vinny Chitluri
ISBN 978 81 207 5447 8
₹ 200

Baba's Vaani: His Sayings and Teachings
Compiled by Vinny Chitluri
ISBN 978 81 207 3859 1
₹ 250

The Gospel of Shri Shirdi Sai Baba: A Holy Spiritual Path
Dr Durai Arulneyam
ISBN 978 81 207 3997 0
₹ 150

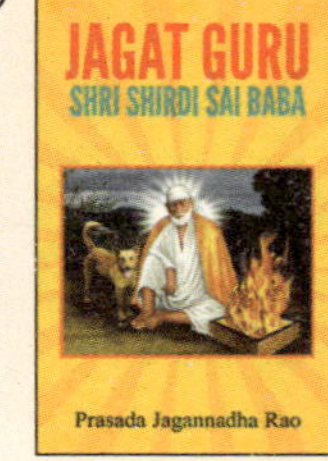

Jagat Guru: Shri Shirdi Sai Baba
Prasada Jagannadha Rao
ISBN 978 81 207 8175 7
₹ 100

Spotlight on the Sai Story
Chakor Ajgaonker
ISBN 978 81 207 4399 1
₹ 200

Shirdi Sai Baba A Practical God
K. K. Dixit
ISBN 978 81 207 5918 3
₹ 75

Promises of Shirdi Sai Baba (The Eleven Precious Sayings)
Bela Sharma
ISBN 978 93 85913 98 3
₹ 75

Shirdi Sai Baba The Divine Healer
Raj Chopra
ISBN 978 81 207 4766 1
₹ 150

Shirdi Sai Baba and other Perfect Masters
C B Satpathy
ISBN 978 81 207 2384 9
₹ 200

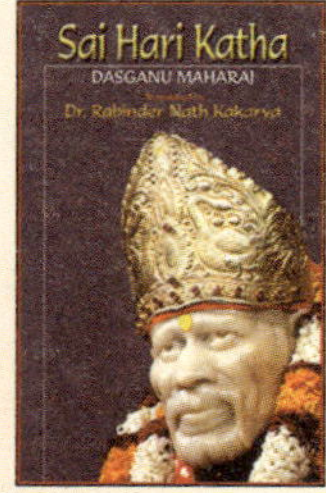

Sai Hari Katha
Dasganu Maharaj Translated by *Dr. Rabinder Nath Kakarya*
ISBN 978 81 207 3324 4
₹ 150

We need Sai forever... at 6, 16 and 60!
Saurabh Khanna
ISBN 978 93 86245 15 1
₹ 190

I am always with you
Lorraine Walshe-Ryan
ISBN 978 81 207 3192 9
₹ 150

BABA- May I Answer
C.B. Satpathy
ISBN 978 81 207 4594 0
₹ 150

Ek: An English Musical on the Life of Shirdi Sai Baba
Usha Akella
ISBN 978 81 207 6842 0
₹ 75

Sri Sai Baba
Sai Sharan Anand
Translated by V.B Kher
ISBN 978 81 207 1950 7
₹ 200

Sai Baba: His Divine Glimpses
V B Kher
ISBN 978 81 207 2291 0
₹ 95

A Diamond Necklace To: Shirdi Sai Baba
Giridhar Ari
ISBN 978 81 207 5868 1
₹ 200

Life History of Shirdi Sai Baba
Ammula Sambasiva Rao
ISBN 978 81 207 7722 4
₹ 250

Shri Sai Baba- The Saviour
Dr. Rabinder Nath Kakarya
ISBN 978 81 207 4701 2
₹ 100

Sai Baba's 261 Leelas
Balkrishna Panday
ISBN 978 81 207 2727 4
₹ 200

A Solemn Pledge from True Tales of Shirdi Sai Baba
Dr B H Briz-Kishore
ISBN 978 81 207 2240 8
₹ 95

God Who Walked on Earth:
The Life & Times of Shirdi Sai Baba
Rangaswami Parthasarathy
ISBN 978 81 207 1809 8
₹ 225

Shri Shirdi Sai Baba: His Life and Miracles
ISBN 978 81 207 2877 6
₹ 35

Shirdi Sai Baba Aratis
ISBN 978 81 207 8456 7
(English)
₹ 10

Sree Sai Charitra Darshan
Mohan Jagannath Yadav
ISBN 978 81 207 8346 1
₹ 225

The Miracles of Sai Baba
ISBN 978 81 207 5433 1 (HB)
₹ 300

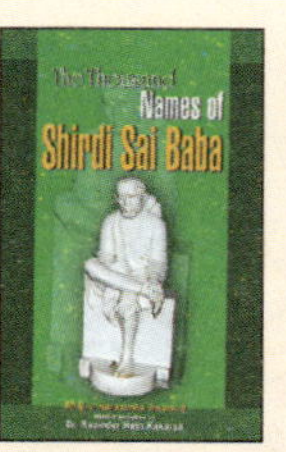

The Thousand Names of Shirdi Sai Baba
Sri B.V. Narasimha Swami Ji
Hindi translation by
Dr. Rabinder Nath Kakarya
ISBN 978 81 207 3738 9
₹ 75

108 Names of Shirdi Sai Baba
ISBN 978 81 207 3074 8
₹ 50

Shirdi Sai Speaks... Sab Ka Malik Ek
Quotes for the Day
ISBN 978 81 207 3101 1
₹ 200

DIVINE GURUS

Guru Charitra
Shree Swami Samarth
ISBN 978 81 207 3348 0
₹ 300

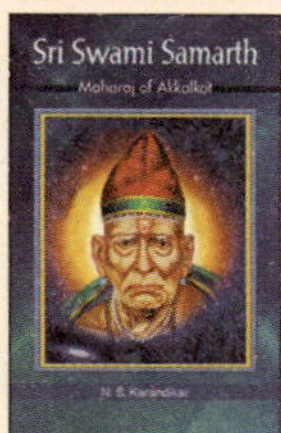

Sri Swami Samarth Maharaj of Akkaikot
N.S. Karandikar
ISBN 978 81 207 3445 6
₹ 250

Hazrat Babajan:
A Pathan Sufi of Poona
Kevin R. D. Shepherd
ISBN 978 81 207 8698 1
₹ 200

Sri Narasimha Swami Apostle of Shirdi Sai Baba
Dr. G.R. Vijayakumar
ISBN 978 81 207 4432 5
₹ 90

Lord Sri Dattatreya The Trinity
Dwarika Mohan Mishra
ISBN 978 81 207 5417 1
₹ 200

शिरडी साईं बाबा नवीन तथ्य
चन्द्रभानु सतपथी
978 93 86245 63 2
₹ 300

श्री साई सच्चरित्र
श्री शिरडी साईं बाबा की अद्भुत जीवनी तथा उनके अमूल्य उपदेश
गोविंद रघुनाथ दाभोलकर (हेमाडपंत)
978 81 207 2500 3
₹ 400 (HB)

श्री साई ज्ञानेश्वरी-महाकाव्य
राकेश जुनेजा
978 93 86245 17 5
₹ 250

हमें साई की आवश्यकता है सदा के लिए 6, 16 और 60!
सौरभ खन्ना
978 93 86245 21 2
₹ 125

साई ही क्यों?
राकेश जुनेजा
978 81 207 9610 2
₹ 200

जेल में साई साक्षात्कार
राकेश जुनेजा
978 81 207 9507 5
₹ 150

श्री साई ज्ञानेश्वरी
राकेश जुनेजा
978 81 207 9491 7
₹ 250

शिर्डी साई बाबा के ग्यारह अनमोल वचन
बेला शर्मा
978 93 85913 97 6
₹ 75

श्री साई चरित्र दर्शन
मोहन जगन्नाथ यादव
978 81 207 8350 8
₹ 200

साई सुमिरन
अंजु टंडन
978 81 207 8706 3
₹ 100

बाबा की वाणी-उनके वचन तथा आदेश
बेला शर्मा
978 81 207 4745 6
₹ 100

बाबा का अनुराग
विनी चितलुरी
978 81 207 6699 0
₹ 125

बाबा का ऋणानुबंध
विनी चितलुरी
978 81 207 5998 5
₹ 150

बाबा का गुरूकुल-शिरडी
विनी चितलुरी
978 81 207 6698 3
₹ 150

बाबा-आध्यात्मिक विचार
चन्द्रभानु सतपथी
978 81 207 4627 5
₹ 175

पृथ्वी पर अवतरित भगवान शिरडी के साई बाबा
रंगास्वामी पार्थसारथी
978 81 207 2101 2
₹ 200

साई बाबा एक अवतार
बेला शर्मा
978 81 207 6706 5
₹ 150

साई सत् चरित का प्रकाश
बेला शर्मा
978 81 207 7804 7
₹ 200

श्री शिरडी साई बाबा एवं अन्य सद्गुरु
चन्द्रभानु सतपथी
978 81 207 4401 1
₹ 90

साई शरण में
चन्द्रभानु सतपथी
978 81 207 2802 8
₹ 150

साई - सबका मालिक
कल्पना भाकुनी
978 81 207 9886 1
₹ 200

श्री साई बाबा के परम भक्त
डॉ. रबिन्द्रनाथ ककरिया
978 81 207 2779 3
₹ 125

शिरडी अंत: से अनंत
डॉ. रबिन्द्रनाथ ककरिया
978 81 207 8191 7
₹ 750

श्री साई बाबा के अनन्य भक्त
डॉ. रबिन्द्र नाथ ककरिया
978 81 207 2705 2
₹ 100

साई का संदेश
डॉ. रबिन्द्र नाथ ककरिया
978 81 207 2879 0
₹ 200

श्री साई बाबा के उपदेश व तत्त्वज्ञान
लेफ्टिनेन्ट कर्नल एम. बी. निंबालकर
978 81 207 5971 8 ₹ 100

साई भक्तानुभव
डॉ. रबिन्द्रनाथ ककरिया
978 81 207 3052 6
₹ 125

मुक्तिदाता - श्री साई बाबा
डॉ. रबिन्द्रनाथ ककरिया
978 81 207 2778 6
₹ 65

साई दत्तावधूता
राजेन्द्र भण्डारी
978 81 207 4400 4
₹ 75

साई हरि कथा
दासगणु महाराज
978 81 207 3323 7
₹ 65

श्री नरसिम्हा स्वामी शिरडी साई बाबा के दिव्य प्रचारक
डॉ. रबिन्द्र नाथ ककरिया
978 81 207 4437 0 ₹ 100

शिरडी साई बाबा - की सत्य कथाओं से प्राप्त - एक पावन प्रतिज्ञा
प्रो. डॉ. बी.एच. ब्रिज-किशोर
978 81 207 2346 7 ₹ 95

दिव्य भजन
डॉ. रबिन्द्रनाथ ककरिया
978 81 207 9505 1 ₹ 125

शिरडी संपूर्ण दर्शन
डॉ. रबिन्द्रनाथ ककरिया
978 81 207 2312 2
₹ 50

शिरडी साई बाबा की दिव्य लीलाएँ
डॉ. रबिन्द्र नाथ ककरिया
978 81 207 6376 0
₹ 150

श्री साई चालीसा
978 81 207 4773 9
₹ 50

शिरडी साई बाबा आरती
978 81 207 8195 5
₹ 10

आरती संग्रह
(3D cover)
on Plastic
ISBN 978 81 207 8940 1
Size: 14.20 x 10.70 cm
₹ 60

आरती संग्रह
(Index Boardbook)
Gold/Silver Cover
ISBN 978 81 207 9057 5
Size: 10.70 x 15.45 cm
₹ 100

आरती संग्रह
(Boardbook)
Green Cover
ISBN 978 81 207 4774 6
Size: 11 x 15 cm
(9 Leafs)
₹ 50

शिरडी साई के दिव्य वचन-सब का मालिक एक
प्रतिदिन का विचार
978 81 207 3533 0
₹ 200

ORIYA LANGUAGE

ଶ୍ରୀ ସାଇ ସଚ୍ଚରିତ୍ର
ଶ୍ରୀ ଗୋବିନ୍ଦରାଓ ରଘୁନାଥ ଦାଭୋଲକର
(ହେମାଡପନ୍ତ)
978 81 207 8332 4
₹ 300

ସାଇ ସନ୍ଦେଶ
ସୁରେଶ ଚନ୍ଦ୍ର ପଣ୍ଡା
978 81 207 9534 1
₹ 100

ଶ୍ରୀ ଶିରିଡ଼ି ସାଇବାବା କଥାମୃତ
ପ୍ରଫେସର ଡ. ବି. ଏଚ୍. ବ୍ରିଜ୍‌କିଶୋର
978 81 207 7774 3
₹ 95

ଶ୍ରୀ ସାଇବାବାଙ୍କ
ଉପଦେଶ ଓ ତତ୍ତ୍ୱଜ୍ଞାନ
978 81 207 9982 0
₹125

ଶିରଡି ସାଇ ବାବାଙ୍କ
ଜୀବନ ଚରିତ (Oriya)
ଅମୂଲ ଶାହାଣିକ ରାଓ
ଅନୁବାଦକ - କିଶୋର ଚନ୍ଦ୍ର ପଟ୍ଟନାୟକ
978 81 207 7417 9
₹125

KANNAD LANGUAGE

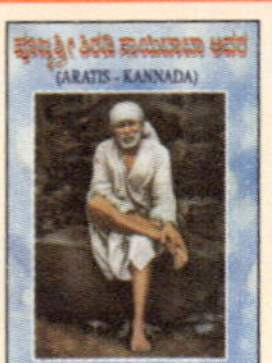

Shirdi Sai Baba Aratis
(Kannada)
₹ 10

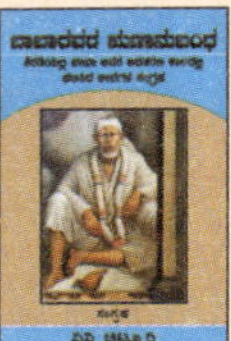

ಬಾಬಾರವರ ಋಣಾನುಬಂಧ
ವಿನ್ನಿ ಚಿಟ್ಲೂರಿ
978 81 207 9500 6
₹ 200

ಪೂಜ್ಯಶ್ರೀ ಶಿರಡಿ ಸಾಯಿಬಾಬಾ ಅವರ
(Kannada)
प्रो. डॉ. बी.एच.
ब्रिज-किशोर
978 81 207 2873 8
₹ 95

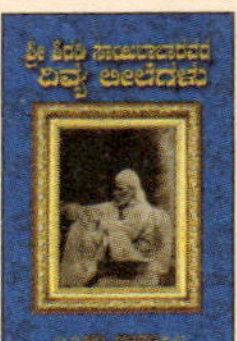

ಶ್ರೀ ಶಿರಡಿ ಸಾಯಿಬಾಬಾರವರ
ದಿವ್ಯ ಲೀಲೆಗಳು
ವಿನ್ನಿ ಚಿಟ್ಲೂರಿ
978 81 207 8930 2
₹ 225

ಬಾಬಾರವರೊಂದಿಗೆ ಒಂದು ದಿವ್ಯ
ಪಯಣ
ವಿನ್ನಿ ಚಿಟ್ಲೂರಿ
978 81 207 9975 2
₹ 200

TAMIL AND TELUGU LANGUAGE

MARATHI LANGUAGE

Life History of Sri Shirdi Sai Baba
978-93-86245-77-9
₹ 250

ஷீர்டி சாயிபாபாவின் (Tamil)
உண்மைக்கதைகளிலிருந்து
பெருமிதமான வாக்குறுதி
प्रो. डॉ. बी.एच. ब्रिज-किशोर
978 81 207 2876 9 ₹ 95

Shirdi Sai Baba Aratis
(Telugu) ₹ 10
(Tamil) ₹ 10

షిరిడీసాయిబాబా
(Telugu)
प्रो. डॉ. बी.एच. ब्रिज-किशोर
978 81 207 2294 1 ₹ 95

शिर्डी साईबाबांची
दिव्य वचने (Marathi)
सबका मालिक एक
दैनंदिन विचार
978 81 207 7518 3 ₹ 200

THE THOUSAND NAMES OF GOD

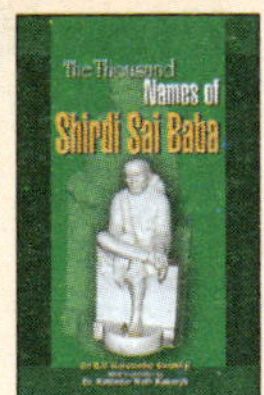

Shirdi Sai Baba
DR.RABINDER NATH KAKARYA
978 81 207 3738 9 ₹75

Shiva
VIJAYA KUMAR
978 81 207 3008 3 ₹75

Ganesha
VIJAYA KUMAR
978 81 207 3007 6 ₹75

Vishnu
VIJAYA KUMAR
978 81 207 3009 0 ₹75

Colouring My Way
STERLING STUDIO
978 81 207 9790 1 ₹50

108 NAMES OF GOD

Lakshmi
978 81 207 2028 2 ₹50

Shirdi Sai Baba
978 81 207 3074 8 ₹50

Durga
978 81 207 2027 5 ₹50

Shiva
978 81 207 2025 1 ₹50

Hanuman
978 81 207 2024 4 ₹50

Vishnu
978 81 207 2023 7 ₹50

Sterling Publishers Private Limited
Plot No-13,Eco Tech-III, Udyog Kendra Greater Noida, Uttar Pradesh, Pin-201308 India
CIN: U22110DL1964PTC211907 GST: 09AAACS0306C1Z1
Phone No : 120-6251823, +91 82877 98380 E-mail : mail@sterlingpublishers.in www.sterlingpublishers.
Prices are subject to change